REDEEMING GRIEF

Abortion and Its Pain

Second Revised Edition

Foreword by Archbishop Barry Hickey

Anne Lastman

GRACEWING

First published in 2013 by
Freedom Publishing Pty Ltd.
PO Box 251
Balwyn, Vic
Australia

This edition published in 2013 by
Gracewing 2 Southern Avenue
Leominster Herefordshire HR6
0QF
United Kingdom
www.gracewing.co.uk

ISBN: 978 085244 821 2

Nihil Obstat: Reverend Gerard Diamond MA (Oxon), LSS, D.Theol
Diocesan Censor.
Imprimatur: Rev. Monsignor Les Tomlinson, Vicar General, Archdiocese
of Melbourne, 4 May 2007.

The Nihil Obstat and Imprimatur are official declarations that a book or
pamphlet is free of doctrinal or moral error. No implication is contained
therein that those who have granted the Nihil Obstat and Imprimatur agree
with the contents, opinions or statements expressed.

Cover Design: Lucas Lastman

Redeeming Grief! Yes some parts are difficult reading, but to persevere through, for a post-abortion sufferer, may well prove a wonderful, life-saving gift from God. Thanks to Anne Lastman, her experience, her wisdom and honesty, and the love she has shared already with so many, are surely gifts from God. Personal contact with Anne is clearly best but just not always possible; there are sadly so many.

This book is a brave and wonderful gift to share with many more, both sufferers and helpers.

Bishop D.C. Moore, MSC, DD, KBE,
Bishop Emeritus of Alotau-Sidea, Papua New Guinea

Anne Lastman explores the psychological, social and spiritual aspects of one of society's taboo subjects: the consequences of abortion. From her own extensive counselling experience, from international research and from the words of women and men who have suffered, she makes a compelling call for the Church to wake up to the issues of abortion and to embrace those who need healing.

Dr Dianne Grocott MBBS, FRANZCP,
Psychiatrist, Victoria, Australia

Redeeming Grief by Anne Lastman is a truly remarkable book which should be in the hands of every bishop, priest, deacon and pastoral worker. A truly remarkable book by a remarkable author.

Rev Fr Raymond Wells PE,
Tasmania, Australia

The book *Redeeming Grief* reveals abortion as a trauma which at times is linked with other traumas that even today are dismissed; and pro-choice lobbies continue deny the fact.

Thanks to the true stories of more than 1500 women counselled by Anne Lastman for post-abortion distress and presented in her book, this is revealed.

Through the pain of the unborn babies and the pain of their mothers – and of all involved people – healing and redemption are possible. *Redeeming Grief* outlines why this grief is a good and redeeming grief.

Benedetta Foà, Psychologist
and post-abortion counsellor, Milan, Italy

This book is not just a bunch of stories, but a beautiful teaching, an entire course, if you like, on the dignity of human life, including the point of view of God, of the abortive women and men, of the siblings and of the whole of society.

As the author so clearly states over and over, abortion causes broken hearts, anguish, fear, guilt, failure and death. Its rippling effects reach to the very ends of the earth and devastate almost everyone whom they touch.

Anna Breheney, Homeschooling mother of four children,
Victoria, Australia

CONTENTS

FOREWORD

The publishing of this second edition of *Redeeming Grief* is most welcome. It is welcome because it is about hope. It offers hope to all women grieving over the experience of an abortion.

Although many will find the reading of this book hard going as it exposes the truth about abortion from one who sadly knows, it is worth it. The inner healing, and the freedom that comes from the counselling Anne Lastman offers, needs to be widely known. It could best be described as spiritual counselling, because it addresses the deep pain, guilt, confusion and self-reproach of women who have had an abortion, and offers not just a sympathetic ear but real forgiveness and a new freedom of spirit.

Her ability to do this comes not just from her experience and personal story, but from her Christian faith which offers the assurance of forgiveness and the love of a God who understands. In this she differs from those counsellors who feel they cannot enter into the area of faith and religion. She does so because she herself has received that forgiveness.

She distances herself too from those counsellors who try to give false assurances that abortion is not a moral issue at all, but a simple medical procedure totally acceptable in today's world.

The stories of the women and sometimes of the men involved are found throughout this book. They tell of the journey from pain and self-recrimination to freedom and self-worth. The book confronts many of the myths currently circulating about abortion that mask the real truth. The features of post-abortion syndrome are outlined here clearly and convincingly, the fear, the guilt, the shame and anxiety, the temptation to self-harm, even suicide, the depression, panic attacks and flashbacks and all the other scientifically identified consequences so often found among women after an abortion, surfacing and lasting for many, many years. Anne Lastman describes them and the ways in which release from them can be obtained.

In addition to all this, the book examines the role played by the sexual revolution of the sixties and the seventies, in creating the permissiveness that has resulted in the exploitation of women and the explosion of the number of abortions since the seventies in most countries of the world.

This book is for every concerned person who wishes to understand the causes of the abortion mentality which has brought so much death and suffering to millions. Please God many readers will resolve to do what they can to change the mentality that results in so much death.

The most important message in this book is hope. This book is GOOD NEWS. It is good news for women in distress because of an abortion. It assures them that healing is possible, that forgiveness is available, and that the courage to seek the kind of counselling that Anne Lastman offers will be vindicated. It is, in a very literal sense, a Godsend.

Most Rev Barry Hickey
Archbishop Emeritus of Perth

DEDICATION

This book is dedicated to the loving memory of Miriam, Joseph, and all the gifts (infants) who were returned to God unopened, unmet, and for a time forgotten and unloved. It is further dedicated to all the mothers and fathers who have experienced and regretted this deep loss and live with the haunting memory of what might have been.

Introduction

My own life, as with all humans, has been difficult and at times most complex, even to today. It is through my experience of grief following my own two abortions that I have come to the belief that it is only through the mercy of God, and my own profound rediscovered love for him, which has brought me through the darker times. It is this knowledge and understanding that allow me to be able to help and show other women how to let their grief, following their abortions, become a redeeming grief. Not a destructive grief leading to self-annihilation but a grief surrounded with haloes. Grief always means love lost, or someone or something special no longer with us. Grief always means a profound loss. We do not grieve for something or someone which is or who is not of value in our lives.

As a Catholic woman with a deep faith in Christ and his Church, I cannot but live my life in any other way than in a Christ-centred way. I am stating my relationship with God boldly, because you will find that my thoughts and work throughout this book reflect this. It is therefore natural that I lean on my God, and use my knowledge of God, and deep devotion, as a tool in my work with women (and occasionally men) who have experienced abortion. One does not have to be Catholic or even a Christian to understand the power of healing and the love of God. I feel sure that this would be the same for other religious beliefs, that is, religions centred or based on a merciful loving God.

Because the term post abortion grief is associated with the word "abortion" it is often thought to be aligned with right-to-life issues. post abortion grief, trauma, psychosis, counselling, are really things that occur after the right-to-life consideration has lost its influence, or benefits, and not been influential in changing a woman's mind. At this point the human life in the womb (or pregnancy) has been terminated and the only living victim remaining is the woman, and in time the male.

Although there is a strong similarity between pregnancy loss and abortion loss, the trauma following abortion is much greater due to the fact of the participation or even volitional aspect of the mother. Although this participation is often little more than the giving of an indifferent consent, at times given under pressure, the guilt component of her emotions, coupled with the eventual realisation of what she has done, becomes unbearable.

The Diagnostic and Statistical Manual of Mental Disorders (DSM IV) specifies that a trauma is more severe and longer lasting when the stressor is of human design, as in the volitional aspect, or consent, to the decision to abort.

It is difficult to imagine that a woman, who is designed by God to be a life-giving and nurturing being, can agree to the abortion of her own child. Yet we know that hundreds of millions of women have done so since the early 1970s, thus not only breaking the invisible bond of love between herself and her offspring, but also negating her own self respect, her womanhood, feminine design and emotional and spiritual well being.

We need to realise that with the termination of the life in her womb, her originally designed womanhood is changed or at least seriously affected, and the person after the abortion is no longer the person she was before. It is almost as if two people die on the surgical table, one physically and one spiritually and emotionally.

Therefore the woman who has aborted is a changed person who struggles with herself, her memories, and her now damaged concept of her own design and, and for a time to come, it is this new broken person in pain and suffering about whom we are speaking in post abortion work.

Abortion trauma and grief do not start the moment a woman leaves the abortion clinic. It can start at any time, even during the decision making process prior to the abortion, or at any time from then on, even as much as forty or fifty years later. Counselling begins after the pain, the memories and especially the guilt become much too great and the woman seeks help, love and understanding. Post abortion grief, trauma and psychosis, leading to breakdown, may begin with a simple trigger in her day to day life. A word, a smell, a sound, a song, a face, a baby, a young woman, a pram.

Post abortion counselling does not lessen the seriousness of abortion nor does it negate its sinfulness. Its aim is to help to return the woman – and more and more as we are seeing the male – to a place of peace, from where with help, they may turn their faces towards God, repentant, and seeking forgiveness and readmittance into the heavenly family, whilst re-experiencing the divine solace which comes from genuine forgiveness through a desire is to return to the arms of the Lord. This can only be achieved after the woman learns of the infinite love and mercy of God and the assurance that her aborted infant is not dismembered waste, or in some limbo of nothingness, but resting in the peace of God. It will never bring the woman back to the same youthful innocence that she enjoyed prior to the abortion, but it will allow her to live with herself in a good and harmonious life in which God is the centre of her space and her knowledge that her infant/s rests in His eternal care.

The right to be born is and must be extended to all human beings. From the moment of conception to the last breath taken naturally, the dignity of human life cannot be compromised. However, the "right to life" as we understand it is mostly concerned with the pre-born and those who cannot speak for themselves. There is absolutely no doubt that a raised consciousness about "right to life" is much needed as indeed we are called to protect all of God's children.

There is, however, a serious unintended side-effect to the thought of the "right to life" lobby, (from my experience) and that is, that its focus is (and probably must be) on the unborn human life and the saving and or protecting such life. All energy and focus is on preventing the abortion. This is their focus. This in itself is a must and very important and it cannot be denied or in any way weakened.

However, in most cases the living victim after the abortion has been ignored and not extended the same "right to life" as the infant she aborted. Perhaps there is rightness to that, and as such there is always the invisible barrier which is raised against the abortive woman. And perhaps even at times it appears that whilst pro life workers utter consoling words to repentant women, there is a much needed empathy required to understand and care for the enormous damage that is done to or by the woman herself, or society, by its pseudo cavalier behaviour towards her. All too often she is blamed for the choice made available through the law statutes, and insisted upon by the boyfriend, husband, parents, career and others. She is (at times) forced into making a decision in great haste and under strong pressure, and at times accompanied by threats, i.e., abandonment, life difficulties, and even at times a personal threat of violence.

There are also many other factors that have a serious effect on the decision making process of the woman, in such a limited time or a panic situation. At times there are further difficulties, and where multiple abortions are the condition, there is the strong possibility of deep psychological trauma due to the experience of physical and/or sexual abuse and abandonment. Furthermore, the deceptive language of the abortion industry, whose use of the terms cell, tissue, embryo and fetus, product of conception, conceptus, menstrual extraction, serves to camouflage the reality of the child's humanity and mislead and denigrate the seriousness of the decision. Further still, the fact that it is a legal procedure creates the impression that it is also acceptable, or worse still, that it is good.

Worst of all, in Australia and perhaps in other Western nations, the abortion process is paid for under government medical schemes which then further devalue the unborn life, by placing the focus of the abortion as a medical procedure and therefore placing it in the category of an illness that requires medical funding. In fact it is not even regarded as elective surgery. Once again, this places the woman in a belief construct where it seems acceptable or even good to have an abortion while the use of public funds to pay for the termination of a life lull people into colluding with the abortion.

It is often not understood, until much later, that these many influences have had an effect on the decision making process of the aborting woman. In many cases a younger woman may be under 18, too young to vote, but placed in a situation where she is forced to decide over the life and death of another.

One can realistically say that many women are victims before the abortion when it is presented or seen as a solution, however wrong this solution may be. Consideration must be given to the age, maturity, spiritual, physical and psychological condition of the woman/girl, not in order to justify the abortion, but to understand the milieu.

This is where the care for women with an abortion experience by pro-life groups becomes especially difficult because we consider and are told that the woman had a clear choice, when the reality is quite different. This particular idea is also promoted by the pro-choice/pro abortion action groups.

We cannot ever condone the abortion and we must continue to assist and pray for the mother and others involved in such a heinous action, a challenging task for all those who work against all odds to promote a pro-life position. For it is difficult to fight the holocaust of abortion and at the same time extend love and care to the perpetrators (abortion providers and abortive women and men). It is for these reasons that post abortion counselling/issues become a rather poor distant cousin of the pro-life movement. Essentially, the right to life movement struggles to extend itself to understand and promote the necessity for the healing of a woman and work for post abortion counselling, as they do working against abortion itself. However, there is a disequilibrium in these priorities.

As Jesus sat with the tax collectors and sinners, the lowest of society, we too must extend our hand in love to those suffering because of abortion and its pain (greatest of sinners). We need to continue to imitate Christ in his work with the poor, broken, marginalised and sinners.

So, even though there is a right to a spiritual life for the aborting woman, post abortion issues/counselling is not a right to life issue per se. It stands on it own and needs to be seen as a separate concern. Indeed a most Catholic, Christian initiative, a parallel but separate initiative to right to life thinking. We need to get away from the blame we place on the women (they do enough of this themselves) and replace this with the compassion of love and healing. We need to help bring about a change from "Eve" (wounded) into "Mary" (radiant) through God's mercy and forgiveness.

At this stage I would also like to say that the first few chapters of *Redeeming Grief* are difficult to read, but I would encourage perseverance. Please. These are very important chapters which set the foundations for the whole book. Yes, they are heavy reading, but important reading. This book is about abortion, pain, sorrow, regret, but over and above this, a grief, which if accepted and handled well becomes a redeeming grief, one which ensures that no child will ever pass by this universe unnoticed. This grief becomes a grief filled with an extraordinary love; it becomes an exercise in appropriation of the beloved lost child/ren. The Christian is promised eternal life if his/ her faith grows to that of Jesus Christ crucified, because through the crucifixion (abortion) and the pain of such it could be said that it becomes a moment for conversion:

"Every time you make a choice, you are turning the central part of you, the part that chooses, into something a little different from what it was before. And taking your life as a whole, with all your innumerable choices, all your life long you are slowly turning this central thing into a creature that is in harmony with God, and with other creatures, and with itself, or else into one that is in a state of war ... and each one of us at each moment is progressing to the one state of the other" (C.S. Lewis (*Mere Christianity*, New York: Macmillan, 1943, p. 86).

Since 1996 I have counselled several thousand grieving women following one or more abortions. After experiencing the redemption of my own grief, through counselling and an understanding of the mercy of God, I gradually came to realise the need for a unique type of counselling for those suffering from post abortion trauma and grief.

In 1999 I established the office for the Victims of Abortion for this purpose.

Clearly there is much silent suffering in the community as a result of universally accepted abortion. The symptoms of the grief are manifold. In *Redeeming Grief* I set out to explain the nature of abortion, the effects of abortion not only on the women involved but also on the wider familial circle along with the demographic winter we are seeing and its effects on society.

Noteworthy is the fact that often sexual and/or other abuse, or neglect and abandonment, are found connected to the abortion experience.

This book offers hope to all who read it, that those who suffer from the abortion experience can 'redeem' their suffering and grief. Often this is easier in the context of religious faith, whereby the suffering is raised to a spiritual level.

Many of the women who have persisted in counselling have experienced forgiveness and healing, and once again returned to joyful living and satisfying personal relationships.

It takes courage to confront the reality of abortion, or the reality of sexual abuse and neglect. It takes courage to confront the evil of abortion and its after-effects. It takes courage to accept responsibility for an abortion and to proceed on the journey of healing the effects of abortion, sexual abuse and other abuses of the spirit.

May this book assist readers to understand the deeper issues of the abortion pandemic. More especially, may this book assist those suffering the effects of abortion, those who live with those suffering, and those who deal with the suffering person. May this book assist in clarifying the issues and effects of abortion while providing hope for redeeming the grief that follows abortion.

1.

Abortion: What is it?

"Before I formed you in the womb, I knew you" (Jer. 1:5)

Abortion is commonly understood to be the intentional interruption of a pregnancy for the purpose of prematurely dispelling the foetus before maturation and before viability is possible. A further definition may be that it is the intentional removal of the unborn child from the womb before he or she has reached the stage of viability.

From both of these definitions the picture is very clear. It is the interruption and the expulsion from the womb of a tiny infant who would (barring accidents or interference) have proceeded to a viable or full term stage, and to natural birth.

The Catholic Church's teachings, found in its *Catechism of the Catholic Church,* are still more specific: "Human life must be respected and protected absolutely from the moment of conception. From the first moment of his existence, a human being must be recognised as having the rights of a person among which is the inviolable right of every innocent being to life." (*CCC,* 2270)[1] It is plain to see that abortion interrupts and interferes with a human process leading to the development of an entirely new creature, a new entity, set apart from and unique from the mother. This new creation and new entity is designed and constructed and brought forth by the power and ingenuity of God. For that reason the Catholic Church acknowledges its personal dignity, right to life and protection from abortion.

It is a presumption to suggest that the new creature is simply the handiwork of the male and the female and at their disposal to do with as they deem fit. Further, it is a gross presumption on the part of the human individual to believe that what is conceived is of his or her own doing. Only God can create life. While the parents provide the body, the vehicle, it is the Almighty who breathes life into the new creation (Gn 2:7). God Himself is present at every new creation. He has a plan for each and every child and that plan is for that new creation to be shaped into the image of his Son Jesus and live with Him forever. He alone endows the new creature with an immortal soul, and in each new creation God is glorified. Each new creation is so special, so important that new structures are put in place to accommodate the new being. The universe changes completely because someone who has never existed before is now brought into existence. In fact so important is the new creature that God commands his angels to guard and protect it (Ps. 91:12). To conceive a child means to become pregnant with a word of God, a desire of God. A "Yes" of God. He has whispered, "let there be a new life, and let my son's image be repeated. Let creation mirror my image again." When a new child is conceived God unites a part of Himself (breath) to flesh (soil) and the encounter edifies and changes both. This is why abortion is so abominable, because it is the rejection of God. Abortion rejects the "something new" envisaged by God.

It must be clearly understood that only God can create or confer life. Uncreated, God can create from his vast desire. Of course what sin can do and has done from the very beginning is to stain and spoil the creative works of God. Perhaps this is wickedness at its genesis. He cannot create and will never create and therefore he can never ascend and be like God. Evil is far from God. He cannot fathom that very unfathomable secret that is "love" and perhaps this is why he has sunk to the lowest "un-love". Lucifer forever remains haunted by a certain memory of his former self and his former place in heavenly glory next to God and desires to continue in this manner. That is why he presents himself as an "angel of light" and is able to convince those who will listen that sin (abortion) will be liberating, will be beneficial, and will be of the "highest good". This is his characteristic. He is untruth personified. As the ethos of God is Truth, so the ethos of Satan is untruth. His hatred is hatred personified. As God is Love (Ps 103) so Satan is un-love.

Whilst "love" effuses from the heart the desires and designs of God, ever creative and effulgent, "un-love" stands enraged. The secret at the heart of God remains always forbidden, always unreachable. Whereas "love" creates anew, "un-love" in its ferocity attempts to destroy.

To be able to understand the evil one's violence and hatred against the creatures of God, one must examine the diabolical, monstrous and barbaric methods used in abortion procedures.

- Dilation and curette: This method cuts, dismembers and shreds the baby while it is still in the uterus.
- Suction method: Suctioning and dismembering of the child still in the uterus.
- Saline Solution: Mostly used for late term abortions, that is, 20 weeks gestation and over. With this method the environment and infant are poisoned and burnt. In fact, the mother undergoes labour and delivers a dead child. (At times a live child may still be delivered).
- Dilation and Evacuation: Crushing and dismembering.
- Prostaglandin: Chemical/violent premature labour.
- Dilation & Extraction, or the procedure known as partial birth abortion: A most barbarous method in which the infant is partially delivered and killed by having its brain suctioned out after a hole is pierced at the base of the skull. This method is used for late term abortions.
- Hysterotomy: Caesarean section followed by the terminating of the infant either by drowning, smothering, or refusing to attend to it, or by any other ingenious method the abortionist may devise.

In all the above methods employed to terminate a pregnancy, a violent, painful, cruel and merciless death of a living child results. Even in the methods used there is a sense of hatred. Yet this hatred is masked by false concern for the "rights" and "wants" of the mother, the father, the grandparents or society. It appears that the "rights" of all others are paramount and are clearly delineated from the "rights" of the child, a separate and entirely new individual. Two separate beings in the one body, yet one has "rights", the other is sacrificed for those "rights".

Indeed society has reached a new level of rationalisation and trivialisation when the value and dignity of a human being is determined by its size (the bigger one), tax paying ability or even perhaps by its ability to make noises. The law of the jungle is being played out in our very modern yet primitive society.

Abortion is ultimately not about rights, or about career, or about reputation, or want, or not want. It is about hatred especially spiritual hatred. It is about the hatred Lucifer bears for God and his creation. It is about the cursing of the seed and the crushing of the head. It is about robbing God of children destined for his Kingdom. It is about wickedness wanting tenants for his own accursed kingdom. It is about violence and degradation. It is about dehumanisation, depersonalisation and death. It is about the mechanisation and finally the death of societal conscience possibly leading to the death of society itself.

Of course the final decision to abort has not been made as a spur of the moment decision. As a post abortion grief counsellor I am constantly coming face to face with individuals whose personal stories can only suggest that the journey to the abortion clinic began long before that particular date.

Without exception those women who have aborted have been on this journey for many years. The actual abortion was the culmination of a lifetime of desensitisation to the sacredness and dignity of life and a lifetime of abused and misunderstood sexuality. For every one of the abortive women whom I have counselled there has been a history in which the Word of God has been totally absent. Irrespective of whether the individual was a Catholic, Christian or of another religious belief or indeed no religious belief at all, the journey to that abortion clinic did not start on the morning of the abortion or even the moment of conception. It started at a distant point in her history where a crisis moment was encountered, and the outcome of that particular crisis has led finally to the abortion.

It is my belief that as the journey towards Calvary did not begin with the conception or the birth of Jesus but was the final act in a long drama beginning with the sin of origins; so too the aborting woman set out on her journey long ago. As I counsel women traumatised by their abortion experience I am made more clearly aware of the depth of pain and degradation into which they have descended. I understand that that abyss has beckoned and bidden and enslaved them over the years. There is more to this abortion or abortions. It is a last act of despair from which there will be either salvation or complete immersion into a form of slavery.

2.

Abortion Aftermath

The question must be asked, "If abortion is such a minor thing, a minor procedure, readily available and socially accepted, why is there so much spiritual and psychological suffering?" The answer to this must surely be that a human being cannot wantonly destroy another human being and then hope to live peacefully from then on.

Psychological sequelae following induced abortion are legion. They include depression, anxiety, low self-esteem, self-destructive behaviour, relationship difficulties, pervasive sadness and substance abuse, suicide ideation, and the list goes on.

Post abortion grief and suffering were first identified over twenty years ago. This condition recognises that the abortion experience has been traumatic and as a result, there has been psychological and spiritual pain. This condition is expressed by behaviour not previously found in the aborting individual and results in a slow changing of the personality. Clearly the behaviours exhibited by the post abortion grief prone woman (or man) indicate that the abortion has not been processed as a death experience and the individual has not dealt with or come to terms with the experience.

Perhaps the best way to understand abortion effects/pain is to place it in the context of what is currently understood as Post Traumatic Stress Disorder (PTSD). PTSD is a category listed in the manual of symptomatology of the American Psychiatric Association and used by professional counsellors. This manual, *The Diagnostic and Statistical Manual*, formerly recognised abortion as a stressor. However, this was removed, thus suggesting a denial or rejection of the possibility that psychological stress can be experienced by aborting women. The removal of this category from the manual has dealt a blow to those who suffer post abortion trauma and grief, because having this category listed in this manual lends strength and more credibility, which also means more research and more programmes for healing become possible. The world of psychology and psychiatry needs to recognise this particular trauma and suffering, and the need for further education and awareness of this trauma inducing procedure.

Post Traumatic Stress Disorder specifies that certain symptoms following a traumatic event must be present for the disorder to be recognised. Following a traumatic event, that is, one outside the range of normal day to day events, the stress experienced is a reaction to the trauma. This is important to understand because the negative reactions experienced following a traumatic event are recognised as valid and requiring treatment. Diagnosis for PTSD requires that at least three symptoms be present. The same symptoms are also to be found in the post-abortive distress prone female. The obvious question could be posed. Why have abortion and abortion grief and trauma been removed from the mentioned manual? It is beyond my understanding.

Some of the symptoms experienced by those suffering PTSD and abortion grief are:

(1) Reliving the traumatic experience, either through nightmares, flashbacks, ruminations about the abortion or the traumatic event.

(2) Persistent avoidance of anything to do with or related to the traumatic event. For the abortive woman anything to do with the abortion issue, or being near someone who is pregnant, e.g., avoiding newborn babies. Being detached.

(3) Hyper-alertness, that is, a very strong startle reaction. The individual feels, and lives on high tension levels similar to a tightly strung guitar.

(4)   Emotional shutdown for fear of feeling too much; so it is
      better not to feel at all.
(5)   The trauma experienced has severely impacted on the
      Individual's life, behaviour, relationships, career,
      family and/or friendships.

While abortion has been removed as a psychosocial stressor, this
does not necessarily mean that abortion is harmless or falls within
the "normal" range of daily human experience. This is true even if
abortions are now an accepted procedure. Abortion is a traumatic
event (at least for some immediately and some later) that requires
recognition as such at all levels of society. With the recognition may
come the realisation that abortion is not the answer to an unplanned
pregnancy. Further, with recognition it may be possible to promote
the healing of individuals who suffer from this syndrome and further
still with recognition more research into this type of grief can become
more feasible.

Trauma, according to this professional manual, is apparently
more severe and longer lasting when the stressor is of human design.
This is important to understand, because abortion or the intentional
interruption of a pregnancy is by human design. It was the intent of
the action and the outcome. Therefore, it is understandable that the
abortion experience can induce the physical, emotional and spiritual
pain especially in those individuals who are more prone to the disorder
and who undergo this procedure.

The fundamental and most characteristic features of abortion after-
effects and grief and associated trauma are denial and suppression.
These two defence mechanisms are set into place, at times prior to the
abortion itself, or immediately following. Denial means to intrinsically
acknowledge and then immediately deny what actually happened, or
deny the knowledge that the foetus aborted was a baby. Suppression
(a very strong defence mechanism) actually helps to almost erase
the experience from conscious memory. These strategies are very

important for the temporary maintenance of equilibrium. They help the individual by postponing the processing of something that is very awful, until a later time, when the psyche is able to deal with it in a more satisfactory manner. However, long term denial and suppression actually serve to create more psychological difficulties. Whilst the event is put in abeyance, by the sub-conscious mind, with the intention that it will be dealt with at a more suitable time, the permanent or long term storing of such trauma, without resolution, will cause the psychological pain to eventuate.

There is a further concern. If abortion is understood and accepted as a minor procedure with a return to normality for the woman, why have studies elicited results suggesting a possible link between abortion and endangered fertility, uterine perforations, breast cancer, suicide, post natal depression, substance abuse, eating disorders, clinical depression, and other factors? Again the answer to this must be that one human being cannot terminate the life of another human being and expect to remain unchanged.

Today we live in a society which seems to insist on being flesh lovers; willing to sacrifice anything that is an inconvenience. Society appears to suffer a collective blindness to the reality of what is actually going on. There appears to be a pathological insistence that abortion is nothing. That it is harmless. That it is a casual experience; therefore no ill effects should be felt. How long will it take to realise that abortion is not "nothing" but is the killing of a uniquely created being? It is the killing of an extension of oneself.

On the one hand the pro-choice, pro-abortion voices parade and sing their death anthem, the social and verbal engineers restructure meaning and political groups seek ever more votes by bowing to the louder voices. On the other hand, abortion grief counsellors and grief counsellors generally, are struggling with the enormity of the problem of grief. While pro-choice individuals believe that the "few" who actually suffer adverse effects do so because of their "Christian" backgrounds and suppressed upbringing, the reality is that even in non-Christian countries (like China and Japan) the findings are the same.

Guilt, shame, regrets, sorrows are not emotions exclusive to Christianity but are part of the natural law written in the human individual and written on the human heart. These emotions assist the human in decision-making. To experience these emotions simply means that the individual has a strong imprint of the natural law written on his/her heart. These emotions express a knowledge that something the individual did went against that deeply etched law. The lie "you shall surely not die" (Gen 3:4) is indeed being retold in every place where abortion is carried out. It is expressed in seductive terminology. However, the truth is that they (mothers, fathers, grandparents, siblings, society) are dying most especially in the psychological and spiritual areas. This Edenic lie "you will not die" resonates within the human person and is believed by those whose need is to remove the evidence of the experience of abortion.

While abortion is touted as the cheap solution to an immediate problem, the reality is that the discarding of a human being, at whatever gestational age, is ultimately a very costly experience. Costly, because the psychological and spiritual health of the woman (and slowly we are learning the male) is permanently compromised. Abortion creates dissonance in the innermost being. It acts as the bridge leading to the crossing over from the belief that all life has its foundation in God and is sacred, to a belief that life is cheap, disposable, unholy and conditional on the parent's benevolence and society's acceptance. It is conditioned to the "wantedness factor. " And when it is conditioned upon this factor then nobody is safe.

The transformation to the acceptance of this "wantedness" factor has been insidious, underhanded and global. It is not a condition of a certain geography with a particular skew to that area, but global. The meaning of life has changed because discard-able humans can then become experiment-able humans simply because they are discard-able and as such have no rights or dignity. The violence against the unborn insidiously introduced itself through a change from "being" to "wanted". It has become an act of violence by the creature against the Creator and creation. It is a new form of violence. It is the making of the statements "I am God" and "I give and take life at my will." It is the greatest form of idolatry because it attempts to usurp God's authority over life and death and relegate God to the realm of the past has-beens.

3.

Lives Touched By Abortion

While pro-choice, pro-abortion voices loudly proclaim their battle cry for unfettered freedom and absolute and unrestrained choice, the reality about abortion is that it does not give freedom or indeed any choice. The reality is that the freedom espoused by these voices is in fact enslavement. It is enslavement because the after-effects, that is, the effects of grief, trauma, sorrow, and anguish – actually paralyse these sufferers. The choice so dearly craved has not been a choice at all. It cannot be a genuine choice because the rhetoric has been biased towards feminist ideology of women first, abortion on demand. No other real choice is offered. Even pro-choice individuals admit that women have little or no knowledge about what is actually involved in an abortion. Most importantly women are not told of the possible psychological, spiritual and physical effects. What possible choices can these be? What type of freedom is this enslavement and paralysis of emotions, which lead to the psychological ill health of whole families and nations? Where are the voices of those calling for choice and freedom when the breakdown of the woman and her family structure occurs?

When God created human beings He designed them in his own image (Gen 1:27). He endowed them with a heart that can love. He gave them a conscience where He can speak directly to them. It is his own private sanctuary where the person and God can meet. He shares his own knowledge and experience with them. He implanted into their very being his own essence "love" (Ps. 103). He covenanted Himself to them. He gifted them with Himself and gifted them with others like them as extensions of themselves and Himself. He became for them the source of all being, including their very being, their very existence.

Abortion is the antithesis of all the gifts from God. It is saying "No" to Him and his gifts. It is the severing of the covenant, which He has established. From the point of an abortion, the journey back to the Father is painful and fraught with many obstacles.

It is crucially important to understand why abortion is so destructive. Why it is not confined only to the aborting mother, father, family, but also wounds God and humanity?

First to be wounded is the Almighty Father from whom the desire and design for the new human being emanates. "Before I formed you in the womb I knew you" (Jer 1:4). From all eternity this new child was beloved of God, known by Him, desired by Him. God is wounded in his justice, in his mercy and in his creativity. Jesus is wounded. His cross becomes heavier. The Holy Spirit is wounded. He has been cheated in his creativity as Lord and Giver of Life. The Spirit has animated the desires and designs of the Father. He has painted on the canvas of the new creation with the master craftsman's brush the image of Jesus the Lord. Through abortion the gift from the Lord and Giver of Life is fiercely refused.

The mother and father of the aborted infant are wounded seriously if not critically. Whilst research into Post Abortion Syndrome suggests that only a small percentage of individuals suffer from this syndrome, it is my contention that without exception *every one* of those who experience an abortion will at some time in their life experience its crippling effects. Why do I make this assertion? Because there is a line in Sacred Scripture which clearly and unequivocally says "I will put my law within them and I will write it on their hearts" (Jer 31:33). This verse does not suggest that only a small percentage of humanity will have the law written on their hearts but *all* of humanity.

The law of God may not be accepted, understood, or believed *but it is written*. It may become blurred, suppressed, weakened or even denied, *but it is written.* Therefore if it has been written and imprinted on the heart of every human creation, then in due course it must exert its influence. With the influencing will come a moment of reflection, a moment of clarity, a moment when the enormity of what was done will be clearly seen, and from this point onwards those involved in whatever way in an abortion will never be the same again. That instant of recognition will become the central point or the decisive point in the life of the aborting women. The history, especially of the woman, will be divided into pre- and post abortion. Her personal history will never be continuous again. Her memory, her psychology, and even her physiology will be fractured. As the birth of Jesus divided chronological time from BC (Before Christ) to AD (Anno Domini – Year of the Lord), so too the abortion will divide time and history into a pre- and post abortion period. Never again will the woman or the father of the child or the grandparents or the abortionists ever know again what it is like not to have had or performed an abortion.

Many reasons are offered in explanation for why the abortion was necessary. However, women who abort are themselves victims of irreversibly tragic events often beyond their control. They become refugees of societal illnesses. This is not to diminish in any way the heinous crime that is abortion, but it is an observation that while it may be very easy to "blame" and find "fault" with the woman herself, it is ultimately the abandonment by society of its weakest members. This abandonment takes the form of deception of the woman by telling her that her role as a mother, nurturer, protector, is secondary to her personal achievement. It is the abandoning of the vision of woman being most fruitful and blessed. It is the abandoning of the belief that a child is the future both now and in eternity. It is horrific abandonment.

For a woman to arrive at the decision to abort her infant child, societal mores, familial mores, pressures, coercion and fear have decreed that final decision. Personal mores developed over her lifetime have influenced the final outcome. It is not to say that only her mores have decreed the outcome but they have influenced the final decision. Often where there has been weakened morality in the life of the individual, abortion is countenanced.

As the evil of the first parents introduced sin unto all future generations, so again evil with the co-operation of others inflicts further death on society.

The destruction of innocence, primal and spiritual, is at the very heart of abortion. The loss of innocence coarsens and blurs the timeless bond between God and his creation. It tyrannises life. I am strongly convinced that the loss of innocence and hence the individual's sensitivity to that innocence are at the heart of post abortion suffering – the hydra that is abortion.

Repeatedly (in my office) I have listened to and counselled women who have had an abortion and who have spoken of nightmares. The same nightmare surfaces with a large number of them. The words, the descriptions and the expressions may vary but the theme is always the same. "I am in a big *white* room. It's pure *white* at first then it's splattered with *blood everywhere."* Or "I can see *pure white snow* I am surrounded by it. Then suddenly there is *blood splattered everywhere"* or "I am wearing a beautiful *white wedding gown* then suddenly it's smudged with *blood* and it's dirty and ugly" or "I'm floating on a beautiful fluffy *white cloud* and it's so peaceful. Then suddenly the cloud turns *red like blood* and I fall." Another dream often retold is one in which snakes attempt to devour the dreamer, or snakes surround the dreamer menacingly. Again the person's bedroom seems to be infested with aggressive, writhing snakes.

Simply looking at the content of the dream would suggest its meaning. It doesn't require a degree in dream analysis to interpret the symbols. The most revealing parts of these dreams are the colours white and blood red. This suggests that the dreamer or woman post abortion perceives at the deepest level what the abortion has meant for her. The colours in particular express her understanding of innocence and guilt. Her innocence prior to the abortion (white) and her pain and abhorrence over her decision to abort, and her guilt (blood red) over what she has done, manifests in this manner.

When we work through, step by step, the meanings behind the symbols, the woman speaking about her dreams is able to recognise and verbalise her feelings about the abortion. Once the dream has been discussed (often repeatedly), it usually stops recurring.

Both religious and non-religious individuals speak of similar dreams. This would suggest that an innate knowledge of what is good and what is evil is imprinted on the human spirit. "I will put my law within them and I will write it on their hearts" (Jer 31:33). The natural law is imprinted on all humanity whether we understand it or not. Further, the response to the violation of the natural law is experienced in a similar way, whether an individual professes religious belief or not.

Evidence of this is found with those women who profess or have a religious belief, who pray, can ask God for forgiveness and ask their child for forgiveness. They experience healing much more quickly than those do who do not profess or want to know about God. Forgiveness from a higher being gives the women permission to grieve, to acknowledge the terrible mistake made, lay the baby to rest and begin the journey homewards.

The journey is painful, yet healing is possible and the Lord God offers his forgiveness even for the most grievous of sins: "Though your sins are like scarlet, they shall be like snow" (Is. 1:18). A forward movement is often followed with a backward step. However, once embarked upon the healing journey, with much courage, trust and goodwill, the Lord ensures that He brings this sorrowful daughter (and at times son) home. He introduces the grieving person to her (or his) child.

The journey to the abortion clinic may have taken many years. So too the journey homewards is not instantaneous but is fraught with obstacles, pain, regret, sorrow, tears and at times hopelessness. But the end is peace. This journey is fraught with fears that require much courage to confront. To face the reality that a mother has willingly taken her child to die is an unhappy prospect. Yet, even in its ugliness it must be confronted so the ugliness does not remain lodged deep within, continuing to wreak its vengeance.

For those who do not know God nor want to know Him it is more difficult. They must learn to forgive themselves. Often the harshest judge is oneself. Implementing recognised models to deal with grief and loss does assist these women to come to terms with their abortion. However, their *joie-d'vivre* is still absent, the sparkle in their eyes is still absent. Invariably I know that that they will be seeing a counsellor again sometime in the future. Next time they will require help perhaps for some other grief or maybe other psychological or psychosomatic issue because whilst "sense" has been made of the abortion, the heart is not appeased or rested.

Those who turn to God for forgiveness and healing become absolutely and convincingly pro-life. Where before they may have been anti-abortion because of the pain they have experienced, now they become fully convinced of the sacredness of all human life. They find a new understanding. They experience the Mercy of God and are humbled by it. Indeed their whole demeanour and life change.

Alternatively, those who do not wish to turn to God for forgiveness and simply rationalise their experience remain convinced "that abortion is OK in certain circumstances such as rape, foetal abnormalities or even for career choice". There is a dramatic difference in the outcomes of the two groups.

"Our sins testify against us." (Is 59:12)

Sally's Story

How do I begin, where do I start.

Many many years have rushed by. In that time I have experienced anguish and pain of unbelievable proportion, crippling emotional and spiritual anguish has surrounded me like a shroud of death. Of course this death shroud is the result of the two abortions to which I chose to have.

I was so young so vulnerable only seventeen, for many years prior to this age I had delved into every kind of life destroying behaviour possible e.g, drugs and promiscuous behaviour. I wanted desperately to leave home but my emotional and spiritual maturity was stunted and self-esteem was nil. I did leave home, the drug use and promiscuity increased along with the desolation and despair of repeated sin. This resulted of course in pregnancy I had to tell my mother and father. Their indignation and shock was palpable. My father did not speak of this. My mother maintained that the child may be disabled and it would be better to have an abortion. I did not argue. I went to the clinic as told to do the feeling was for all of us to sweep it under the carpet, forget it.

From that moment in time my life stopped and nothing has been the same, nothing has meaning. My behaviour continued but with the added edge of suicide in mind. Death was like a chain around my neck. A few years later, another pregnancy, another abortion. Oh God. My then boyfriend did not want a child so again I chose abortion. I had finally hit rock bottom. God in his mercy a few months later allowed me to meet the man I was to marry. Some of the pain was dulled, but of course the wedding was rushed because you know, I was pregnant again, thank God I had my fiancé's support otherwise I would have repeated the atrocities.

Ironically the fear of a child with a disability did eventuate and life from then on became confused with self-blame. I was sure this was God's punishment because of the abortions. The sins of the past came to me as a son with multiple disabilities Another loss, another burden. But the love I feel for this child, this injured imperfect human being has been the greatest love of all. He has brought me through life with capacity to find dignity and value in every human being.

Many years of searching to be healed of my pain and loss over the abortions followed the birth of my son. Maybe God in his wisdom wanted me forever healed. So I searched psychiatrists, psychologists. The unending humming will haunt me forever. My son has a severe disability, so much so that he could no longer live at home and we had to make the decision to place him in care. The weekly seeing him and then saying see you next week, went on and on. I searched to be released from the mourning death wish and the how do I make it through the day? Thank God I had my four beautiful other children to dull the pain.

Now twenty-three years down the road finally I came into contact through a dear friend and great Christian woman who described the work of Anne Lastman. Even though she did not know my history, our Lord did and he knew my anguish. She gave me a newsletter. In that edition Anne spoke about the great spiritual damage abortion brings. post abortion grief and the true feelings of being crazy. She knew! She knew because, she had been there. At this time when Anne's name was told to me I was at a very low point in my life, my loss and feelings of grief for my babies was becoming increasingly difficult to cope with. I really don't know if I would have coped for much longer. The feelings of death, guilt, horror, loss and deep anguish were overwhelming me.

After years of searching finally I have encountered the miracle of Anne Lastman. For the first time through prayer and Anne's help, a healing of spirit and mind is occurring. Through prayer God has granted me the privilege of seeing my two beautiful sons Michael and Gabriel. They shine with purity and appear to hold no malice toward me. When I first met them they sat on the green banks of a lazy river together, my two golden haired boys. I sat with them, I was with them through prayer and God's grace. During subsequent prayer time they moved towards the gates of heaven. When I finally said goodbye they entered into heaven. They are safe with Jesus forever resting in his goodness and love.

I see them there through this realm I have been given texts from the bible to read and to be healed. My babies' names await the entry into the book of life through a special mass, which Anne will organise. The plaque in which their names will be etched will be placed in a special memorial garden. They will be acknowledged as having life and being a part of our lives if only for a short time. I found a healing is underway even concerning the great chasm which was left between my mother and me over this terrible tragedy

This treatment which Anne has devised in consultation with Our Lord Jesus Christ is miraculous. Only through the healing of spirit can my babies and I be finally set free. Thank you, God. Thank you, Anne.

4.

World or Divine Anchored Humanity

Repeatedly efforts are being made to anchor human value and human dignity horizontally rather than vertically. By this I mean world approved values and world approved dignity. However, in doing this, the fabric of humanity weakens because world values and world dignity are transient. They are passing and weak. They belong to a time and an era. Further, by such anchoring we misunderstand the nature of human beings who are designed in the "image of God" (Gn 1:27) and are destined for a relationship and an eternity with Him.

The horizontal anchoring pursues and speaks a language alien to the human design. It is committed to entertaining the mundane world and all its offerings and speaks about life as a temporary mechanism to be enjoyed, lived, and terminated according to individual whim. Horizontal anchoring denies the sacredness and the origins of all life. It denies the sacred and invisible reality. Only what can be seen, touched, felt, smelled, has any value. The unseen world of God, the eternal destination, is viewed as the nonsense of the feeble-minded.

Horizontal anchoring idolises the "self". Thus it is able to select what it sees as "good" and therefore is fit to live and what is "not good" is summarily disposed of. In this atmosphere no-one is sacred. Therefore no-one is safe because only those with a world recognised value may live, while those who do not fit according to the world reckoning (the sick, elderly, disabled, and foetus) are a disposable commodity. Horizontal anchoring creates the scapegoating phenomenon whereby selected individuals are sacrificed to the god "society", to the god "convenience", to the god "choice", and to the god "rights".

This scapegoating phenomenon is not a new reality nor an invention of the twentieth/twenty-first centuries. However, beginning in mid-twentieth century it has taken on diabolically sophisticated dimensions. In biblical understanding scapegoating meant sacrificing an animal (goat) on which had been laid the sins of the community or of its individual members, in the place of those who sinned. "Aaron shall lay both his hands on the head of the live goat, and confess over it all of the iniquities of the people of Israel, and all their transgressions and all their sins, putting them on the head of the goat and sending it away into the wilderness by means of someone designated for the task." (Lev 16:21) The modern "goats" to be sacrificed by horizontally anchored society are the weak and marginalised. They are those without a voice, especially infants in the womb. Like the biblical scapegoat the modern scapegoat is banished to the realm of the societal desert where death is assured.

With this type of anchoring, the societal psychic fabric must also change to accommodate the emerging coarseness and desensitisation, which must accompany it.

Vertical anchoring, on the other hand, graces the human being with an inestimable worth. In the words of the Psalmist we are told that "You have made them a little lower than God and crowned them with glory and honour" (Ps 8:5). Vertical anchoring sets the human individual at the apex of divine creation. The human person is the last and ultimate work of God. Within each new creation there is a majesty which only God is capable of giving. Therefore vertical anchoring serves to allow us to view all of humanity as an ever new and divine initiative and as a gift where no one has more "right" to be than another, because the other's dignity is equal and guaranteed.

God-centred anchoring (vertical) honours the works of his hands. All works. Whereas world centred anchoring (horizontal) seeks to accommodate the self, the fit, the convenient and woe to those who do not fit into a specific mould. God-centred anchoring does indeed allow us to be our "brother's keeper" (Gen 4:9) and not be "conformed to this world" (Rom 12:2) It allows us to love, accept and rejoice in our littlest pre-born neighbour, our sickest neighbour and our neighbour who may be different in any way. Vertical anchoring (God) understands that the very real essence of the human being rests in its relationship with God. St Augustine joyfully proclaims our being created for God and we are unable to rest until our rest is in Him.

World-centred anchoring blinds individuals and societies and lulls them into an apathetic mindset where intrinsic values, dignity and life become changeable and disposable. This is the mindset that is able to pick and choose who lives and dies. God-centred or vertically anchored humanity is not trivialised. It understands the eternity factor, while world-centred humanity collapses into a deep moral malaise and eventually condemns itself to extinction. The "now" factor is only temporary.

Perhaps the greatest tragedy that faces modern society is not the possibility of another world war; nor even nuclear war, nor germ warfare, or even global terrorism. The greatest tragedy that faces the modern human is the ever-increasing collective muteness in the face of such evils as abortion and the rising tide of voices calling for legalisation of euthanasia, embryonic stem cell research, and perhaps the final assault against God, cloning. These evils speak a language of death and yet are passé by modern thinking.

A further and greater tragedy and treachery is the societal march towards deification of itself, thus committing the most serious of crimes against God. This is idolatry, and idolatry has always been severely punished.

"In arrogance the wicked persecute the poor." (Ps 10:2)

5.

Moral Malaise

At the very heart and root of abortion will be found a pernicious moral malaise, multiple losses, suffering, fear and a negative or absent relationship with God. There is a loss of the sense of the sacred. Abortion cannot happen otherwise.

Perhaps before we look at what goes into the moral malaise Pandora's Box, it is important to clearly understand the terms "moral" and "malaise". The dictionary defines "moral" as concerned with being able to make a distinction between goodness and badness, or with the distinction between right and wrong conduct founded on the moral laws. The word "malaise" means, bodily discomfort, especially without development of specific disease; a feeling of unwell ness. Combined, these two words give an indication of the state of society at the present time.

There appears to be an uneasiness and confusion, especially in the area of morality. There is a sense in which society has changed from certainties about beliefs and conduct to uncertainty and disarray and confusion. An attitude shift has left society bereft of higher wisdom and hope. We now see a new paganism which has resulted in a decline of the sense of the sacred and which has in turn led to a loss of the awareness of God and his created order. There appears to be a persistent and certain pressure to call good evil, and evil good, thus insidiously changing the structure and moral order of things. The verbal and social engineers have over a short period of time succeeded in convincing humanity that past beliefs and absolutes were restrictive and inhuman and set about, with the help of all forms of media, to change the existing order.

The past seventy years, whilst free of general world wars, have been witness to more pernicious warfare. This era has witnessed the introduction of television worldwide with its at first softly, softly approach to change. (Now there is no longer a need to tread softly.) Television today blatantly parades its perversions through storylines designed to manipulate the mind of the viewer to its way of thinking. This era has succeeded beyond its expectations, including the Internet, with its offering of available pornography and other perversions. It has witnessed space travel of unprecedented magnitude. It has been a passive witness to previously unknown scientific findings. It has witnessed the introduction of the contraceptive pill resulting in the sexual revolution with its immeasurable negative effects leading to a moral decline on a grand scale.

We have witnessed unparalleled change, some good and some appalling. Amongst the changes has been the rise of the feminist movement both in society and the Church. This particular movement has been one of the powers and strengths behind the demand for liberalised abortion and has fought hard and achieved its goals.

The feminist movement in many cases has been helpful in raising the awareness of past injustices on women, ameliorating the lot of the modern woman. However, it has also contributed to the loss of dignity of the feminine and the feminisation of the male, and erosion of the male identity leading to a confusion of roles and identity. The loss of dignity of the male has in turn led to the weakening of fatherhood, where today a father can actually insist and takes his pre-born child to be killed.

Past moral definites have also suffered at the hands of the new social engineers whose benefactors and supporters have been strident in their demands for equality in all areas of human endeavour including the liberation of all sexual behaviours. Of course this sexual liberation with its agents of change has not ultimately bettered the lot of the woman. In fact it has resulted in a loss of sense of self-worth, the loss of her intrinsic value as a woman. These so-called bearers of change have in fact dealt the human species a tragic blow, with both male and female being the sufferers.

Perhaps the most tragic of all the assaults on past definites have been the ravages these changes have wrought on the family, the centre point and stable hub of humanity. This invasion into and assault on the family is not a localised phenomenon but appears to have infected every nation, tribe, culture and race. The newfound ideology of the social engineers, of the feminist brigade, together with media compliance, has found its disenchanted and therefore willing servants to implement and carry out the changes in a most subtle and nefarious way. The changes have not wrought a new, higher and more equitable moral order but the insecurity of moral sterility, a moral jungle without set standards.

In his encyclical *Evangelium Vitae* (1995)[2] Pope John Paul II rightly calls today's society one immersed in a culture of death. It may be appropriate to look at past times and societies and see why today, more than at any other time, we have the dubious honour of living in a "culture of death". A look at three past societies and their moral beliefs and truths may help us to see how sophisticated, deadly and expendable we have become.

The attitudes, feelings and beliefs about death issues such as abortion, euthanasia, infanticide, and fratricides are not new, and they have existed since the first sin in the Garden of Eden. We have not invented anything new. What we have done, however, is to improve on methods and techniques to carry out these deaths.

Ancient Greece with its pantheon of gods and goddesses permitted abortion and euthanasia (Greek word meaning *good death*). Ancient Greek doctors knew how to remove the foetus from its mother's womb by using either herbal concoctions or surgical procedures. However, whilst abortions were carried out, there was a sense that it was wrong and that the child was precious. The only acceptable reason for an abortion (for them) was to save the life of the mother.

Euthanasia simply means an earlier death than through the natural course of events. Its proponents would suggest that it is death or dying gently and with dignity. Perhaps a more emotive term for euthanasia is the one used to justify the act: *Mercy killing.* Where mercy comes into this is beyond understanding. There is no mercy in knowing that someone, who is supposed to be loved, chose to, or is encouraged, to terminate his or her life prematurely or for convenience. Naturally, the reason given for euthanasia is to alleviate the suffering of the dying or very ill person.

Suffering is part of life; we inherited this when Adam and Eve sinned. However, suffering experienced in its reality is difficult for all concerned. It is difficult to watch and difficult to experience. This does not mean that we have the moral freedom to alleviate it at all costs. Again, as with abortion, so with euthanasia, there is stealing involved. What is stolen is stolen from God. Both with abortion and euthanasia human beings usurp God's authority over life and death. A very wise person spoke these words about suffering: "You know people don't like to suffer. They don't like to suffer in their own lives but especially they don't like to see suffering in someone else, especially if they are not suffering at the time." A special friend of mine said, "To watch someone suffer and be helpless disturbs our notion of how things should be. Suffering says that things aren't perfect and in fact suffering says to us that we are finite." This particular friend, after much of her own suffering, is now with her Lord.

Another ancient society with strong views on abortion was Assyria where any attempt to terminate a pregnancy was deemed a crime and the woman was sentenced to death by violent means. Whilst Assyria was very obviously anti-abortion, ancient Rome on the other hand permitted it. In fact a husband had the right to demand that his wife have an abortion if he so chose. However, the philosopher Tertullian was opposed to the idea of abortion and viewed it as murder.

Ancient Greek and Roman cultures were very much in favour of euthanasia. It was even deemed a morally correct act especially if the individuals involved believed that they had outlived their usefulness and were a burden, or it was a way to end life if the pain was too much. It is interesting to note that ancient pagan cultures (including their philosophers) in some ways condoned some form of termination of pregnancy and euthanasia. However, the monotheistic religions condemned the practices, believing that all life is sacred and belongs to God, the Lord and giver of life, the Author of Life.

Whilst different cultures tolerated intentional death, especially for a particular reason, modern society was awakened to its employment by the Hitler regime of the 1930s and 1940's. Under this diabolical despot euthanasia clinics were set up and victims chosen because of their illness or inability to work. In fact the very weak, disabled or very ill concentration camp internees became candidates for the clinics, together with those who opposed the Hitler regime or who were already on their death list.

The 20th century witnessed many atrocities including two major world wars and hundreds of smaller localised ones. It saw the attempted extermination of a race of people (Jews) simply because of who they were, euthanasia clinics with unlimited candidates, the almost worldwide legalisation of abortion on demand and the re-emergence of the call to legalise euthanasia, Today we see the cloning issue, the embryonic stem cell issue. Further, the last one hundred years have witnessed the de facto legalisation of homosexuality, now demands for recognition of this through same-sex union legitimisation or same-sex marriage, rabid feminism, increase in suicide rates, especially youth suicide, and the AIDS virus. As the Holy Father John Paul II has said, it is a culture of death.

A culture of death does not develop overnight but evolves slowly and insidiously. For modern society, the contraceptive pill has fuelled this culture of death. The introduction of this weapon meant that control over life and death was wrested from God and placed into the hands of mere humans who then proceeded to devalue the very thing over which they sought control.

The introduction of the contraceptive pill and other contraceptive devices served to slowly cheapen and demean sexuality, reducing it to a mere tool for pleasure or leisure time activity. This device for controlling the nature of sexuality and making this most sacred and intimate of human activities mundane was only the precursor to the further devaluation of the dignity and essence of life. The sacredness of sexuality had to be deeply obscured, erased, calumniated; and freedom to self-destruct had to be encouraged before moral malaise could develop.

The moral malaise of a society infects and affects families, individuals, children, legislators and legislation, and renders them vulnerable to demonic machinations. Moral malaise also brings with it a unique kind of suffering, abandonment, and a society with hedonistic aspirations leading to absolute devaluation of all that is sacred and holy. Where a society becomes a society of flesh lovers it is only a matter of time before its value is grossly diminished and the sins of abortion, euthanasia, homosexuality, lesbianism, murder, rape, and so on become part of the existing panorama.

Where the weakening of moral definites and structures takes place, the loving union between a man and a woman becomes the lustful union, master of those involved. Rather, the union in lifelong marriage between man, woman and God, leading to children whose value is intrinsic to the wellbeing and happiness of God and humanity, is not fulfilled. The lustful union cannot tolerate intruders to destroy self-gratification, the "self" pleasures. Because it cannot permit intruders it must by definition remove all traces of anything that may interfere with its ongoing destructive force. In a society that values hedonism, "life" becomes not only cheap and expendable, but of necessity transient.

If we understand that sexuality, the most intimate, precious and creative aspect of life, is also the most vulnerable, then perhaps we can understand that evil influences consistently and strongly target this area. Sexuality is where a man, a woman and God act co-operatively to generate a new creature for the kingdom of God. Lucifer in his fury cannot create new creatures for his kingdom because he himself is a created being and therefore is unable to create without the co-operation of God Himself. Man and woman can only become co-creators because they have been given the mission and mandate "to be fruitful and multiply" (Gen: 1:28). Satan has no direct commission and therefore cannot be fruitful by his own power. However, he can be fruitful by touching the fruit already created by man, woman and God and spoiling its image. Satan's fury surely must be that creatures lower than himself have been commissioned to perpetuate the work of God whereas he has been reduced to a mere caricature of his former self. Man and woman co-operate with God to continue the work of creation and expansion.

Understanding the sacred nature of sexuality leads to an understanding that when this area is compromised indiscriminately by a hedonistic society wounds result which are very difficult to heal. These wounds become the entry point or doorway for "unholy" and unwholesome sexuality – sexuality at odds with its original design. The evil one knows that where there are wounds and scars attached to sexuality, other areas of the individual's life including relationships with others and God will be affected. By damaging this most intimate aspect of a human's life Satan knows that he strikes at the very heart of society.

It is important to try to understand why abortion is so destructive (apart from the death of the child) to woman, man and society. To do this we must revisit the Creation story in Genesis (Gen 1-3) and follow step by step the creative works of God. He moves. He creates. He calls into being each new creation, beginning with the largest then gradually to the smallest and most exquisite until last of all He created the "woman" (Gen 2:21-25). With tenderness and consummate care

He created one to be a companion, lover, wife, mother and co-creator with Him of future humanity. He enclosed within her spirit the secret, which is "love". He enfleshed and enmeshed within this last creative act His own plan and hope for humanity. In the creation of woman He created his masterpiece, his joy. Knowing this, is it any wonder that abortion will cause a change in the psyche of every aborting mother and hence change the original design of her? It would be surprising if this were not so.

How can we equate abortion with the sin of Genesis? Simply because the same lie is being told and retold approximately 40,000,000 times a year in connection with abortion, and the same lie continues to be believed, "you will not die" (Gen 3:4). Again man and woman and society are being manipulated and deceived and again she (the woman) betrays and surrenders that most exquisite area where God has imprinted his secret "love".

Abortion shatters and destroys the primal innocence of men and women and violates and exposes crudely that secret of God, "love", planted at the very heart of their being. A further reflection of the Genesis saga reveals the role of the male both then and now with the issue of abortion. How weak the male appears as he passes the blame: "The woman whom you gave to be with me, she gave me fruit from the tree and I ate" (Gen 3:12). Today, those same words and actions (I hid) are replayed daily as the men (husbands, boyfriends, fathers) march docilely, or alternatively, aggressively, towards the abortion clinic and wait idly by while their child/grandchild (the fruit) is destroyed. How tragic it is to see these males abandon their child and not even voice their opinion or lift a finger to prevent their baby from facing a lonely and cruel death. How tragic that the infant dies without its male parent even murmuring a noise of protest.

Pagan Rome is being revisited. Rome, where the father had the right to kill or cause his child to be killed because it was his wish to do so. Today it is perhaps more monstrous. All too often it is not only the father, but more likely the mother, the nurturer, who chooses and is given the legal right to terminate the life of her child, while at times the father is given no choice in the matter at all.

Abortion today is spoken about in terms of "rights". Within the abortion industry everyone has "rights". The only one who does not have any rights is the child or "victim" whose own "right" to life, selfhood, and self-determination are summarily snuffed out.

Truly with abortion we can see the ultimate form of sexual abuse and exploitation of women and men and the ultimate form of abuse of children. We can also see the ultimate rejection by humanity of its future. We see humanity on the road to self-destruction.

Today's society could and would teach pagan Rome some lessons. In today's society it is the mother, the nurturer, the safe haven, who demands the right and is given the right and affirmation, that to dispose of her own child is empowering and beneficial for her. Yes, pagan Rome and pagan societies could learn much from this new paganism.

The greatest irony of this new society and societal mores is the perception that women have been freed from past tyrannies and accorded the respect previously unknown to them. How ignorant is this really? And who believes this nonsense? Women have been freed from or even robbed and cheated of the function for which they were exclusively made. They have been accorded "equal rights" in the arena of employment. Their life and burdens have been lightened by innovations designed to alleviate hardships but at what price? The respect demanded by them has been given but it is a "gilded" respect. Gilded to appear as gold but in reality the cheapest of metals, because to achieve this respect they have surrendered their exquisite design and become womb-less automatons without compassion for the treasure (child) of their own womb. To call this respect for women is to add insult to injury. The modern Eves who bellow "non-servium" have dealt a death sentence not only on themselves but also on society present and future.

Grace

To my darling daughter Grace.

Well I am finally am able to do this – it has only taken eight years, as you well know.

Eight years of anguish squashed and denied, manifesting itself in all sorts of strange ways. And all along it was you my darling girl – letting me know you were there and telling me in your own way that I would have to acknowledge you one day if I was ever to heal and give you the goodbye, on this earth, that you truly deserve.

As I write this the familiar pain, the tightening in the chest, the lump in my throat – it's all there still and I guess it will always be there, but there is no anger anymore angel, just a lingering sadness. The type of grief only other mums of terminated babies could ever understand. The guilt is passing as I embrace you as my baby and express the love I have for you in my heart – as I set myself free to do that.

I know now that you are there, Grace, in Heaven with God and being looked after and protected as you should have been on earth. It is the saddest thing in the world that you are not here with me today – a happy eight-year-old with the world at your little feet – but you are not. How do I know you were a girl? I don't – it's just a feeling, an instinct, and its always been there. So I have named you in the way you should have been named and found you after all these years. And I am getting better-as you want me to.

I love you my baby. I am sorrier than words could ever begin to touch on for failing you in my duty as a mum and for rejecting you when you were there. Your little heart beating, your tiny, tiny body growing, waiting to be nurtured. Expecting to be welcomed. There are no excuses, no reasons, no explanations that can really change anything today-I did not believe I would be a good mum and that decision has haunted me until today.

Grace there is no greater pain than the realisation that the most terrible mistake of your life can never be undone and we will never have the chance, in this life, to know one another as mother and daughter should-you know that. Still now, the magnitude of what I have done, the sheer reality of stopping a life which was mine to nourish, the rejection of a gift from God that so many are never blessed with – it is almost unbearable – but I do.

I love you now as I never did then – in the way that I love my three children on earth, your brothers and sister, you are my baby as they are and I will always hold you in my heart. I cannot physically hold you. I cannot see you – but I am finally free to love you, and I believe you are wrapped in my love. I believe that you love me too and that you forgive me. That you want me to smile when I think of you, safe in the belief that I will see you again some day and that I will know you. That we will have our chance.

It has taken me what feels like forever to get to this day Grace, and so much has happened since the short time you were with me. I can now thank God for all that happened, good and bad, for the history that led me to where I am today – three beautiful children and a wonderful husband – a life to be proud of. You helped steer me here little girl, so thank you. It is because of you that I am now the mum I always wanted to be. There will always be a void, but that's OK, I can live with that now and I have reached some sort of peace – it is vulnerable and shaky on days, it is fragile when I think about you for too long, but that's OK.

I don't know that there is much to be gained from talking to you about what happened all those years ago but I will try. It was the most terrifying moment of my life, to discover that I was pregnant with you. I think my mind knew instantly what I was going to do. So my lifelong objection to abortion went out of the window – I found a new way to look at it. A scientific explanation I could grip onto – a way to deny you the little soul that survived.

I used phrases to myself like, "mass of cells" and I wrote a long letter at the time, attempting to justify your fate – it was all very dishonest. I have since destroyed the letter, not believing a word of it really. I told myself that I was not ready, and I wasn't, that it was not the right time, and it wasn't. Your dad was not the right man, and he wasn't. I would be no good at it – who knows? Does it really matter now – I didn't even try.

I said at the time that you deserved better. So instead of a privileged life surrounded by a loving family, I let them suck you out from the warmth of my womb where you were nestled, discard you like rubbish and sent me on my way. I still cannot drive down that very busy road in Melbourne, little girl – it's where your life ended and mine changed forever.

Everyone close to me was affected by that awful day – none more so than you and I though. We were in this sad nightmare together, weren't we? I felt very depressed after I let you go – many days were hard to face, some I didn't. I told myself it was hormones. I was told to expect this by the terribly cold staff at the clinic – the ones that sent me into a tiny cubicle with a pad, a paper gown and said "wait till we come and get you." They don't even look at you in the eye. They don't seem to know your pain, and I hope that they really don't understand what they are doing.

They put my legs in stirrups and got out their vacuum but forgot to tell me how much I would miss you. How this day would never go away. How I would dream about you eight years after that day. They forgot to tell me how I would get to the day when even to make a cup of tea would make me cry because the memories refused to go away. But I don't really blame them Grace – it was me.

After a few months I went into denial – a very important thing really, if someone is to get on with their life. I can't tell you what I thought in the many years in between – the truth is that I tried forget. I tried very hard not to think about you at all. You crept up on me at times and sent me into a spin, but only temporarily – I would shut down and move. In my heart I knew you were always there though.

So why now Grace? I guess only you can answer that. Was it because I had a little girl? Is it because my family on this earth is complete? Or was my time up? I don't know the answer for sure; maybe it was all these things.

As I started on the road to healing, I had no inkling of how to go about it, but you guided me. At first it seemed crazy to name you – see even then I didn't want to give you an identity for fear it would undo me. But I did it. Grace seemed the natural name for you. I said it without even pausing to think. It is the middle name of your great grandma and your sister and I really believe it was the name God had already chosen for you before even your mother could bring herself to give it to you. I hope you like it.

Soon I will go to Church Grace and say goodbye to you before God. I think you are waiting for me to do this so that you too can move on, so please help me be strong because even though I am your Mum I am more scared than you. There are some very good people out there who understand the grief of mums like me – I think they are Angels sent to help our spirits to heal and I could not have reached this point without them (here I mention especially Anne who has journeyed with me and helped me to get to this day.)

They will allow me the Mass I did not ever think I deserved and I am so grateful for that. You will have a plaque of your own as a living memento that you have existed, even if only for a short time, in this world and that your soul lives on – and that you are loved.

More than anything Grace, I am grateful to you for not giving up on me. I love you baby girl, and I will see you again. You will always be in my heart and your soul will be forever with mine as it should have been from the beginning and for the rest of our days …

Love Mum.

6.

Humanae Vitae

Pope Paul VI's encyclical, *Humanae Vitae*, "On Human Life" has as its focus the sacredness of human life. It reminds me very much about the biblical story of the institution of the monarchy by the Israelites.

When the people of Israel demanded a king "to govern us like other nations" (1 Sam 8:5), God warned that a human king would not be a just king. He would enslave them, their sons and daughters and take what belonged to them so that their lives would ultimately become unbearable (1 Sam 8).

The people of Israel refused to listen to the words of God, spoken through the prophet Samuel, so God relented and permitted an earthly king to be enthroned where previously He had reigned exclusively. Of course his prophecies came to pass.

While the monarchy or rule of David and Solomon were reputedly glorious, they also set the scene for the future destruction of the people of Israel. The division of the kingdom (North and South) in the tenth century was followed by the exile into Babylon and the enslavement of the people in the sixth century, and the destruction of the temple. The division began a series of events leading to complete and utter control of the people by different ruling dynasties, e.g., Persians, Greeks, Romans. Each new ruling dynasty changing, controlling and weakening the already tenuous life and spirituality of the people of the covenant. To my way of understanding, *Humanae Vitae* has the same prophetic dimensions.

Humanae Vitae was issued in 1968. However, cultural changes towards marriage and family had become obvious during the 1950s and 1960s. While the seeds of this change were planted much earlier with Malthus and Darwin's theory of evolution, the middle of the twentieth century saw the rationale gain momentum. This period was a period of discontent, post-World War II confusion, followed by the Korean War and then the Vietnam War. The explosion of the sexual revolution occurred at the same time and was followed by the emergence of the drug culture.

From this melee emerged Vatican II and the prophetic *Humanae Vitae*. *Humanae Vitae* was a warning direct from God. We know the Holy Spirit inspired it because humanity's immediate response was to rebel against the document. No past or future papal document elicited such a response, as did *Humanae Vitae*. No document has caused such divisions both inside and outside the Church.

To look back from the vantage point of forty-five years, it is clear to see how prophetic the words were: "It is also to be feared that the man, growing used to the employment of anti-conceptive practices, may finally lose respect for the woman and, no longer caring for her physical and psychological equilibrium, may come to the point of considering her as a mere instrument of selfish enjoyment, and no longer his respected and beloved companion " (HV, 17).

The anti-conceptive devices and practices opened up the door to enslavement. No longer was sexuality something sacred but a leisure time activity to be engaged in by all irrespective of state in life. The anti-conceptive devices and practices opened the doors to a liberalised sexuality that promised to bring previously unknown pleasures to those who had felt burdened by past sexual mores. Further, they opened the doors to rampant teenage sexuality, an explosion of STDs, followed by unplanned pregnancies leading to an enormous and monstrous escalation in abortion rates. The prophecies of enslavement had begun to be fulfilled.

As I studied *Humanae Vitae,* more and more I became convinced that this was a document of immeasurable value and the most important document by a pontiff. The timing of the promulgation was exquisite. Its release was so appropriate and timely. The 1960s with its spirit of rebellion and change needed stabilising.

Into the cauldron of change from past moral definites, past certainties, past ideals, the Holy Spirit attempted to infuse and reawaken the knowledge and notion that God was still in control. The Holy Spirit was using the document to alert modern society that the new morality was seeking to eliminate and dethrone God as King and enthrone the creature as "king". He was giving the warning that to remove the sacred from creation would lead to idolatry of the worst kind.

Humanae Vitae arrived at the most appropriate time. It attempted to curb the sexual revolution; it attempted to warn about the future breakdown of family. It warned that fertility control in the hands of individuals would lead to mass destruction of other unborn individuals. It emphatically warned that relationships between male and female would forever change and that the female would be the greater sufferer. It warned that to cheapen life at its very genesis would lead in a short time to the call to cheapen life at the end of its span. It warned that marriages and children would be placed in jeopardy by a society whose sexual morality was confused and weakened. It warned that anti-conceptive devices and practices meant a big NO to God and to children and to future society. It meant that it would lead to further degradation of man and woman and marriage. It would lead to calls for irregular unions. It would lead to complete breakdown of society.

Humanae Vitae sought to warn that there was a plan to re-invent humanity and the culture of the human species. The re-invention required that old mores had to be discredited and abandoned and a new understanding of the benefits of liberal sexuality both inside, outside, and parallel to marriage were to be seen as good and desirable. In this newly re-invented society children were to be sexually active and free from constraints especially from parents, and contraception and abortion were to be free and available in order to complete the picture. Indeed as we review the past 30-40 years it is possible to see that this diabolical plan has not only found root but has mushroomed into a deadly cocktail leading to the culture of death.

It was into this miasma of change, both spiritual and secular and much suffering that *Humanae Vitae* was announced on the world stage. *Humanae Vitae* was the document which came out against the social engineers. It attempted to sound the warning bells about possible future disasters. Very sadly it was a document not embraced either by the Catholic world or society in general. Hence the rampant spread of unbridled sexuality, unholy sexuality, contraception of unimaginable order, abortions in unprecedented numbers, overt demands for homosexual acceptance as a "normal" lifestyle leading to demands for same-sex marriage, and the slow and insidious disintegration of the family.

I began this chapter by saying that the document *Humanae Vitae* reminded me very much of, and had the same prophetic quality as the first book of Samuel. It still does so. God warned the people both times that doing a specific act would result in wholesale breakdown and destruction. In both cases the warnings were not heeded and the outcome can only be described as tragic. In the immediate past we have been able to see in one generation that trying to usurp control over life from God would lead to societal suffering and ultimately death. We still have not seen what the end result will be. The prophetic word in First Samuel took centuries to unfold; however, sin appears to have escalated at an incredibly fast pace. Today in just 45 years (one biblical generation) we have witnessed the prophetic words of *Humanae Vitae* being fulfilled.

The message of *Humanae Vitae* was not made known or obeyed or believed. However, the prophetic words, "... a man may finally lose respect for the woman and no longer caring for her physical and psychological equilibrium may come to the point of considering her as a mere instrument of selfish enjoyment and no longer his beloved and respected companion*"* (HV, 17), have found fulfilment. Indeed the anti-conceptive practices have contributed to the male losing respect for the woman. Today this is evident in all areas of life, most specifically in the area of abortion. Truly in this area the male uses the woman as an instrument of "selfish enjoyment" and when conception occurs, cares little for the woman or their child. This is clearly manifested in the abortion rate worldwide and the fathers who take their child to be immolated, while they wait passively for the procedure to be completed.

Whilst it is impossible to convince those who have decided to abort their child that there will be long term suffering both psychological and spiritual the facts are clear on this. Abortion grief is real and it exists. It is undeniable. Abortion pain and grief are one of the various death merchants in our society at present. These peddle death through broken hearts. Through anguish. Through fear. Through guilt. Through failure. Post abortion trauma, grief, regret, sorrow, can be deadly because it is silent. It brings death in silence, perhaps just as the death of the infant occurred. The psychological and spiritual death bought at the time of the abortion is the legacy of society's failure to accept *Humanae Vitae;* failure to accept the warning that human beings were attempting to rebuild the Tower of Babel again.

7.

Rachel's Women

A voice was heard in Ramah wailing and loud lamentation
Rachel weeping for her children
She refused to be consoled because they are no more.
(Mt 2:18, quoting Jer 31:15)

To be able to understand the above biblical quote it is important to understand who Rachel was and the reason for her anguish and tears.

Rachel was the daughter of Laban, the brother of Rebekah, who was married to Isaac, the covenant son of Abraham, who was the founding patriarch of the House of Israel. Rachel's story is a love story. Jacob, son of Isaac, had to work very hard to win Laban's approval before he was able to marry her. Fourteen years he had to work to prove his love for her. Whilst Abraham, Isaac and Jacob were patriarchs, Sarah, Rebekah, and Rachel were Hebrew matriarchs.

The above quotation refers to the lament of Rachel, matriarch and ancestress who prophetically weeps for her grandchildren Manasseh, Ephraim and Benjamin and their children, who are killed, deported and/or exiled by the Assyrian dynasty.

Perhaps a more apt application would be the tears wept by the matriarch Rachel over the slaughter of her innocent descendants at the hands of Herod (Mt 2:16-18). Perhaps in a moment of clear sightedness or clear vision Rachel saw the tragedy that would befall her people because of the continuing sin of the people of Israel. Perhaps Rachel glimpsed the bloodied path that her people would continue to walk and which would result in more anguish. Perhaps Rachel clearly saw but did not understand the death of the innocent Hebrew babies which would herald the birth of the Messiah. She saw his entry into the world marked with the blood of the innocent and knew with foreboding what this meant. Perhaps because Rachel was unable to conceive more than two children (and children were considered a blessing in her day) she wept at the wanton slaughter of the babies by order of King Herod.

Perhaps the Old Testament matriarch (Rachel) and the New Testament Matriarch (Mary) weep because babies are no longer considered a blessing from Yahweh. Perhaps through the centuries the matriarchs continue to mourn the generations never to be born. Perhaps, down through the centuries the matriarchs will continue to mourn for the babies that no one will mourn for, or even remember. Perhaps their grief will be the catalyst for the redemption (through grief) of the aborted women and men never born.

Grief is associated with the process of attachment and separation and is usually a very healthy sign. When grief-work and behaviour are present when necessary, it means that the individual is attentive to the reality of the death that has occurred, and is not employing denial strategies, which can and do at times create a completely new set of difficulties. Grief-work ensures that the process of letting go has been commenced and the emotional pain is expressed rather than stalled.

The grief experience is a process by which we realise, adjust and come to terms with a significant loss in our lives. The loss may occur through death; however, grief can be experienced due to a divorce, separation, change of locale, loss of friends or close relationships, loss of career, loss through a miscarriage, loss of long held dreams, loss of possibilities, and loss through abortion. Any sudden loss will elicit grief reaction to some degree. However there can also be deeper persistent grief for "something" lost that was anticipated but due to circumstances never came to fulfilment. Of course the deeper the relationship the stronger the grief reaction.

Whilst grief is acknowledged as a sensitive issue, it has the capacity to affect profoundly the behaviour of those suffering the experience. The behaviour may take many forms such as aggression, depression, weeping, social withdrawal, anger, confusion, embarrassment, deterioration and withdrawal from normal lifestyle activity, sleep changes, daydreaming, fear and anxiety. Indeed the list is endless. Any one or a combination of any of these symptoms may be seen in an individual experiencing grief reaction.

Grief is an in-built response designed to first assist and then promote a return to a normality once a crisis or separation has been faced and dealt with. Grief allows the individual a time of grace, a time to re-gather and reopen the ancestral memory bank and add to this bank more bits of information regarding this newest ancestor. It is a time when our internal life is revisited and eternal life really hoped for. It is hoped that indeed all those "things" we know about heaven are true. Grief permits the grieving individual to be totally vulnerable and to surrender control even if only just for a while. It is a time and reaction of innocence. So we can see that grief is an important function of life. It is important for human recovery. It is vital that when the need arises grief is experienced, expressed and permitted. The absence of this capacity to grieve can occasion the development of malignant syndromes that may, and often do, result.

As an abortion grief counsellor, speaker and writer on the abortion issue, I am at times confronted with individuals who sincerely believe that women who abort their baby do not, and cannot, have the right to a grief reaction. According to them the "choice" to abort has automatically disqualified the aborting male or female from having any emotion about the procedure. Of course this is not so. Far from it; it is normal.

Grief and weeping help the individual come to terms with the loss of a significant one in their lives. However, in the case of abortion neither grief nor weeping is generally permitted. This becomes

"Disenfranchised Grief" (K. Doka, 1989) The aborting woman, child's father, family and society all decree that abortion is a minor procedure, quick, simple, and problem-disposing which requires no psychological processing other than as an inconvenience. *This is not so! Abortion is about death and requires processing as a death experience. Abortion is not the removal of a wart but the violent and premature removal of an infant from its mother's womb for the sole purpose of causing its death.*

For the non-abortive person who has lost a loved one, there are family, friendships, groups and strategies in place to assist during the grieving times. These serve to assist not only with the immediate practical requirements but also as far as family is concerned there will be long term support, compassion, and love. It is understood that the death of a loved one is a sad and difficult time for all concerned. It is expected that grieving will occur and that it may take a long time before a return to as close as normal can be expected. The loneliness and desolation are expected and accommodated. It is our way of acknowledging to the grieving one/s that the one they lost was important and will be missed. The work of grief writers and researchers has greatly helped us to understand that grieving is essential for continued mental health. Experiencing the grief (when the need arises) is as important as love, laughter, joy, silence, and companionship. All are needed to maintain our equilibrium.

For the woman who has aborted, it is an entirely different situation. Beginning with a society that has decreed that abortion is acceptable and is "the choice of the woman" the same society then proceeds to build and maintain social taboos about this procedure. This leads to a collective silence. Into this silence enters the abortive woman who must then live according to the rules, which govern the society with its taboos. That is, she acquiesces to the hidden-ness of her abortion and so must remain silent about any emotions that she may experience about the event.

Because the abortion has been her "choice" alone, or her "choice" with the assistance or coercion of others close to her, it is believed that there should not be any grief associated with the experience. Therefore no grief will be experienced or grief-work required. *This is not so.* Abortion is a death experience. A death has occurred. A violent death has taken place and a life has been summarily terminated. In actual fact two deaths occur when an abortion is carried out: the death of the infant and the death of the woman's primal innocence. Two losses have been sustained and must be dealt with as losses, especially if the woman is to retain her emotional and mental health.

Where there is no grieving the unexpressed grief can paralyse, because it remains unresolved, unacknowledged, leading to psychological impairment. We must clearly understand this because from research we know that denial and suppression are two features most prominent in post-abortive women. Unresolved grief has been suppressed grief and the result of suppressed grief is mental pain.

By denying and suppressing any emotions a woman has about her abortion, the woman (males at some time also) sets into place defence mechanisms guaranteed to protect her from intrusive thoughts which she knows intuitively are too painful to bear. Intrusive thoughts about "baby" have the potential to destroy her "psychological equilibrium".[3] The woman knows that she is unable to cope with the notion that what she aborted was her infant; therefore for her (she considers) it is better to not think about this at all.

To continue feeding the denial factor, the aborting woman learns to become an expert at avoiding anything to do with the issue of abortion. She remains silent and alone battling that "thing" that needs to be dealt with. Her shame and guilt guarantee her silence. Her survival tactics are refined over time, and using these tactics she tries to move on with her life. Of course the repressed event cannot remain neutral and works imperceptibly to change forever the individual's beliefs, understanding of the nature of things and her freedom to live fully as a child of God.

The psychoanalytic theory founded and developed by Sigmund Freud posits that individuals develop defence mechanisms in order to protect the ego or "self" from destructive behaviour. Some of the known defence mechanisms are repression, which is the conscious suppressing of, or restraining of, intrusive and disturbing thoughts. These thoughts are actively suppressed so that they cannot invade the conscious memory and cause anxiety. Of course constant suppression requires enormous amounts of energy leading ultimately to weakened physical and mental state. Denial is another defence mechanism whereby the individual refuses to accept a certain reality. This also requires energy utilisation and diversion leading to mental health issues.

Other defence mechanisms are projection, reaction formation, regression, intellectualisation, rationalisation, and displacement. Post-abortive females employ all of these defence mechanisms. However, some are more prominent than others. Ultimately the role of defence mechanisms is to protect the individual from the impact of reality so that the truth of the reality may be dealt with at a more appropriate time. These defences in effect act as guardians against intrusion of reality and in fact imprison the individual behind a wall of unreality. Continual strengthening of this wall of unreality may eventually lead to psychosis and at times death.

Because defence mechanisms are constructs set in place for self-protection and meant to be of a temporary nature, long-term use of these mechanisms will serve to change the psychological makeup of the individual. Further, there are times when leakage from the subconscious memory about the suppressed or denied trauma work their way into the conscious memory and this spillage serves to cause further suffering. These flashes of memory awaken in the abortion grief prone woman (and male) the enormity of her action (abortion), which in turn engenders new fears, anguish, weeping, and self-loathing. Depression becomes part of her life.

It is also important to understand the loss of the woman's primal innocence if we are to understand grief following an abortion. Primal innocence is the innocence inherent in all humanity. It is the innocence enjoyed by all human creatures before a rupture changes the design. It is the innocence that speaks of sameness of the human species. Primal innocence recognises that all human beings are inter/intra related, unique, and inviolable. It is an in-built mechanism to prevent injury to a like individual. The human species has depended upon this primal innocence for its continuation and survival. This mechanism had to be in place otherwise the original murder of Abel by Cain would have resulted in the destruction of the species.

The destruction of the woman's primal innocence leads to further destruction in relationships. It leads to the destruction of male and female relationships because a barrier must be erected between them (hence those who do not understand post abortion grief), between men and men, (hence violence against children and others), women and women (hence those who reject women who have undergone an abortion).

Those who abort, their partners, or parents of the girl who insisted their daughter take their grandchild to die, must after an abortion, create a new and flawed manner of relating if their relationship is to continue. A conspiracy of silence must be imposed. However, from research into abortion after-effects, abortion grief, sequelae, we know that there often occurs an irreparable breakdown in relationships where an abortion has been jointly agreed upon. Often the couple embark on a series of destructive relationships leading to more anguish and suffering. Abortion actually violates the invisible attraction that exists between males and females, parents and children, and demands that "fig leaves" (Gen 3:7) in the form of self-destructive behaviours be sought. Like the loss of the primal innocence in the Garden of Eden, the psychic connection, once ruptured, can only be restored or repaired by God.

Abortion also severs the permanent covenant imprinted in the human person. Covenant in biblical terms means "relationship", "sacred bond", the intimate and binding "something" or agreement or commitment which acts to safeguard and protect those in the covenantal relationship. For the woman her most intimate covenant is between herself and the one she is designed to protect, that is, her offspring. Following an abortion, that which is sacred (her innocence and her covenantal role) is also violated. Hence her own experience or intuitive knowledge of salvation and/or relationship with her creator, which is situated in the context of her covenantal role as mother, is also broken. The indefinable something that existed before the abortion is gone. No longer does she feel innocent. For most women, even non-religious ones, the sense of loss of any mystery or the sacred is gone.

Often it has been said to me during counselling sessions: "Now I understand what sin is and what sin does". Until this time the sense of sin had not been an issue. "Sin" was what religious fanatics spoke about which others committed. As I listen to these and other similar words I am filled with hope, as I see that the spirit's travail for this loss can be the energiser for future hope. I can really see that sometimes God allows what appears to be an abhorrent evil to happen in order to achieve a greater overall good. While this may appear as decidedly unjust, we can only admit that only God can see the complete picture. The canvas on which every human blueprint has been etched can only be seen completely by the master craftsman. He knows the nuances and their meanings.

Because mourning by abortive women is socially forbidden, validation that something traumatic has happened to her is also absent. In all types of loss, society and individuals can and do acknowledge the existence of the "lost" one. There are memories, images, stories, history, anecdotes, and so on. These ensure that the one who has died is remembered and that the "lost" one was involved in relationships with others. There was a beginning, middle and then an end and a closure to that life. For the abortive woman (and man) there are no tangible "things" to mark their experience of having participated in the creation of a life and definitely no evidence of the death and culmination of that life. There was a beginning to the story but no middle and no ending. There has been no closure. There is no remembering that someone passed by in his or her life that was very important and is no longer.

Added to this there are two most destructive emotions to contend with: guilt and shame. These emotions heighten the depth of grief because they clearly spell accusation and point the finger back onto the self. The pain is all the more difficult because the knowledge is there that this death could have been prevented and for whatever the reason it was not. Mother Teresa was absolutely correct in her understanding of peace when she said, "abortion is the greatest destroyer of peace". It truly is.

Juliet's Story

I guess the biggest realisation of my journey with Anne has been realising that I'm a mum. And that will never change. Having very strong ties with my own mother, and experiencing the unique connection, adoration and respect there, I almost feel the same sense of pride for a daughter I simply can't see.

Hi my name is Juliet and I am a mum. My daughter lives in heaven because six years ago I made an irrational, ill-fated and uneducated decision, which meant I would never meet my daughter Madeleine. But we dance in my dreams – me 30, her 5 – and she spins around dancing and singing, and my heart sinks when she stops and grins at me. She looks like me. And like her father. She has my dark brown hair and eyes, but a gentle whisper and musical voice like her father. This is where I've come to know her. Visualising her as a five-year-old-full of innocence and joy. Although I allow her to live in her reality and me in mine-this is our special place, that is and will always be very sacred.

It hasn't always been this easy to write about my daughter Madeleine, let alone share with you, a reader and complete stranger. It's also never been easy to admit the details – that I am a mum, I have a daughter who would now be five, that she has a name, a face, a body and that if I had said yes to life-she would be here dancing around in my reality.

But my story is not going to centre on the negative. I've come too far in my journey of forgiveness and hope to think along these lines. I'll just say this; that I wish that I had the wisdom, courage, and respect that I have now, six years ago. I wish I had my daughter in my arms. Despite my professional achievements – nothing can fill that hole. I also wish that I had trusted my family enough to tell them that I was pregnant. I wish that I had enlisted their eternal love to help my daughter and me. Although the strength of their heart has always been obvious and cherished, the discovery and telling of these events to them has only deepened my understanding of their eternal protection, love, commitment and faith. Not for one moment have they left my side, both physically and emotionally since telling them about the abortion over the past 12 months. The terror I had dreaded then (six years ago) and since then has never emerged. I expected them to hate me. I expected them to look at me differently. To love me less. To respect me less.

But they didn't. My mum held me in her arms and wept, when I told her. It came out unexpectedly on a park bench, on a footpath, near my house. It was about midnight and raining. Of all the places in the world – here we were. My body by this stage had had enough. It couldn't handle the suffering and the silence any more, which started becoming physically obvious, as my menstruation cycle began playing up and I became very irregular. So on this night it all came out.

For about six months mum had sensed that there was something wrong with me. She had never seen me so moody. So teary. So pained. After six long years of carrying around my secret, I'd had had enough. I had trouble telling her but she assured me that nothing I could tell her would make her love me any less. That was a huge relief. However, I suggested that we should not take bets on that because what I had to tell her was going to rock her world. And why I hear you ask? Because my family is Catholic through and through. Generations of good practising Catholics on both Mum and Dad's side. Irish Catholics too! I had grown up in a pro-life family. A family that had adopted a young boy, who was told as he was growing up that his mother must have loved him so much because she never aborted him. So these factors and many others had compounded my inability to tell my parents that I was pregnant. And then after the abortion, I decided that I would simply never, ever tell them.

So anyway here we were on the park bench and I tell my mum.

She held me and we cried together. The next day she told my dad. And we all cried again. They were simply devastated that they had a granddaughter whom they had never met. They were also devastated that their baby (me) had been agonised for such a long time. If you are reading my story and feel you are at this point – please don't try and carry the cross on your own. Jesus may have but in that He taught us that we don't have to. We have Him and our families for support. Before ever looking at abortion as an option, talk to your family. I didn't trust them enough and look where I ended up. It's simply not worth it.

So since telling my parents and them getting over their initial shock, they have been like a rock either side of me, making sure I was a survivor of my ordeal. The other two rocks in my life over the past seven months have been my counsellor and friend Anne, Jesus and His blessed Mother Mary. The latter I know have never left my side, and by acknowledging as a rock now, I mean their presence in my healing has been very visible and very appreciated.

Anne on the other hand has been my tour leader through this journey of healing. She's led the way through the thick forest of my emotions, my past and my pain. She's drawn back the branches and swept away the debris to help me see inside myself – to hear, witness and relive the steps, the pain, grief and agony. And then to come through the other side- she's stood behind me, waved me on and then waved me goodbye, the forest behind me and the clear path ahead.

I didn't know what to expect when I first started with Anne. I'd seen a counsellor before. Two in fact. Much to my pleasant surprise the counselling with Anne didn't just deal with the post abortion guilt and pain, but also every other pain in my life since day dot. Interestingly, the night after my first session with Anne I went home and wrote a list of every time I had felt let down in my life. Either betrayed by others or myself. I couldn't stop writing. It started with not getting a little baby girl we tried to adopt when I was six, through to my cousin dying, through to issues with my grandmother. It was the best thing that I had ever done and gradually Anne and I worked through my life thus far.

I liken Anne to a tour guide because I understand now only you yourself can work through the healing. But she pointed out the beacons of hope and trust along the way. She's encouraged me to take the back roads, dig up and nurture other pains. She's helped me take road trips to the hearts of others and ask for their forgiveness. She's picked me up when I tripped. And she has shown me that there is a light at the end and promised that I would find rest there. This especially during the times when I wanted to run and hide. She's confronted me like a mirror on my soul and urged me to dig deep for the answers only I know exist. She's challenged me, held me, cared for me and been the counsellor I never knew existed and I never knew I needed. Without her devotion and belief in a better world where would we be? I thank God every day for sending Anne to me and I ask Him to give her the strength, fervour and determination to continue her work. May she know that her reward lies ahead at the gates of heaven.

I have one chapter yet to finish and then the book is complete. That is to again meet with Madeleine's father Kenneth. I've recently told my brother my story and having survived that much-dreaded occasion, the final step of seeing Kenneth seems more achievable. I feel it is important to complete the story with Kenneth and to close the door. I complete the journey that we began together but finished apart and somehow never quite finished. I think it is fair both to him and to myself. This then would allow me to be free to love again when love knocks at my door.

One of the big things that I have learnt is that abortion is not just about the woman – the mother. It's also about everyone connected with that story. Immediate family, cousins, uncles and aunts. Its about an unseen, unknown tremor that can unsettle a family – sometimes a secret tremor, but definitely one that must be tamed, forgiven and healed in that generation. I've learnt about the sins of the father through Anne, and this is one piece of knowledge that I will take with me through my whole life. I will not allow any demons, unspoken hurts or anguishes to languish into the next generation.

So back to Kenneth. I will ask for his forgiveness. He never had a choice in the matter. I made the decision to abort, for both of us. I want him to know that I am sorry. That I have paid a high price but now I have come out the other side. And I am feeling wonderful. All four wheels are working again – I am physically and emotionally back on track. I'm healed and invigorated with a new passion for life – a passion that has merely flickered over the past six years. I also want to see if he is ok. How he's been? Has he felt similar pain over the years? I understand my interest and contact with him will seem sudden. God give me the strength to say enough, and not too much. I believe its important to give him the opportunity to speak. Either now, or down the track.

Kenneth had a child to someone else not long after my abortion. It was a tangled old mess – something that would take another chapter to explain. And as much as I have detested this other child's mother for so long, I've now come to feel shame for thinking such thoughts. I've come to realise that I have no reason to hate this woman, just because she said yes to life. And in doing so, she had a child to a man I loved very much. She has since married someone else and had other children. So it's time to put her, their child and Kenneth all to rest and in the past where they belong. I've carried them all around in my life for too long. Time to use this energy in other areas of my life.

In concluding I would like to add how amazing it is that my journey and experiences are now helping others. Since telling my family and having counselling, I have been able to touch other people's lives. It's amazing how many girlfriends of mine have had abortions. And in seeing me take action, they too are facing their own pain. It also amazes me how taboo this subject is. How taboo the individual makes it. How as women, we think that we can just forget about it. Pretend it never happened. When all that the ignorance is doing is ripping apart our very being. Abortion goes against the innate ability to conceive and bear children. It's our design purpose and to abort goes against this grain. As much as its also pure murder, and I hate to think of all the little ones discarded, I feel so strongly for the survivors. I am delighted that my story and experiences are now helping many other people, maybe even you, the reader. Good night.

8.

David's Lament

"O my son Absalom! O Absalom My son, my son!"
(2 Sam 19:4)

Under the reign of King David, Israel prospered beyond dreams. However, with prosperity also came corruption, disillusionment and intrigue so that the possibility of insurrection was ever present.

David's third born son Absalom took advantage of the seething discontent and intrigue at the time, in order to both avenge the rape of his sister by their oldest half brother Amnon (he had him killed) and to secure for himself succession to his father's kingdom. Amnon as David's firstborn was, until his death, the presumed heir of David.

Of course the murder of David's eldest and heir (Amnon) sent ripples of fear through Absalom and he fled Israel for several years of exile. On his return after reconciliation with his father David, Absalom again set out to plot against his father with the intention to cause a rebellion that would deliver his father's kingdom into his hands. Of course the rebellion planned by Absalom failed because of the loyalty of David's fighting hierarchy and Joab in particular. Joab was David's chief commander, who killed Absalom (against David's explicit orders), thus leading to David's lament for the son whom he had loved dearly. David was known to love all his children even when, like Absalom, they sought to hurt him or the kingdom.

The Old Testament is littered with references to the value of children and the blessing that they are believed to be. Even as we see with the story of Absalom, who attempted to forcibly wrest the kingdom from his father, he was still loved and deeply mourned and an attempt was even made by his father to ensure that his child's life was spared. (2 Sam 18:5)

Fatherhood in biblical times was understood differently from fatherhood as understood in this modern and 'enlightened' era. Whilst a union between a man and his wife may have terminated, or the man may have felt the need to have more than one wife (as was then the custom), the children of unions were none-the-less loved, and when there was a loss, greatly grieved. Abraham and Sarah were childless. They had a deep desire for a child. Abraham and Sarah's devalued sense of self-worth was caused primarily because they had no offspring. This clearly indicates that fatherhood and motherhood were the greatest achievements understood by these people.

Human fatherhood is a concept difficult to understand. It is the extension of self, yet it is different. It is a total giving or gifting away of a whole "self" to be united to another different whole "self" in order to form a completely new, different and separate "whole self". Fatherhood initiates the process of transmission of the "essence of maleness". Fatherhood is strictly maleness. It is not only the transmission of DNA or transmission of cells but in essence it is the transmission of what it is to be "me," male.

The very terms "father" and "fatherhood" have an ascribed meaning attached to them and universally understood, which immediately describe not only the essence but also the relationship in its unique design. Fatherhood has ascribed to itself various meanings e.g., provider, protector, progenitor; but its very essence is yet beyond these metaphors because the role also embraces and incorporates behaviour, emotions, leadership (both spiritual and secular) and presence. It is all these and more. Fatherhood ultimately is supposed to mean male love enfleshed.

Abortion frees and/or denies the man the responsibility of fatherhood; and it dishonours the very essence of maleness whose design is to be attracted to and receptive towards the one whom he has engendered and who is an extension of himself.

Research into post abortion grief and after-effects in females has been, while not necessarily adequate, steadily on the increase. Research into the male response to abortion, however, has been not only inadequate but also abysmal. The reason for this imbalance is uncertain, although it could be suggested that the new type of male/female understanding of relationships could be a reason why the male is not permitted to express his thoughts and feelings about the death of his child. What is certain is that indeed some fathers do experience much suffering at the abortion of their infant.

The freedom which liberalised abortion has given to males and females is often touted as liberating and enhancing. However, that same freedom from responsibility has also meant that the man has been freed from and denied any rights in relation to his child, and dealt the male an almost irreparable blow. The abortion of his child has meant that his "fatherhood" or his "essence" was unwanted by her, and/or rejected by him. This rejection has demeaned the man whose very design is to be drawn and protective towards the one whom he has engendered.

Abortion has meant many things to males, females and society. I believe, however, that what has mostly been damaged, loosened, weakened, is the invisible cord which holds individuals and families together. Abortion has weakened "maleness" and all that this means. Even with one intentional lost "fatherhood" the whole structure of the male of the species is weakened. Perhaps here we may be reminded of the domino principle, that is, when one falls down then the rest go down. In a society where millions upon millions of infants are aborted annually, then the fabric of this society is surely corrupted and into this corrupted society fatherhood must have its blueprint perverted. Its original design then must be altered to accommodate violence, rejection, weakness and abandonment. The design must be transformed from one that was sublime to one that is malignant and must incorporate new structures, which are deformed by default.

Studies into abortion grief experienced by males suggest that only "some" males are affected. However, even if it is "some" males who are afflicted with potentially destructive and malignant reactions, these males then bring to their society and environment their reactions and responses. This must then affect those with whom they come in contact and they in turn affect others so that like the ripple effect a large segment of humanity is affected by that one act of violence. Therefore when we consider that over the past 30-40 years there have been millions upon millions of abortions worldwide, the enormity of the damage to modern society can only be described as astronomical or even incomprehensible.

It is important that we try to understand why it is that some men do in fact suffer post abortion trauma/grief whilst others appear to sail through the experience untouched. Understanding the impact that abortion has had on society, the change in perception and expectations, together with changed mores, may help in some way to explain this new and emotionless breed called modern "man". This new breed of man takes his spouse/partner to the abortion facility, pays for the abortion and actually leaves the premises for several hours whilst she is left to undergo the procedure on her own. It is at times mind-numbing to read the callousness in the body language. Indeed this new breed of male has had a massive transfusion of abandonment, blindness and malice. Only this could explain the ease with which they deliver their child to be destroyed.

A further reason may be posited for the abandonment by the male of the female whom he has impregnated. This reason may be suggested as the result of the endemic societal malaise, which appears to have overshadowed the last two generations. These last two generations have somehow permitted a culture to develop, which is decidedly anti-God and anti-human. In this atmosphere of emotional and spiritual detachment an insidious strain of death wish appears to have taken hold.

Whilst abortion has been with us since time began, constraints have always existed which ensured that abortion remained outside of civilised society. In past eras morality was also understood and practised differently. Sexuality has been with us since creation and understood as blessed by God (Gen 1:28). Sexuality was also understood as creative, mysterious and life-giving. Even in a perverted sense the vestal virgins and temple prostitutes of ancient times understood that sexuality was exquisitely precious and was something entirely owned which they could offer to the gods. Human beings have always known that the sexual act could result in the creation of another creature. Both genders of the human species knew/know this and most cultures promulgated and protected this creative gift and its fruit.

This is not to assert that past societies have been honourable in the areas of life and death. However, no past society has been so brainwashed as to believe that human life is so disposable as the society which has emerged over the last forty years. A slow, methodical and well-resourced movement has arisen which has changed the understanding of what have always been known as certain absolutes. This movement has replaced this understanding with a monstrous caricature of the former.

Past societies have at times practised euthanasia and abortion, and in primitive cultures even infanticide (when it was felt there was a need because of shortage of food), but no society or culture has practised these to the extent that it is done today, and further, no society has practised these because of a hatred of children, a love of self, and a belief that it is a "good" and a "right" and enshrined into legislature. A new attitude has arisen, one which sees nothing sacred, and life is disposable or a commodity to be used or discarded at will. It is a frightening vision of a future culture where all, except the "appropriate", will be disposed of without emotion. A eugenic society perhaps?

The ease with which unrestricted abortion has been facilitated into the world community must be questioned, and the change from creative protection to abandonment queried. What happened that so quickly changed the emotional component of the male so that he can so readily abandon his partner and child/children? What measures of accountability have been put in place so that men and women are responsible? Conception has not changed. Pregnancy has not changed. The question must be asked, "What has changed to turn the male and female into unsocialised, almost primitive beings who mate and hate? What has contributed to this irresponsible sexual behaviour resulting in millions upon millions of deaths annually?"

Margaret Mead, after years of studying the sex roles within societies, came to the conclusion that human fatherhood is a social invention. However, to enhance and maintain this invention, Mead argues it is important that the desire of the father to contribute to the welfare of his children must be firmly established and deeply instilled. Where this notion of caring and providing for the welfare of his offspring has been firmly established and imprinted, it is also understood that this link is of vital importance for the preservation of a viable and functioning society:

> Every known human society rests firmly on the learned nurturing behaviour of men. This nurturing behaviour, this fending for the females and children instead of leaving them to fend for themselves, as the primates do, may take different forms ... But the core remains. Man, the heir of tradition, provides for women and children. We have no indication that man the animal, man unpatterned by social learning, would do anything of the sort ... Men have to learn to want to provide for mothers and this behaviour, being learned, is fragile and can disappear rather easily under social conditions that no longer teach it effectively.[3]

Perhaps Margaret Mead has one answer. That is, that the male has removed himself (or has been removed) so far from reproductive responsibility that he has not learned (or what little he knew is forgotten) about the "want" or "need" to provide and nurture his offspring. The loosening of moral structures in the sixties and onwards has served to remove the past understandings about what men and women intrinsically knew about morality and its effect. The society which has emerged over the past four decades is a composite society but it is a composite made up of different shapes and sizes and none fits perfectly. This composite is free of guidelines and definites so that the anything goes theory is applicable. Sexuality in this new society is not sacred but a drive/instinct. It is not creative. Sexuality is not for reproduction or the joy and intimacy between two people, a man and woman, married and committed to a lifetime relationship, but a leisure time activity without meaning, something done for something to do, in any combination. With this understanding and into this milieu, abandonment and abortion are foregone conclusions.

Perhaps there are many, and yet maybe no answers to the questions, but unless we find answers the vision of selective, mechanical breeding is a very close possibility. The scenario of selective breeding opens the doors to death as required by the powers that be. It is a frightening prospect that because of societal acceptance of death as something owned and negotiable, we would let the genie escape from the bottle. The same genie will absolutely refuse to go back into the bottle even if told that this is good for her. To recapture the genie the male must take control again. This does not mean the male must become the bully but must take control of his family and especially become a father to his children. He must re-learn and understand what fatherhood means in the full sense of the word.

Fatherhood in its truest sense means reproduction or an extension of oneself in body but above all in spirit. We have a clear image of this in the Genesis story of creation. God moulds, shapes, and breathes life into the newly fashioned figure. Up to this time no one had existed who could keep company with God. Now there was one designed "in our image" (Gen 1:26). Someone who could love God in freedom just as He loved. God loved so much that He breathed into that inanimate shape a part of Himself. From out of the desire of God and into the mouth of man was transferred a divine essence which in turn was so energising that it enlivened and animated the new body. He covenanted Himself to the one that He had created. We know this because man and woman were enjoined to continue the same works: "Be fruitful and multiply and fill the earth and subdue it". (Gen 1:28)

Modern understanding of fatherhood fails to capture the importance of the bond between God and man and man and child. There is transference of something dynamic in the transference of a father's essence into his son or daughter. The moral, physical and spiritual bond and the acceptance of this bond make the human being very different from the other created species. Modern fatherhood, whilst acknowledging that the generative act is important, has sabotaged its essence. Modern fatherhood (understood out of context of permanent marriage partner) has been neutered. Modern fatherhood is despised because sexuality, lifelong marriage, family and children have become tradable commodities. The understanding, therefore, of the sacredness of life and "essence" transference has had to undergo a change also.

In its original design the essence of fatherhood presupposed a great honour and a unique relationship based on "sameness". The father's likeness was reproduced in the offspring. Added to this the ongoing nurturing of the child and hence the relationship presupposed an ongoing and permanent love bond between the father and the one he has generated, which ultimately meant the fulfilling of covenant responsibility to take care of and protect the one he has been covenanted to. Covenant love. For the male who blithely takes his child to be aborted, covenant love and covenant relationship do not have a meaning. Covenant love, covenant knowledge cannot be found in the life of the male (and female) taking their child to be killed.

Abortion is fatal to fatherhood because it is a perversion of the very essence of being male. Abortion can be likened to *Original Sin;*

because the father, like Adam, is absent when "the bone of my bones and flesh of my flesh" (Gen 2:23) is being destroyed just as he was absent when Eve was being manipulated and tempted. It was the same demon who could persuade the woman that God lied, who can now persuade the modern woman that her baby is disposable, while persuading the modern male to turn his face away while his child is being sacrificed. The same demon continues to tell the lie and the creature continues to believe.

It is vital for modern man to recapture his own self-knowledge about what it means to be a "father" and to enliven a new creation. How mysterious is the fashioning of a new creature. We know that the instant of conception is so mysterious, sacred and holy, that it must remain hidden in the depths of sightlessness. Every new conception proceeds silently and in the darkness of the mother's womb. Only God is to be first witness to new life because He has whispered words of "love", words which said, "let there be life" in the silence of that womb, words that commanded the new creation to take shape.

The engendering (not enfleshing) must proceed silently and must be covered by mystery, as even Adam was unconscious or even in deep ecstasy when Eve was fashioned. Adam himself was fashioned from inanimate created material and wakened from the depths of God's own design. So exquisite was to be this ultimate prototype that it was to be left until the very last creative work. Each of the previous creations became more and more refined until at last the human creature! The Creator, who fashioned the complex universe and all in it, did so from the depths of his own hidden and vast desires which overflowed into life.

The Father (God) who engenders his own Son (Jesus) does so in order to show humanity what it means to love. He (God) introduced his Son Jesus as the One, who was and remains, an extended likeness of Himself. The Father (God) has engendered his own Son, watched over Him, and knew Him as only a father and son can know one another.

Indeed the child more than anyone else is nearest to the father's heart. The child awaits the father's breath to animate him, ransom him, rescue him, and ultimately to be given his heritage, that is, his identity as a son/daughter of the heavenly father imaged by the earthly father.

Without the father's love and animation of the child, he or she remains a voiceless, powerless, emotionless creature whose presence remains hidden from the world. If it is not hidden then it is a lone traveller in the world, always seeking the lost "father". The father's seal must be passed to the child in order for the child to "grow" and when fully grown to be able to be a father himself. It is the most essential spiritual and psychological need of the child to know that his/her father is a good and loving person in order for that child to progress healthily and happily. Interruption of this development will result in the child seeking the father that he/she should have had. The child will be unable to say as Jesus does, "eternal life is to know you" (Jn 17:3) until there is intervention.

A man who has participated in the abortion of his or someone else's child will not feel "good", and cannot by nature be a good father to an existing child, having the knowledge that he has taken another child to be immolated. The guilt involved with abortion ensures that the father will not, and cannot father his son according to his original design. The flaw will mar his fatherhood.

However we may choose to interpret the Incarnation, the event is about the sowing of the divine seed, not in heaven, but here on this earth. God so respected and honoured his laws of governance of the world that He chose to enter into the created order through the medium known to the human species, that is, via conception and birth. He, the Son (Jesus), took on vulnerability and in doing so imaged his own Father (God) who in fact made Himself vulnerable by giving his creatures the freedom to choose, or free will. In the history of Jesus and his Father, God, we have been given a clear picture of the intended love between father and child, where the bond developed because of the extension from one to the other is clearly evident. The bond of love according to God's design transcends all else.

When we compare human fatherhood with divine fatherhood we can see that something has gone wrong. Human fatherhood is so far removed from the ideal that at times it must appear like a caricature. However, human "fatherhood" while flawed is still the mandate inscribed on the male psyche. If human "fatherhood" is now flawed it still remains the divinely conceived strategy to perpetuate the creative works of God. By his "fatherhood" the male co-operates and assents to his calling. He is called to an act of total unselfishness and giving. He is called to "give" away a part of himself so that someone new can come into being. Fatherhood is at the core of God's plan for humanity. Abortion then must be understood as the violation of that very essence of masculinity. Abortion is the antithesis of the blueprint which must be amended in order to accommodate something that was not in its original design.

In fatherhood, the father's task begins with the generation of his child and must continue with the rearing of the child. The ongoing deep relationship that exists develops into an everlasting bond, which goes beyond the physical into the spiritual, which is the element separating the lower animal species from the human and divine creation. It is the moral, spiritual and eternal bond, which ultimately makes true fatherhood complete and elevates the relationship from the animal realm.

Abortion wounds the man at the deepest and most intimate level, because the wound is rooted in his innate knowledge of his masculinity and its actual meaning. This wound suspends the man's covenantal role, which is situated in the context of "fatherhood", and derived from the fatherhood of God. Fatherhood is rooted both in the divine (spiritual) and natural (physical generation), order and cannot be circumvented without suffering the ramifications of perversion

For the male who is the father of an aborted child, personal suffering, frustration, helplessness and at times destructive behaviour propel him towards behaviour consistent with self-loathing and emotional shutdown. Alcohol abuse, substance abuse, dangerous pursuits, violence to self and others, suicide ideation and suicide behaviour are the external manifestations of an internal personal war or dis-equilibrium. The anguish of failure, the sense of loss or even the sense of foreboding is the male's response to the violation of his covenant, and only God in his infinite mercy can restore peace and equilibrium. Only God can enter into his conscience and remove that enemy of peace. It is only through God's mercy and forgiveness that a man can regain his lost sense of worth, his apostolate of fatherhood and his masculinity. To be able to return to the Father (God) the abortive father must acknowledge his own lost fatherhood and seek renewal of his relationship both with the divine Father and his own child so that at least he can spiritually reclaim his aborted child and renew their relationship.

Post abortion grief is monstrous in character because of its destructive and merciless intent. Consciously or unconsciously the male who experiences post abortion trauma designs a sophisticated strategy to inflict self-punishment. His slow but persistent change in personality and behaviours ensures estrangement from existing and future relationships leading to an isolation, which can become impenetrable. "I don't deserve to live and I don't deserve to ever be happy again," said a twenty-three-year-old young man (James) whose girlfriend aborted their child. For this young man who fought valiantly to save his infant the abortion outcome was disastrous. Their engagement was terminated and he embarked on a lifestyle which would ensure his early demise.

For this young man the baby was not a foetus or a "bunch of cells" but his son. He had ascribed to his infant human characteristics and had already developed a personal relationship with his "son". For men who see the pregnancy as personal and ascribe meaning to that pregnancy an abortion decision is simply devastating. For these men depression, guilt, anger, sadness and shame become the norm. To further heighten their helplessness, the male whose child is aborted without his consent is often told that the pregnancy and abortion are "women's business" and therefore not "his business as to the outcome". The law has ensured that even if he wanted to protect the life of his child he is unable to do so and indeed cannot interfere in the outcome.

The grief of the post-abortive father is compounded by the fact that societal stereotyping has the male needing to behave in a particular way when trying to cope with grief. Where a woman can weep, the man must endure his pain with strength. This self-understanding then leads to silence because this is what is expected of him. Social taboos about abortion (though de facto accepted) also ensure that he remains silent. His own needs and beliefs have to be suppressed because society has promoted that pregnancy and its outcome are entirely women's choices. The matriarchal mentality reigns in the abortion arena. His powerlessness over this life and death decision renders the male impotent. His *raison-d'être,* that is, to be a protector and provider is removed from his control and his sense of masculinity is fractured. Indeed this is why the abortion experience leaves in its wake a panorama littered with broken relationships.

While speaking about abortion and its effect on the male it is also important to try to understand why a huge number of men appear not to experience any regret with regard to the abortion of their child. In actual fact it appears that a larger percentage of males (boyfriends, husbands) actually coerce their female partner into the procedure, or alternatively offer no support and leave the decision to them. The question must be asked, why this refusal of responsibility? What has happened to the male psyche to change the order of understanding of how things should be? A further comment encountered in my counselling room has been "he told me it's my problem, and to deal with it". Perhaps the most common and pernicious threat is that unless the "it" is dealt with, then their relationship is over. This threat is deadly because it is made when the woman is most vulnerable (hormonally, emotionally) and the fear of abandonment is palpable. Under these conditions it is of course understandable why the woman resorts to a decision that she may not have otherwise made.

The answer to the "why?" may be found in the new sexual norms espoused by modern society. These sexual norms have introduced a false "equality" into the collective conscience. The ascendancy of the feminist movement through the powerful women's lobby has led to the diminishing of respect for the male. The march towards self-reliance and autonomy by the female, combined with the sexual revolution and the contraceptive device have liberated the female from the fear of pregnancy and turned her into a wombless predator who is (like the male) freed from commitment. Like the new male the modern woman need not commit herself to a lifetime spouse/partner but is free to roam until she determines that "this" is the right person.

Of course the response of the male to this new freedom from responsibility has been to relish the new status quo. For the male whose tendencies are towards "love them and leave them", the new freedom means that his sexual activity is not tied to commitment and relationship but to "conquests". The thrill of the chase, followed by seduction is thereafter followed by abandonment because he senses in her the same predatory instincts as his own. His devaluation of her as a woman begins with societal acknowledgement that she is free to be his equal in all things, including and especially sexuality, and continues with his demand for an abortion (if the need arises). Otherwise his interest wanes and he is off on the next chase.

The introduction of the contraceptive pill and development of the contraceptive mentality have unleashed upon society a monstrous weapon for the perversion and dehumanisation of the creature of God. It has also served to change the natural order of things. When women decided that conception was in their control and contraception was their choice the males rejoiced. From this point onwards responsibility for sexual acts and their consequences was handed over to the women with the comment, "It's your problem, you deal with it."

In times past when a pregnancy occurred the male was expected to at least do the "right thing" (which implied both duty and dignity). Today he is at most expected to drive the woman to the abortion facility and occasionally pay for the procedure. It is not even required of him to remain at the facility while the procedure is carried out but he is encouraged to return at a more appropriate time, "after it's done." The irony is that even very pro-choice women have seen the connection between contraceptives and irresponsibility, and yet women continue to take into their bodies these poisons which are actually fertility retarding agents.

For the uncommitted man and woman abortion is simply a temporary inconvenience or an alternative when contraception fails, and then they can move on to other pastures. The relationships do not need to be strong or lasting and are not geared towards bonding for life. For the male whose inclination is towards the "love them and leave them" philosophy, the sexual freedom without the need for permanency (marriage) is ideal. His detachment has been slowly programmed and practised to lead to irresponsible, immoral behaviour.

For the modern woman detachment from her infant is also an objective. However, because of her biological makeup the detachment achieved by the female is nowhere as predominant as that of the male. Because of her design, that is, to love and nurture, and to be loved, the woman has difficulty in reaching the same level of detachment. Where it appears to have been achieved, the result is monstrous. The results show a woman whose femininity has been compromised and ridiculed. She becomes a caricature of what she should have been and this in itself results in a new form of suffering.

The availability of the ungodly dyad of contraception and abortion has, I believe, led to an insidious alteration of the "face" and conscience of society. Unrestricted abortion has not only dealt a terrible sentence to innumerable millions of infants but also contributed to the masculinisation of the female and feminisation of the male. This androgynising of the human species has progressed with such precision that one has to be blind not to see that there is a hidden agenda. The availability of contraception and unrestricted abortion has not equalised the genders but has in fact diminished both the male and the female.

The big "YES" to contraception and abortion has resulted in the decline in respect for human life, for women, for men, for children, for the elderly and infirm. Unrestricted abortion has not meant reproductive freedom, but reproductive suicide and societal suicide. Unrestricted abortion has not meant unity for men and women but alienation. Their roles become blurred, with neither of them clear about what their role is meant to be and how they should behave as man or woman.

Unrestricted abortion has not meant enhancement of the woman, but absolute and undeniable exploitation. He has the sex; she has the abortion – his moments of pleasure and her lifetime of anguish. Unrestricted abortion has not resulted in unwanted pregnancies but in disposable children or abandoned and abused children. Ultimately, unrestricted abortion and contraception have not been the saving of an overpopulated planet but its possible destruction, because men and women have forgotten what it is to be men and women and instead are more and more becoming creatures who mate and hate.

A new type of violence has entered society; violence against the extension of self and this type of violence can only lead to annihilation unless the Almighty God intervenes in some radical way. Abortion or the terminating of the child in the womb is Satan's ploy at attempting to dethrone God. It is at the heart of the culture of death, which has been Satan's legacy to humanity from the very beginning. Sadly in our generation, both male and female offer the sacrifice to Moloch.

Divine Fatherhood

To conclude this topic of "fatherhood" I would like to look at the "function" of the father as imaged in the parable of the "Prodigal Son".

The role or function of the father is important to the spiritual and psychological development and formation of his child. The link with the father is not only that of physical generation, but also of establishing a spiritual bond. It is through this bond that the "son" or child gains his identity as "son" just as surely as God is identified as Father, through the generation of his Word Jesus.

As the human father confers on his human child his nature and personality (all that it means to be human), so too the divine Father confers on his Word his own nature, which is divine. God's Word establishes the fact of "sonship". "You are my son the beloved" (Mk 1:11) and "You are always with me" (Lk 15:31) are the identifiable characteristics and promise between the Father and the Son. For it is true that the Son has been within the Father always, forming an extraordinary and indissoluble bond.

The parable of the Prodigal Son is extraordinary because it shows the "son's" or the "human's" misconception of God the Father. This is clearly evident in Old Testament Scriptures where God is portrayed at times as ruthless, tyrannical and someone who required appeasement, obedience and detachment. This imagery is also evident with the son's desire to flee from what he thought were strict confines of his father's house. However, in his wanderings he discovers that the image of his father was false and that instead his father's house meant freedom from any kind of want.

In this parable Jesus skilfully wove the true image of his Father on the tapestry of the human story. With this parable Jesus reverses past beliefs about God's attitude towards his creation. Jesus clearly shows an image of his Father which was previously unknown or vaguely hinted at. The mercy of God the Father previously only alluded to, is incarnated in visible form so that it could be understood by all who heard. The mercy and compassion shown by God (father figure in the parable) is constant, even in the weaknesses of the child. God is ever vigilant for the son's return and knows the humiliation and baggage borne by the child are heavy. In his solicitude He (God) lightens the burden by running to meet his still distant child, his child still weighed down by his sin.

Perhaps this parable is most appropriate for today because of the diminished role of fatherhood, which in turn has led to the diminishing of the enjoyment of the Father and his house, the Church.

Graeme's Story

Ann you have asked me to write my thoughts about how I felt about the abortion of my "son" whom I have called John. I know that you are not going to like what I say but you did say that I could write as I felt so here it is:

First of all thanks for seeing me at first as an emergency and then weekly for I don't know how many weeks. I was referred to you by a woman friend of my family who has heard of your work. By the time I rang you I was ready to do myself in. But I'm glad someone had your name and you thankfully saw me immediately.

I cannot say that you helped me much because there is not much anyone can do to help me and how I feel about my girlfriend's decision to abort our baby. I don't think there is anyone who can console me, though you helped me immensely by patiently listening every time I came in to see you. I know I behave irrationally and even blamed you at times, but this was because you are a woman and you seem to make allowances for those women who abort. I understand that you probably see only women who have been forced by their partners to have the abortion, but NOT all of us men want our babies aborted. I didn't. I offered everything under the sun for my girlfriend to have our baby, but she wouldn't. She kept saying she wasn't sure she wanted to be a mother. Her mother wanted her to abort. Her friends thought she should abort, and I am sure even the milkman had a say in her decision, EXCEPT ME the father. I was the only one who wasn't listened to.

Well she went through with it. She took our 13 week baby (I was sure it was a boy) and she had him killed and for this I will never forgive her. In fact I never want to see her again. I can't see her as I used to see her. I can no longer see a future together. In fact I don't want to have a future with her, because I couldn't trust her with any of future children. I would live in fear that she could go off and kill the babies if and when she wanted to, just because she can.

You know Ann, the morning she went to the abortion I got blind drunk; I just didn't want to be thinking while it was happening. I didn't want to be conscious.

The worst part of the whole damn situation was the fact that I could do nothing to protect my son. He needed me and I couldn't do anything to stop what was going to happen to him. I don't think I want to have any children in the future because maybe I won't be able to help them when they need me, as I wasn't able to help John.

I am angry Ann because it didn't have to happen because we could have managed. We could have got married and had our own family. We wouldn't have been rich, but we could have had our little family and slowly things would have got better.

I hope I never see her again because I am not sure how I will react towards her. At this moment I think I hate her. I certainly have none of the feelings that I had for her before this. I had seen us together for life. Not anymore.

I am also not sure that I could even be civil towards her.

Will I ever forgive her? Absolutely NOT. Not now or ever. She willingly took our baby to be killed. I don't want to be involved with this kind of person and certainly wouldn't trust her with any of my children again.

Thanks for asking me to write about my feelings, I know it's probably not what you thought but these are my thoughts and feelings.

I have appreciated your care for me. I have appreciated your calm especially when I felt no calm inside of me. Thanks for the many cups of tea you made for me. Thanks for the kind words you have had for me. And no I don't want a plaque for John. I carry him in my heart and mind and when I go he goes with me. There is no one else to mourn him except me.

9.

The Family and Society

The family is the original cell of social life. It is the natural
society in which husband and wife are called to give themselves
in love and in the gift of life.[4]

Abortion and its attendant after-effects are monstrous because it not only affects the men, women and children in a family but also the society in which the family is situated.

At times I have been accused of stretching the bow too far in my assessment of societal change due to abortion. It is my contention, however, that even one abortion has the power to negatively alter the status quo. As I counsel more and more males and females who have participated in an abortion, I am made aware of the suffering, dissonance and fragmentation of that one act on the individual and those within their social sphere.

The family has been designed by God to be the safe haven for human beings to grow, to be nurtured and learn to love, and then extend that life farther afield to incorporate new individuals. Through this extension love is diffused, new families are formed and society flourishes. However, abortion acts as a barrier to that extension not only because children who would have formed new structures are not born, but also because those already in existing structures lose the ability to love, nurture and then let go. The fears, loss of serenity, sense of doom or alternatively sense of impermanence, are conduits for further fragmentation.

The family, and hence society, both on the small and large scale, are permeated with a sense of loss. The idea that their intrinsic worth is gauged upon their worth in the market place rather than upon their worth as uniquely created beings, slowly conditions mothers and fathers in the family and society. This new "worth" is a replacement for the "loss" of conscience and the loss of personal value as human beings. The family as a temporary stopping point replaces the traditional family, once measured in terms of a "quiver full".

At the risk of sounding morbid and pessimistic, from observation and from my experience with post-abortive men and women, it is clear that abortion has significantly altered societal ideals and expectations. This acceptance of abortion and its proponents have managed to erode the certainties and truths inscribed in the human heart and replaced these truths with lies and false promises. Let me explain.

The promise is that abortion is a minor procedure, a removal of the inconvenient, and a return to normality. To the woman experiencing an unplanned pregnancy, these promises are attractive. However, what is not promised or even inferred is the fact that what is removed, her baby, will not leave her unscathed or untouched by the experience. Irrespective of the language used to convince her that what is removed is a "bunch of cells" or "some tissue," at the intuitive level she knows that what was removed was her baby. This knowledge causes the deepest of wounds and her thoughts are played out by her actions, either immediately or in the future. This knowledge will not return her to the state of pre-abortion but will now place her in a state which I call "stagnant". It is a stagnant state and like stagnant waters this state is poisonous. In the quiet of the night, in the silence of self, this one act has forever changed her design and no matter what efforts are made to continue "as before", even she recognises that this cannot be. She cannot be the same again.

This intrinsic knowledge of change then serves to propel the woman towards a remedy for the uneasiness and emptiness which pervade her being. Something is not right. Something is missing. Of course the "something" cannot be named, just feared, and the memory of this "something" that is feared must be erased. Hence the self-destructive behaviour she embarks on. Her self-destructive behaviours can at times be seen as positive attributes, that is, they appear as actions leading to fulfilment of life's dreams, however, these life dreams have been fuelled by a restlessness of spirit, a debilitating relentlessness. She needs to justify her action as having been the right action. A need to erase the memory of her action, a piece of her narrative history, by seeking temporary fulfilment via any means. A need to forget what was done; therefore, a life lived just for this moment. The behaviour of women who have aborted their baby is characterised either by frenzy or apathy. Each of these is equally destructive.

For a male who either encourages, forces, or participates in an abortion decision of either his or someone else's child, the result is similar to that of an aborting woman. His own history will no longer be the same. He too must, in his own silence, in his own space remember that his child or a child within his sphere has died. He also cannot return to the place pre-abortion because whether he appreciates it or not he is a "father". He is a father to a dead baby. He also intuitively knows that what was aborted was not something incomplete or foreign but his own baby, his own flesh and blood which he was mandated to protect. His life, together with hers, has now entered into a new phase of the profane. He has taken an innocent lamb (his very own innocent lamb) and offered it to the god, society. He has enacted his priestly role and offered sacrifice, however, it was not a sacrifice offered to God but to Satan. He seals his covenant with Satan with the blood of his own child.

Every tribe, clan, and nation has now been affected with the scourge of abortion and within these tribes, clans and nations are families who have offered this sacrifice thus tainting their own generational conscience. Where a nation has legalised this abomination the collective conscience of the nation (unseen) must deal with the fallout of the consequence. A nation, which legally mandates that its future citizens may be murdered, has also covenanted itself with death, because it (the people) has attempted to wrest sovereignty over life and death from God, and placed it in the hands of *Caesar* (Satan). Having done this, it cannot then hope to justly govern its people. Those who have forced the legalisation of abortion cannot then rest because what has been enacted must be protected, and so further abominations must be deemed necessary in order to justify the original act. Thus late term abortions, infanticide (a new term coined post-birth abortion) patricide, fratricide, matricide, euthanasia, same-sex addictions, demands for deconstruction of marriage and demand for same-sex marriage must follow. Beginning with the killing of weakest infants slowly the moral order must collapse.

Perhaps it may help to understand why every tribe, nation, clan, family is affected by an abortion decision. With over fifty million abortions carried out annually worldwide, not too many families will be left untouched by this death experience. As we are slowly beginning to find out, abortion trauma is the result. It silently works its deadly poison on the individuals involved. These same individuals must then attempt to deal with their internal dissonance by whatever means available to them, which in the case of young people, is often destructive behaviour, and indeed at times the most permanently destructive, that is, suicide.

It is known from studies into abortion trauma, that this syndrome is malicious because of its mode of presentation. Post abortion grief may present itself immediately as sorrow, regret, anxiety, fear, weeping and a host of other symptoms. This grief may at times lie dormant until a significant triggering event. Until this time individuals may have continued their life experience without seeming to change until the triggering event. This clearly indicates that the abortion has not been forgotten but has been "placed on the back burner" where it has been quietly simmering. It is the quiet, slow simmering that has produced a new mentality, a new understanding of how things should be.

Because of our increasing knowledge of post abortion trauma and its effects on men and women, and because of the large-scale slaughter of preborn infants, we can safely say that the moral "glue" holding societies together is losing its adhesive power. As more and more abortions are carried out in the name of "reproductive rights", "women's rights", "privacy rights", "population control" and "right to choose", the more we can expect not a strengthening and growing society but a slow disintegration of the same society. The unseen adhesive, the superglue that is the family, will become more and more endangered and corrupted because within the hearts and minds of those forming family groups, there will be unresolved guilt, grief and trauma associated with an abortion. New forms of "family" will be demanded because the "natural" family has been deconstructed. There will also be the burdensome baggage of life lived at odds from its original design. A heartless and emotionless people whose blueprint has been corrupted will in turn not be able to be present to and raise future healthy individuals who will strengthen their own society.

As more and more parents fail to parent, abandoning their children, (at least those who have been allowed to live) to the care of others in order to pursue self-satisfying paths, then more and more we will see a society peopled by refugees from that self-same society. Children who have been left to the rearing by strangers cannot hear the voice of authority of their own parents but different voices. The voice of their mother or father was absent during the formative years and cannot be replaced at a later time when it is considered necessary for rules and regulations, for behaviour to be adhered to. This voice of parents is absent and the young will not respond to a voice unremembered and unrecognised.

Traumatised, wounded, abandoned, broken people can only parent in the style known to them. Males (as it appears to me) seem to have lost their sense of being strong, masculine and protective, whilst modern women have been wooed and seduced by the notion that empowerment comes from denying their design and becoming emasculated. The notion that a woman's design to give life, teach that life, nurture that life, love that life is demeaning, and will lead to the psychological, spiritual and physical neglect of that child or children, leading to further disintegration and loss.

The family *is* seriously affected by abortion. Not only the immediate family, but all families because as more and more abortions are carried out (at times on very young girls) the corporate effect will spread so that most families will be in some way touched by this experience. The death of the weakest members of society cannot but desensitise and toughen the conscience of those who have called for the death. The connection between abortion and failure, abortion and depression, abortion and suicide, abortion and family breakdown has been established. Yet still the call is for more abortion, more sexual freedom, and more freedom to self-destruct. It would appear that there is a spirit of vengeance at work and this spirit allows for no survivors. This spirit of anti-life is the same spirit which declared "you will not die" (Gen 3:5). It lied then and continues to lie. It had its followers then, and it still has, and more so today.

The family is under severe attack from many fronts. I believe, however, that the most insidious, most cunning, most destructive front is the lethal assault on children by their own parents. The children, the bond of the flesh between a man and a woman, are now the most vulnerable members of society because in the womb they are unseen, unheard and unprotected, and those designed to protect and love them have become their executioners. The family of those who abort their child/children has its adhesive, its love, and its *raison d'etre* compromised.

The question must be asked, "Is there hope for the future?" The answer must surely be, *yes,* because God's mercy is far greater than any human transgression. God's mercy, though, is always mediated through the human person. His mercy, while deep must be appropriated and acted upon. God can and does forgive. He can and does heal and renew but He won't force, nor will He tolerate indefinitely the wholesale slaughter. In justice and with mercy He must act on the society, which has attempted to wrest from Him his authority over life and death. How the society fares will depend upon the response against this abomination. Will we respond by returning to Him his control and asking for mercy, or will this society vanish from the memory of future societies.

Past history tells us that those societies where children were offered as sacrifices to the gods have indeed perished and then vanished. Perhaps our society with its technological advances has indeed become the most primitive because our technology has not protected the value of life but rather has made it dispensable while deifying technology. The collective guilt has instilled a projected self-hate, provoking individuals and groups to inflict more death on others. Truly it is those who escaped the net of death who are calling for the extermination of others, especially those who are most vulnerable. The crippling sense of collective guilt has led to flight via the medium of first denial and then ego satisfaction.

The reality of the deep sense of societal guilt is a reality many fail to recognise. This failure or recognition of the malaise leads to escapist behaviour in order to flee from persistent inner conflict. The moral dereliction, which is guilt, manifests in societal solidarity with sin. Blindness over the sin of abortion and our corporate responsibility over this abomination unite all, and serve to lessen and diminish our sense of compassion. In order to escape the sense of corporate wrongdoing and relieve the unbearable sense of guilt, new and more sophisticated horrors must be engineered to confirm solidarity with existent guilt.

Ultimately what can be said about abortion and the family is that it (abortion) destroys the very structure called "family". Just as the family of God is held together through the love of the Father, Son and

Holy Spirit, so also the domestic family is bound together with love. The destruction of the human family is brought about by the violence of its parents against their children, who are meant to be future parents. Further, at the very heart of the destruction of the human family is the attempted wresting from, and destruction of, the family of God. Abortion can only be seen as the attempted annihilation of God's supreme gift of life and of his design for the protection and continuation of that life.

Abortion is symptomatic of the spiritual death present and occurring in these days. To bring to birth a new child is to bring to birth one designed in God's image, to grace all of creation with another whose image creation mirrors. It could be argued that violence done to a child is technically done to God the Father and to Jesus as the Son and to the Spirit. Abortion also can be seen as an injury to Mary as Mother of the same Jesus and our Mother.

Every child who dies is denied the life intended for him or her, but they also cannot bring future generations to birth to form inhabitants for this earth and for the Kingdom of God. A child is born so that it might fulfil its own destiny, which is inscribed in him or her. Abortion thwarts God's authority and plunges humanity into a new state of de-civilisation, primitiveness and tyranny. The society or generation which turns its back on God and God's earthly institution, the family, is the humanity which experiences dissonance, discouragement, delinquency, despotic behaviour and finally destruction: "Brother will betray brother to death and a father his child" (Mt 10:21).

Leigh's Story

I thought the nightmares would never end

It all started after I had my first child, a son. He was born with a disability. His father and I were happy we had a baby but also saddened and confused about what was to be our future.

I still lived at my parent's home and so did he live at his parent's home, as we were both very young. I was 18 years old and he was the same age. Six months after the baby was born I found that I was pregnant again. There was much pressure put on me to abort the baby just as there was pressure with the first pregnancy. While the parents of my boyfriend were happy that I was pregnant my own parents were not because they thought that I was too young to be having another baby. So when I told my parents that I was pregnant again, you can imagine that they did not take it very well. In fact this time even my boyfriend was upset and he disappeared for a few days without telling me where he was going or what he was doing. My own parents were really upset because they thought that it would be up to them to help me bring up this other baby and they couldn't cope. So the only solution that they could see was to have an abortion.. I didn't know where to go for help and my first son needed weekly treatment at the children's hospital. I even needed my mother to help with this because I needed help to get my son to the hospital for treatment.

I wondered how I could cope because my boyfriend didn't stay around because he didn't want another baby so soon. In the end my only choice was the abortion. This was carried out at a large women's hospital. They didn't say anything to me they just did the operation. My boyfriend took me in and was no support to me at all.

When I came out of surgery all I wanted was my baby but everyone told me not to be so stupid because it even wasn't a baby (I was 11 weeks pregnant) and if it was a baby it was dead now. My parents picked us up from the hospital and took us home. He stayed with me for about an hour then he went.

Eventually I became pregnant again (this time we had split up but were seeing one another sometime because he had someone else). When I knew I was pregnant I pleaded with him to get back together so I wouldn't have to go through with the abortion. But he didn't want me back and my parents again pushed and pushed and with no one to help me I conceded to another abortion.

After this abortion I swore I would not ever see him again but somehow I did and again I became pregnant (8 months later). By now I didn't care very much I didn't care how I looked, what I did, what anyone thought of me, and I didn't want or care if I didn't use contraception. I think I was punishing me and I didn't realise that I wasn't punishing just me. When I again went to my boyfriend and told him I was pregnant all he said was "you know where to go and what to do". By this time I thought I would go crazy because I had begun to think of myself as a murderer. I felt like a monster who killed her own babies and I couldn't believe that I kept doing it.

Even my parents were now totally disgusted by my behaviour and my irresponsibility.

After this third abortion I went on a downhill spiral. I hated myself and my boyfriend but I couldn't stop seeing him. It took another three years before it all came to an end.

What eventually happened was that I started suffering not only severe depression, crying all the time, I started having panic attacks. In fact I couldn't even leave the house. I was terrified of people. I felt that people could tell that I had killed so many babies. I also felt that I was really mad. I couldn't control anything in my life and I had this terrible fear that my first son (whom I loved a lot) was going to die. I was scared that I was going to die. I kept having so many nightmares. In fact I kept seeing my babies dead and broken in bits and I would wake up crying and spend my day crying.

Eventually I found a self-help group and went there for nearly three years and have gone to counselling about the same amount of time. However, for the last 9 months I have been seeing a lady called Anne and she has been counselling me about the abortions only. Without her help I think I would probably have ended it all. In fact I was thinking seriously about suicide the day that someone gave me her phone number. In fact I didn't really want to go to any more counselling because the other counselling hadn't helped so I didn't see how this one was going to help. All I could think about was if I committed suicide then everything would be finished. As I said I was very depressed and my self-esteem was destroyed through the abortions and drinking and affairs since my first abortion.

As I said I didn't really want to see this lady called Anne I didn't want to tell another person my story all over again and nothing happen, but today I am glad that something pushed me to ring. To give it one last try. The work that Anne has done with me has been amazing because she has introduced me to God again and has helped me believe that even someone as awful as me can be loved by God and the day that I really started to get better was the day that Anne said that God loved me and my babies didn't hate me. That day I cried a whole river of tears. It was almost like someone was washing me clean of something so dirty and ugly. After this time I really began to feel better. Little by little. I have now had a Mass said for my three aborted babies, gone to reconciliation and I know that their angels brought them to the Mass that night so that I could say goodbye to them. It is important to understand that on the night of the Mass and the many months of counselling and spiritual direction I had with I was able to forgive myself because God forgave me first. It has taken many years of suffering and pain but I have finally reached a stage where I am free of the awful pain in my heart.

I still have days that hurt me and when I remember what I did to my beautiful babies I feel great horror but I no longer think of suicide in fact I look forward to life and I also try and not blame myself all the time. I think it's important to understand that I didn't know any better so I did what others told me to do. I also am grateful that my son is coming along really well even though he is disabled he is a great joy to me. I also stopped being promiscuous because I know that God loves me really and I don't have to look for false love. I still hope that one day I will meet someone nice who will love me and my son and who will want to have children with me and who will not abandon me. This is my hope and I know it will happen because God loves me.

10.

Abortion Grief and Trauma – Why?

It is useful to attempt to understand post abortion grief and trauma and some of its characteristics and why these symptoms occur. This may help us in understanding how "right" and one might say "worthy" are these external manifestations of internal conflict.

It's mistakenly understood that where a woman wants to have an abortion (for whatever reason) there should be no psychological and or spiritual dissonance. It's believed that she understands her situation and has acted according to the reasoned dictates of that situation. However, it is not understood that over and above the rational mind there is the spirit, the soul, the emotions, which are also part and parcel of the person's system. Her emotional life, that is, the affective, and her spiritual life, are as paramount to her wellbeing as is her cognitive, rational being. Together these independent yet complementary aspects unite to form the complete, balanced, fully functioning being. Too much of the rational, or too much of the emotional results in a person who is "unwell".

Abortion trauma results because the psychological and spiritual are assaulted. It's not because they (women and men) have seen the baby. In most cases the abortion is carried out within the first trimester of pregnancy so there was not even movement. Post abortion trauma might be better understood where the pregnancy is advanced, as the changes within the woman ensure that she has formed some kind of attachment to the baby. Therefore it is possible to imagine that trauma would be present. However, what is most intriguing and most interesting is the fact that post abortion trauma is found in and is as severe in cases where the pregnancy is in its early stages (2-6 weeks). One must then ask the question. Why? After all, emotional attachment has not had the opportunity to be formed. So what could possibly have triggered the sorrow, the regret, the anguish, the despair? If it is not the "law written on the human heart" (Jer 31:31) what could possibly cause the emptiness of heart, the sense that "a part of me has died"?

As a post abortion grief counsellor I encounter these comments, this behaviour, the anguish and regret. After listening to very many stories I have formed the opinion that abortion grief is the response to, or knowledge of one's own contribution to another's death. The intent or volitional factor. The human response to a violation of one's own and another's life principle. The solidarity, which an individual has with another human being, not merely a blob of tissues, has been severed. It's the awareness of consenting to something so awful and so outside of their range of "normal" behaviour, that deep fear and anxiety are activated. The guilt induced is so strong that to face it is impossible, therefore an attempt is made to cleanse the self from dissonance by behaviour which is aberrant and unexplainable and rooted in the *thanatos* desire or death wish.

The immediate response to this guilt is to hide oneself first from the reality, from self and then from others. This is achieved by changing their being from that which they are, into that which they are not. The loss experienced leads to diminished sense of self, health, capabilities, faith, family and friends and at times the sense of loss is so deep that a need to permanently lose oneself through psychosis or suicide is experienced. Only a scintilla of existence remains, and it is the last straw to hold on to.

The question, "abortion trauma and grief why?" can be answered at many levels but first and most important of all it must be understood at the deepest level, that is, the essence which is the human being. It must be answered at the level of the individual's own behaviour barometer, the conscience. It is at this level where the damage of abortion is at its deepest and most destructive. We cannot hope to understand abortion trauma unless we first attempt to understand conscience and its relationship to the human person. This invisible barometer of wellbeing, when compromised, either individually or corporately, leads to illness both of the mind and the body or the whole of society. The conscience cannot be manipulated by prevailing ideologies and therefore when an attempt is made to inscribe on it alien principles, it rebels against the assault by making individuals and society very sick. The language of a dulled conscience is one of alienation, confusion and erroneous judgement.

As an example of this I suggest that we look at the rampant sexual activity of the young (and not so young!) who go from sexual partner to sexual partner, mating and leaving until a ravenous hunger for sexual intercourse is developed but never satisfied. Every new partner is acceptable for a time and then boredom sets in requiring a search for a new one. In this scenario the conscience becomes confused. It no longer recognises truth, restraint, respect and restfulness. There is a sense of the loss of "something" indefinable. Something is missing and needs be found. Of course the search is not for something or someone but a search for peace of heart and mind (or conscience) which has been lost. The frenetic pace of a life lived at odds with itself is a sure sign that the internal radar or barometer has been damaged.

Conscience

For the Catholic, as for all Christians and people of goodwill, the belief is that sincerity, truth and freedom are important components in the development of conscience. However, whilst these are important in themselves, they are not supreme. To suggest that sincerity and freedom are supreme is to suggest that no higher authority, except the "self" exists. This is dangerous ground because the human being is notorious for self-protection and self-deception especially when this means adjusting a moral truth to suit one's own personal situation.

A Catholic understanding of a well-formed conscience is that in its formation, the individual follows the prompting of the inner voice, or commanding law written on our hearts. This is guided by the Holy Spirit, and subservient to the same Spirit, and leads us to do what is good and avoid that which is evil. Hence the outward manifestation of that inward guidance results in actions and behaviour which are both Christ-centred and neighbour-centred. That is, love of God and neighbour is evident. Further to this, a Catholic conscience is formed in accordance with the teachings of the Church, which is authorised to transmit the teachings of Jesus and his divine laws.

Actions contrary to divine laws act as catalysts for rebellion against nature and cause the conscience to formulate its judgements, and consequent actions, according to corrupted input.

Perhaps we can see that where a conscience is continually renewed and maintained with divine inspiration, truth leads to righteous judgement and behaviour. However, where conscience is muddied with erroneous input and then judgements made according to that input, it can only become coarsened and over time lose its pristine sensitivity to hearing the Authoritative commands. The conscience, as the direct radar to God, fulfils its function by listening to the voice of Him who Is and directs actions according to the received inspirations. The conscience cannot do so when it has been subjected to continual judgements and actions contrary to its design. A muddied conscience can only make muddied and confused judgements and decisions leading to behaviour alien to it.

A conscience formed and guided by the Holy Spirit and divine laws is a conscience formed in truth, love and freedom and not guilt. Truth always gives freedom. However, a conscience formed according to human machinations must by its nature accommodate variations to the truth. Conscience formed from habitual errors and according to intellectual judgements alone must learn to manipulate truth. In the development of conscience, it is clear that the human person must acknowledge accountability and responsibility. Correctly formed, it is clear that the development of conscience leads the human person to be truly human. While the conscience is fragile, it is also the aspect of the human being, most capable of being truly Christlike. In the development of conscience *Truth* is always supreme – *I am the Way and the Truth and the Life* (Jn: 14:6) – and conscience bows down before it.

The conscience is a most extraordinary faculty of human creation. It enunciates its un-ease by insistent dis-ease. It refuses to rest while the legacy of sin and deviation remains. While time and/or suppression may erase the memory of sin, the indelible mark left by the sin acts to bring a sense of guilt to the individual and society. Extended further, this sense of sin and guilt must then be expiated via means available to the corrupted reality.

A healthy and unsullied conscience is the essence of a human being. When this instrument is maintained finely-tuned, it allows the person to hear God and to hear neighbour. To feel God and to feel for one's neighbour. To have a dulled conscience means to be deaf to the pain of the other. It means to be able to engage in acts of pain and violence against God and neighbour. It means to have no remorse, no inkling of pain inflicted on God or neighbour.

Abortion acts as the sharpest of instruments against the conscience. Repeated acts of violence and death against the conscience serve to blind and nullify its discrimination for good. With over 50,000,000 abortions annually (globally) individual and societal conscience appears all but dead. Its function, to conform human beings to the moral law designed by God for the good of his creation, has been blurred and its guidance of the human will is so compromised by habitual sin, that even as it attempts to forewarn of error (by guilt) the message is distorted.

The effect of abortion on the conscience is clearly discernible even where there has been no religious formation. It is extraordinary to see, even in women and men professing no religious persuasion, how traumatised are their consciences. How restless is their spirit! How an indefinable "something" causes them anguish. How an intangible "something" causes them distress to the point of illness. Indeed it is true what the Psalmist says, "my soul is struck with terror." (Ps. 6:3)

Human beings were not designed to abort children. They were designed to fulfil a desire to give birth, therefore the damage which abortion does cannot be repaired by psychological or psychiatric measures (although these measures can help) but by God Himself. Only He can repair the damage to the sacred sanctuary where He encounters the creature of his desire. The healing of abortion grief comes when there is an encounter between the sinner and God. When this reconciliation is facilitated then solidarity with God and neighbour (including the aborted infant) is re-established and reintegration into the human and heavenly family is achieved. Failure to reconcile abortive humanity with God can only lead to these words spoken by the Holy Father, John Paul II, in his homily on the fifth Sunday of Lent, 1981:

If a society concedes the right to kill a human being when still in the womb, then that society starts down a slope with incalculable consequences in the moral order. If it becomes licit to take a human life when it is weakest, wholly dependent on its mother, on its parents, on the strength of human consciences, then what dies is not only an innocent human being but also human conscience itself. And who knows how widely and quickly the cancer of this destruction of conscience will spread.

11.

Post Abortion Syndrome
and its Symptoms

"I am deeply grieved even unto death" (Mk 14: 34)

The impact of a trauma-inducing event like abortion, if left unattended, manifests in a myriad of ways and results in a change towards negative behaviour.

A syndrome is usually understood to mean a group of associated, similar or interrelated symptoms, at times individually or concurrently present. For a syndrome to be accepted as a "syndrome", consistency over time, individuals, language or expression, or behaviour should be identified. Post Abortion Syndrome fits that bill. A typical list of Post abortion grief and trauma symptoms follows. Individuals, who do not know one another and whose only commonality is abortion, display similar elements of the list. It includes guilt, shame, fear, low self-esteem, chronic depression, suicide ideation, sleep disorders, eating disorders, relationship difficulties, internalised anger, flashbacks, alcohol/drug abuse, sexual frigidity/promiscuity, panic attacks, psychological numbness, child abuse, atonement symptoms, anniversary reactions and absent relationship with the spiritual. Many of these symptoms are self-explanatory. However, I will explain several of them so as to clarify their interrelationship,

But before I do this I want to speak a little about the latest study into the effects of abortion on women. This study was carried out by Professor Priscilla K. Coleman, 2011, and published in *British Journal of Psychiatry* and found that overall, of all mental health problems of women, 10% are related to abortion and the increased risk of severe mental health problems rises by 81%. Imagine 10% of 50,000,000 women (globally) who undergo the procedure every year. This equates to 5,000,000 women every year affected by abortion related mental health issues.

This was one of the largest ever studies on this topic using 877,181 participants out of which 163,831 had had an abortion. This study took care to avoid all data which could lead to the mantra "bias" by its stringent criteria for inclusion/exclusion of previous studies which were deemed questionable.

Professor Coleman, who has done much work into this area of mental health issues in women, presents the most comprehensive study to date and according to her this study was carried out in order to offer the best and most valid information to those seeking abortion and for women to be clearly informed and to make informed decision when deciding whether or not to abort.

This study showed some astonishing figures: 34% increase in anxiety disorders (e.g., OCD, panic attacks and some of the symptoms experienced over time like sadness, uncontrollable weeping, loss of concentration, loss of joy of life).

110% greater risk in alcohol and substance abuse, leading to other self abuse as a result of being under these influences.

155% greater risk of attempting suicide and suicide ideation (persistent thinking about suicide).

This is a study which is not old or antiquated but is a new and reliable one using and analysing other reputable studies (meta analysis) by reputable researchers without the "religious mantra." This study says clearly please watch out, abortion seriously hurts women and men and babies and society. If the health of women is something we are all interested in, which then leads to health of society, then abortion is not the answer. A woman will never be able to "live" with herself either in the immediate of, or in the future post an abortion. Something within her remembers the child that was not born, but should have been. The intentional factor in which she was a contributor weighs heavily on her. Her conscience is more than a refined "superego"; it is its link to its creator and it's the place where God and creature speak with one another.

While the "Superego" of psychology fame appears to speak or warn of right and wrong it does not know why it's right or wrong and settles with "learned behaviour." Conscience speaks of refined reason for not doing a wrong so the more refined a conscience the more "right" and Godlike judgement made. And thus it is at this place or level where the pain following abortion begins because something in the "inner me" knows that the judgement was wrong and like Adam in the Garden hides behind words and actions for fear of being found out that "I" had no right to do what I did. "I had no right to destroy another "I" who was also gifted and meant for a life to be lived" Abortion is not accidental but intentional and conscience cannot rest in this untruth.

Death through abortion remains a near kinsman of the death of Abel (Gn.4:8).

Some of the Symptoms experienced by those suffering post abortion grief and trauma

FEAR

Fear is a highly aversive, negative emotion, uncomfortable, unpleasant, and requiring urgent attention and elimination of its cause. Fear is aroused when a threat or perceived threat or danger to oneself or a significant other is confronted. Fear results from the notion that pain may be experienced. When anxiety is aroused due to some subjective stimulus or threatening memory, fear is aroused due to an objective stimulus and or memory. Fear is the response to a memory of pain. The fears of a pregnant woman who believes she should not be pregnant at this time are manifold. There are all the "what ifs" and into the "what ifs" basket fall such questions as: "What if he leaves me?", "What if I can't make it?", "What if I lose my job?", "What if my husband, boyfriend, parents, friends, peers, school abandon me?" The list of "what ifs" is endless so that the reality of a living, breathing human life, a child who is "a part of me" and dependent for its total protection is able to find none. These are the pre-abortion fears. Post abortion "fear" wears a different mask. Pre-abortion, the fear felt is related to the situation that the woman finds herself in, and the difficulties that this situation presents; post abortion fear is more abstract and appears to me more metaphysical.

Without exception all those who have sought help for post abortion trauma speak of a "deep sense of fear" as if something within them is waiting in a continual state of arousal, for a punishment to be meted out. They appear to live in a perpetual state of doom. The guilt experienced by their action has placed them in a hyper alert state. Their internal dissonance not finding an outlet goes into overdrive and remains there until the issue is resolved. Fear needs to be confronted because fear causes the imagination to seriously misrepresent reality and this will affect the life of the individual to the point of leading to debilitating mental health illness or even phobias.

GUILT

During the course of human socialisation individuals learn that certain actions and decisions may hurt others and, in doing so, inflict pain. Empathy develops as a result of being able to relate to another, to see or feel the pain experienced by another, and one is moved by the experience. Over time human beings learn that to cause pain to another result in self-pain and self-diminution. The internalised ideas about right and wrongdoing develop and strengthen until a personal set of norms and rules is established. Indeed empathy and conscience together form a solid barrier against the destruction of like species. The idea of murdering another human being is abhorrent to most people, hence the notion that responsibility for all is upon the shoulders of each and every person. Indeed we have an intuitive knowledge that we are our "brother's keeper" (Gen 4:10). It is in this context that guilt develops. Chronic or acute guilt develops when an individual fails to live up to personal moral standards and is sustained in its intensity by self-hate and crippling self-rejection.

Perhaps the best way to describe guilt is that it is an emotion which has as its fruit self-destruction. It is an emotion, which demands escape rather than interaction and it is an emotion entirely aversive in its ugliness. No other emotion has the potential to be as self-damaging as guilt, and no other emotion has the capacity to poison an individual's personality. Guilt induces severe psychological and spiritual suffering, because it points the finger at the self and ceaselessly accuses of wrongdoing. Yet it points also to something else. It points to a time pre-guilt. It points to a time of innocence, and so guilt accuses the person of the loss of innocence.

Guilt following an abortion occurs as a result of the woman or man's own set of moral certitudes being compromised. Regardless of the reason for the abortion, the sense that a very deep wrong was done, induces such self-loathing that to run from it becomes the only escape mechanism. Hyper alertness becomes the continual mode of existence because guilt increases the sense of doom. Hyper alertness means being on the go all the time so that the sense of being "found out" is diminished. The guilt of the abortive woman or man, like the guilt exhibited by Adam and Eve in the garden, urges the individuals to run and hide from life. Life and God become very threatening. One hides from something serious.

The state of hyper alertness and strain then leads to the employment of psychological strategies in order to cope with the persistent need to hide what is shameful. Symptoms of guilt, e.g., hand-washing, ritualised movements, avoidance of anything related to the abortion, anniversary symptoms, that is unconscious remembrance of date of abortion or anticipated birth date, have their origins in a traumatised spirit. Buried guilt has its own peculiar expressions. They include explosive temper, argumentative personality, uncontrollable and erratic weeping, erratic behaviour, substance/alcohol abuse (in order to expedite one's own demise), strong aversion to children or alternatively over-protection of children and a constant and strong demand to be acknowledged as worthy, lovable, pleasing. These form part of the "guilt syndrome".

Guilt is a universal emotion. It is not limited to the religious or to the West but is experienced by all cultures and races, when a perceived wrong is done to another. However, continual wrong has the capacity to blind individuals and society to the effects of pain, leading to dehumanisation and ultimately to a perversion of Truth. Further, guilt serves to alienate and to exclude human beings from the freedom of God, and to attach them to the bonds of sin. Guilt taps into that primal sin of Adam and adds to that primordial rebellion, leading to an increase of societal suffering and thus the nagging, persistent, malaise. Corporate responsibility for sin unites all (we have a debt to pay) and slowly but surely diminishes the capacity for compassion, and helps to form an unholy solidarity.

Abortion, euthanasia, suicide, genocide, infanticide, bestiality, homicide, substance abuse, can only happen because of the tacit approval by the silent community. It is the silent majority that does not want to intrude on another's privacy, or to question another's rights, that gives permission for these atrocities to continue. However, it must be understood that whilst human rights and societal rights are important and good, over-exaggeration of these rights obscures the concept of duty, which accompanies the rights. Rights always equal duties in equal measure, except that with the abortion issue only one side has "rights": that is, the bigger and more vocal of the two parties. The child being aborted has not been consulted over his/her "right" to live, so it appears that only the most vocal and the strongest has the so-called "rights".

Whilst individual responsibility for abortion cannot be denied, communal responsibility and ideology must also not be diminished. Abortion today has a corporate dimension, hence the experience of corporate guilt. This surely must explain the headlong rush towards isolation. Within that imposed isolation, society can then protect itself against reaction to guilt. In this way society does not have to deal with the knowledge that another group of millions of infants have died in the past year. Isolation can also be a protective measure against the psychological and spiritual confusion of this age.

The poet Kahlil Gibran expressed this beautifully:

> *And as a single leaf turns not yellow*
> *But with the silent knowledge of the whole tree*
> *So the wrong doer cannot do wrong*
> *Without the hidden will of you all.*
> *And when one of you falls down*
> *He falls for those behind him*
> *A caution against the stumbling stone*
> *Aye and he falls for those ahead of him*
> *Who though faster and surer of foot, yet*
> *Removed not the stumbling stone.*[5]

It would be easy to lay the blame for abortions at the feet of the aborting mother, father, or abortionists. It is my contention, however, that the community in which these holocausts occur is also very much responsible. The community, in which the aborting woman lives and is an integral part, must bear some responsibility because the aborting woman is part of that community, and is a reflection of the prevailing and unspoken attitudes and beliefs. Abortion is a community issue because at stake are the mother, father, grandparents and a dead infant who would have been a member of that community. It is the community, which has allowed abortion to flourish. Abortion has now become so accepted that it has become unstoppable. What caused this flourishing menace? I would suggest apathy, individual self-interest, unbridled ego-centricism and a false notion of privacy. Unbridled individualism rejects community and communion and builds barriers of isolation where all manners of evil and perversion then become possible.

SHAME

Shame is both a negative and a positive emotion, which announces that something within us has experienced a loss in our hearts. It demonstrates that something has occurred which has instilled a fear into our being, something not present before. Shame is connected with dignity and integrity and it results from the endangering of these two vital and life-sustaining attributes. Dignity and integrity are vital for our connection with another and to our very humanity. When these two are endangered "shame" presents itself as a cover-up. The absence of dignity from our being tells another that we have experienced a loss and that while this loss exists we are unable to love freely, to move freely and to behave freely. The experience of shame removes freedom from freedom. Shame introduces loss of freedom because shame now places conditions on, and boundaries between, the other and the self. Shame also places a barrier between love and life, and can be also expressed as a loss of grace.

It's of particular interest to try to understand the subtle difference between guilt and shame because it is in the difference that we can then see the resultant behaviour. The inherent instinct of guilt is to try to escape from any personal pain, struggle, responsibility and failure, and to project the guilt (blame) onto someone else other than the self. There is always a need of a scapegoat to take on the sense of wrongdoing. The hallmark of guilt is blame. Shame on the other hand seeks to cover the loss by withdrawing and trying to find fig leaves to cover up. Shame tells the other that "my essence" has been violated and "I am no longer the same as I was before". In the eyes of the other, the "I" is now less and there is a need to cover this loss with flight. The "self" needs to feel valued and affirmed for itself. When this does not occur a fear emerges which seeks to put the "I" into flight. The hallmark of shame is flight.

ANXIETY

Anxiety arises as a response from some internal barometer, or stimulus, memory or perhaps some internalised fear, terror, un-ease. Anxiety is the grossly exaggerated form of un-ease. Whilst it is a response to the illumination of some internal negative self-belief it requires an external stimulus to activate it. However, the important thing about anxiety and the activation of this is the reality that in the activation, other linked scripts are also activated, such as other fears, terrors, wounds, hurts, disappointments and so on. This is especially true of those scripts that have had a deep impact, and have remained unaddressed. These "wounds" have found a niche within the psychology of the individual and have become established there and remain outside the periphery of immediate consciousness. Anxiety and fears are conditions which find their genesis in situations where the individual's own perceived sense of safety was threatened and where personal integrity was violated or threatened with violation.

Anxiety, a human and unavoidable condition, is an indicator that something different from what was there previously, has occurred. It is a fear of this difference being discovered that arouses the anxiety script.

Anxiety and guilt and shame are correlated and share links to something which the person considers "wrong". It is the self-knowledge of the state prior to the "wrong-doing" and the self-knowledge following the "wrong-doing" which is understood, because the anxiety script has been activated. Self-esteem, which is also a subjective experience, is threatened when anxiety is experienced. Self-esteem, the self's own guide to sense of self-worth and therefore mental health, perceives in anxiety a negative attribute. An attack on self-esteem does not pass by without leaving behind a permanent imprint of its passage.

SUICIDE

Today we live in a society in which death occurs in different ways. The youth suicide rate is rising, as often reported. We are told that the suicide rate among young males is increasing as are the modes of violence against the self. Yet abortion is not countenanced as a root cause. Government and private task forces work diligently to find the cause of this epidemic. Yet, they do not include abortion among their considerations.

Suicide is the total absence and rejection of love of self, of love of the gift of life. Self-rejection has reached the degree that there is revulsion against one's own life and a refusal to accept this life and one's history. It is the ultimate refusal of self.

The abortion/suicide connection has been known for a long time and recently in her latest work Professor Priscilla K. Coleman in a study, together with past studies, has found that abortion increases the risk of attempted suicide by a huge 155%. Imagine a huge 155% risk of suicide and still the connection is not even countenanced or discussed and an individual presenting with suicide ideation or attempted suicide is not asked about an abortion history. What does it take to link the two together? How many more deaths will it take before the abortion/ suicide connection is made and dealt with appropriately?

Over the past 25 years most nations have experienced a dramatic increase in suicide rates and in some cases statistics cited have been extraordinarily high. Specifically some nations like Australia have witnessed dramatic increases in male suicides, whilst European nations witnessed an increase in female suicides. The increase over the last 25 years is most interesting as this is also the period in which abortion on demand has galloped forward. Family breakdown has also increased markedly. Substance abuse began slowly until today it is out of control. These anti-life activities appear to have developed a momentum which is out of control.

The abortion-suicide-substance abuse 220% increased risk following abortion (Coleman, 2011) link has been known within the medical literature for many years, yet it has been suppressed. Is it compassion or perhaps is the media not interested in the abortion-suicide connection? Is abortion so politically "hot" that the media refuse to become involved? Yet for anyone who has eyes it is not difficult to see the connection.

Abortion after-effects can be slow in developing, though at times abortion grief, which manifests at times prior to the abortion or immediately following is identified and connected to the event and easier to treat. Post abortion grief is easily identified and with some help the individual can learn to integrate and live with the act. However, Post Abortion Syndrome (PAS) is different. PAS is silent and deadly. It is unresolved grief over the abortion, which may have happened many years earlier. At a conscious level the incidence may even have been forgotten. However, at the unconscious level it has remained active and working its deadly poison. The complicated nature of PAS ensures that it remains hidden until a triggering event forces the trauma to the surface.

Whilst the reality of Post Abortion Syndrome (PAS) remains barely accepted, generally unacknowledged and therefore untreated, it works to change the sufferer's personality and life. Where an individual was happy and carefree pre-abortion, after the abortion and development of PAS the same individual shows a marked change. Depression, weeping, unhappiness, loss of joy and withdrawal lead to self-imposed isolation and self-designed punishment regime. For those who deal with post abortion trauma and who understand the nature of Post Abortion Syndrome, it is not difficult to see how suicide ideation, suicidal behaviour and completed suicide can occur. The emotional pain following abortion is at times unbearable. The sense of regret, helplessness and loss, can at times appear insurmountable. The deep sense of loss is especially acute around the anniversary date of the abortion or anticipated birth date of the child. These times are critical and PAS sufferers are most vulnerable around that time. For the post-abortive woman (or man), suicide is the escape from pain but it is also, in a sense, a way of being reunited with the child that they aborted and have since achingly missed.

DEPRESSION

Depression, following an abortion, is very common and may be diagnosed as either chronic or acute. Depression may begin at some point before the abortion itself when the decision is being made. It may begin immediately following the abortion (after the initial relief) or it may develop over time as the woman (or man) attempts to suppress the abortion event. Contrary to popular opinion post abortion depression is extremely common. Its development and duration may vary, but its existence is undeniable even where the abortion was sought for what were thought to be good reasons, or by an individual who did not originally want the baby.

Understanding the reasons for the depression and its manifestation may help ease some of the pain involved. Depression occurs because the woman (or man) comes to an understanding that the abortion was final. There can be no going back. It was a completed act from which there is no return. Perhaps the finality factor coupled with the enormity factor propels the woman (and man) into a state of psychological shock from which it is difficult to emerge unscathed. A depressed individual cannot usually emerge from this without help. To emerge from this place of darkness requires much mercy, love and patience because individuals reach a stage where they possibly don't want to return to normality. They see their suffering as just, and deserved, and at times struggle against returning to a healthy condition. There is the deep sense of atonement. By their own pain and suffering they feel that they atone in some way for the pain which they have inflicted on their unborn children.

Depression, post abortion, manifests in a myriad of ways. Commonly there will be very low self-esteem, lethargy, explosive temper or alternatively over-compliance, frigidity or promiscuity, weeping (at times uncontrollably), panic attacks, indecisiveness, numbness, difficulty with relationships and more. Typically, the depressed person feels and believes that joy, laughter and happiness are not for her. Her world is often peopled with other depressed and unhappy individuals or alternatively she lives an isolated existence. Studies into post-abortive depressed individuals indicate that the low self-esteem factor is very strong, and preoccupation with self-destructive behaviour is also very strong. Perhaps the strongest and most telling sign or symptom is her/his withdrawal from normal day-to-day activities at a functioning level, which is permanently set on autopilot. Her sense of reality is compromised and this individual learns to move from day to day in a surreal state. He or she is lethargic. There is a marked absence of sparkle in the eyes and the person cannot respond to daily emotional demands such as joy, love, anger etc.

Medical and mental health professionals often misdiagnose depression following an abortion, leading to misdirected or inadequate treatment. A depressed individual is one whose spirit has retreated. The client may have been biologically well treated but the spiritual factor is missing.

ALCOHOL/SUBSTANCE ABUSE

The relationship between abortion and alcohol and substance abuse has been established and studies appear to clearly indicate a strong correlation between the two. Researchers who have studied the correlation have found that those women who abort their babies have a higher risk 220% (Coleman, 2011, Reardon, 1987, Fergusson, 2006, Gissler, Hemminki & Lonnqvist, 1987-1994) of using alcohol or hard drugs as a measure for pain relief or escape. Substance abuse has been cited as a cause of addiction, post abortion.

Perhaps it should not surprise us to learn this because unresolved abortion grief causes deep pain and deep pain requires pain management. It is the sense of shame, guilt, loss and pain which usually the abortive woman is not permitted to express, and which she must endure alone, that leads to the use of substances which create an avenue of escape. Alcohol and other substances may be taken privately. Whilst these two substances have a social dimension, for the abortive man or woman it is not the social aspect, which leads to the initial introduction, but rather the need to alleviate the pain of loss or guilt. Alcohol and or substance abuse serve two purposes for the abortive individual. The abuse alleviates pain and sets into motion the path to self-destruction. At the deepest level the individual knows that this deadly cocktail is dangerous, yet still continues, because of the unconscious sense that this is what she deserves.

Of course the initial introduction to substance abuse may have occurred simply as a measure to deal with the recurring nightmares, flashbacks about the abortion, sleep disorders and depression. Indeed there are studies which have found that a large number of women who had aborted later became addicted to alcohol.

I have encountered young women (as young as 14 and 16 years of age) who are drinking and drug-taking in order to sleep without nightmares, and without hearing the baby's voice crying out, or because "I keep dreaming about dead babies" (Melissa). Alcohol and substance abuse are used as anaesthesia to blot out the memory.

Today as we hear of more and more young people becoming addicted to substances, which are harmful to themselves and tragic for their families, I am convinced that for many, abortion lies behind their death wish. Although many projects embark on finding a solution to this diabolical agent against youth, the one confronting us (abortion) is continually ignored. What will it take for abortion to be considered a risk factor?

PANIC ATTACKS – INDECISIVENESS

It should not be a surprise to learn that after an abortion the woman most often will have difficulties with panic attacks and decision-making. I place these two together because I believe they are related. Professor Coleman, (2011) in her study found 37% of post-abortive women suffer increased risk of anxiety disorders (e.g., OCD, panic attacks) and 37% increased risk of depression, sadness, uncontrollable weeping loss of concentration loss of joy of life.

Panic attacks may be severe or less severe. Severe panic attacks immobilise and virtually psychologically paralyse an individual into a state of twilight existence. This means that the individual experiencing severe panic attacks becomes so terrified of a certain action, movement or smell that they shut down and are unable to function especially in a specific area of their life. If panic attacks remain undealt with, in due course the individual's whole life will become isolated.

What is a panic attack? In layman's terms it simply means a shutting down or psychological freezing at the recall of a memory of something traumatic. The event may not even be overtly remembered, or it may be a smell, colour, word, indeed the person cannot even think what it is causing the shut down. However, at a deep unconscious level, something about someone or someplace evokes deep emotions about a past traumatic event, which has caused pain and has remained incompletely healed.

Panic attacks are serious because over time, unless resolved, these have the capacity to seriously affect the life and quality of life of the individual to such an extent that the individual may become almost paralysed with fear, and ultimately housebound and isolated for a panic attack is fear of fear. Any trigger may cause fear to return. This serious because the person is afraid of having another panic attack and because of this fear actually brings on annother attack so to avoid the triggers, any triggers, isolation becomes the answer. To the person suffering panic attack the reaction is toxic.

Post abortion, Leeanne was unable to drive her vehicle. She experienced deep terror, shivering, nausea and disorientation. Indeed, this young woman had become so paralysed with fear of others "knowing" about what she had done, that she was unable to drive her other three children to school, shop for the family, or even go to the corner store. The car, to this young woman, represented something so painful and so awful that she reacted violently against it. When someone else drove Leeanne, she experienced no reaction. She could not even sit in her car alone. Over many counselling sessions it emerged that she made the final decision, to abort, whilst driving in her car. She even insisted on driving herself to the clinic (her boyfriend went with her to drive them home after) and all the way there she kept hoping for an accident to happen. These two events, that is, the definitive abortion decision made in the car, and her willing herself to have an accident so that she would not have to go through with the abortion, left on her heart and mind an indelible mark. After the abortion itself, the fear remained that she might still have an accident, especially when she had her children in the car. She had lost complete confidence in her skills in driving, coupled with guilt about the abortion and "his" (God's) anticipated punishment of her through her children, led to her panic attacks. Much work was done to re-establish her confidence in God and herself and today after many months she is able to drive again.

Linda's very first panic attack occurred three days following her abortion. On her first outing to the shopping centre Linda experienced a classic panic attack. Her words to me were, "as I entered the shopping centre I began to feel uneasy. I didn't know why. Then I remember standing in the middle of the centre, and suddenly I felt that everyone was looking at me and they knew that I'd had an abortion. I could see it in their eyes that they knew and that they were judging me. I just froze, I wanted to scream at them that I knew I'd made a mistake, but I couldn't fix it, so I just stood there. I guess I deserved their awful judgement." From this time onwards Linda was unable to go anywhere where there were crowds, including parties, because she always felt that the people were looking at her and they knew that she had "killed my baby". Linda's guilt was so strong that she froze, and by the time she received counselling, panic attacks were a feature of her life. Linda also could be helped and today she is able to function normally.

Indecisiveness is also related to the abortion experience. This I believe is related to the actual decision made, that is, to abort. The woman who believes that she has worked through the reasons for abortion, and satisfactorily come to the conclusion that it was the right decision, then finds herself grieving seriously over the decision, and becomes afraid. It is a fear based on the actual decision made and not on the process of decision-making. This particular individual exercised the rational aspect of her being but suppressed the emotional. Post abortion the emotional aspect is heightened and the loss she feels leads her to the belief that the decision she made with utmost care has let her down. From this time onwards, her decision-making will always be coloured by this experience leading to doubt, hesitancy, indecisiveness and procrastination. Over the long term this then leads to lowered self-esteem, insecurity about self, and an almost paranoid fear of anything which requires her to make a decision. Phobias may also develop from this. Indecisiveness can be ameliorated and ultimately cured but it is a long, slow and at times painful process.

FLASHBACKS

Nearly all my clients have reported flashback memories, although they may have used different expressions, or experienced different types of flashback. Flashbacks are the instantaneous reliving of the entire abortion event, or a certain part of it. This seems to indicate that the abortion, even though it may have happened many years earlier and has been suppressed, has remained active at the unconscious level. Kelly's flashbacks were triggered when she heard a particular song on the radio. Maria's flashbacks were triggered by a particular smell. Sally relived the abortion experience when in a twilight stage of sleep. Anna relived her abortion experience at Christmas when she saw Santa arrive in the shopping centre. She recalled that her children would never sit on Santa's knee and have a photo taken with him.

It appears that a triggering event will and does activate a deeply held and suppressed memory. The triggering event (whatever it is for the individual) acts as a cue, which unlocks (temporarily), the door behind which is to be found the "demon". In many ways flashbacks, whilst painful, have the capacity to lead to healing of deep-seated wounds. They act as catalysts for help because flashbacks will continue and strengthen in intensity and frequency until the event is dealt with. Flashbacks literally ensure that the one experiencing these relives the event in its entire and total intensity. The person relives all the emotions, thoughts, pain, doubts and anger as she experienced them on that particular morning/afternoon of the abortion.

ANNIVERSARY REACTIONS

Professor Anne Ancelin Schützenberger has much to say on the theory of anniversary reactions (conscious or unconscious) which are very common among abortive females.[7] Anniversary reactions are identified reactions such as sadness, weeping, and attempted suicide, self harm, usually at or near the anniversary date of the abortion or near the expected birth date of the infant which was aborted. Valerie attempted suicide every year in the month of June. For five years Valerie's mental state would begin to decline (she was under psychiatric care) until in desperation and pain she would attempt to take her own life. This young lady wanted to die to be with her aborted infants (three of them). The mental health and medical profession should investigate anniversary reactions seriously. Where a patient shows a history of repeat attempted suicides it is important to investigate closely the possible causes, including and especially an abortion history. Strong anniversary reactions will not disappear over time, and may continue (at times tragically) until the root cause (abortion/sexual abuse) is openly dealt with. Grief around the anniversary date is often profound and requires open expression in order that it may be brought to a satisfactory conclusion.

Anniversary reactions speak volumes. When we consider that those women and men suffering abortion after-effects have most often suppressed either the event (abortion) or the emotions connected with the event, then the anniversary reactions speak of something requiring completion. Further, when we consider that anniversary reactions occur around the time of the due date of birth, then this seems to me to imply that the body, mind and spirit are attempting to complete a process begun and interrupted prematurely by the abortion. There appears to be a deeply held psychic memory of a pregnancy and the hormonal changes needed to complete the pregnancy. Further, it appears that whilst the conscious memory works to suppress the deviation, the unconscious (or spirit) memory works towards concluding the process according to its design.

RELATIONSHIP DIFFICULTIES

Global studies clearly indicate that abortion is disastrous for relationships. They clearly show that where an abortion is procured, especially to save a marriage or relationship, it invariably is the catalyst for the final disintegration of that relationship. Studies appear to strongly suggest that weakened relationships do not survive an abortion decision and even in relationships that appear strong, an abortion clearly indicates that the relationship is troubled. Where an abortion decision is forced by one of the partners it really sounds a death knell not only on the baby but also on the existing relationship.

Perhaps the most telling aspect of the death of a relationship following abortion is the barrier which is placed between the couple, even when both made the decision to abort their baby. It appears that "something" destructive enters into the relationship and it will in due course exert influence. A sense of distrust enters where it never existed and weakens the bond between them. It appears like a deadly parasite entering into the relationship, slowly worming its way deep into their bond, utterly destroying it.

What seems to add to the difficulties in the relationship is a sense of rage, which was never there before. Hannah spoke these words to me: "After the abortion I just hated him. I had wanted him to take control and tell me that he loved our baby and me. Instead he couldn't wait for the abortion to happen. It was like nothing to him, but to me it was our baby. I'll never forgive him! He killed our love and our life together." More disturbing than Hannah's comment was Jerry's comment: "I can't understand how my wife could do such a thing. We didn't have money problems. We didn't have family problems. Our two existing children were at school so there was no reason why we couldn't have had the third baby. Except that she didn't want it. Something died in me that morning and I can't see my wife the way I used to see her. I don't know if we can survive this." In fact Jerry's marriage did not survive. He left shortly after.

Frances, a young mother of two children, who aborted her and her husband's third child, reacted exactly the same as Jerry. In her own words she said, "He abandoned me. He abandoned our conceived baby and our two other children. He betrayed what we had. I can't stand him touching me anymore. I hate him!"

Perhaps what can be said about abortion and relationships is that a procured abortion is not conducive to maintenance of a relationship and appears to hasten the demise of an already unstable one. Further, where there has been a stable relationship and either or both parties agree to an abortion (for whatever the reason) the relationship is destabilised leading to a breakdown. Guilt, depression, sadness, anger and a sense of loss introduce into the previously healthy relationship an obstacle, which appears insurmountable.

Today we live in a society where traditional values and certitudes have been eroded and a type of hedonism has taken hold. With marriage breakdown and the family break-up continuing to increase, and childcare handed over to one parent or a succession of de facto parents, (including paid childcare facilities) a stand-off situation seems to have arisen. The standoff is between the parents, with children suffering the consequences. A deep animosity appears to have developed between males and females, and the result of this alienation is the death of children pre-birth and an increase in physical and sexual abuse and abandonment post-birth.

Parenting, that once noble profession of both men and women, has been devalued to the extent that now both males and females actively seek the termination of their child. Where a child is permitted to live, parenting tends to become conditional. A parent will be a parent for a specific time (e.g., three months after birth) and then will return to a more satisfying pre-pregnancy occupation. Often a parent then leaves the ongoing, long-term parenting to others who do not always have the best interest of the child at heart. Parents are generally designed to understand their child better than anyone else. There appears to be an unspoken language between parents and their child and only a parent in tune with his/her child is able to respond according to that need.

Parenting children is no longer considered worthwhile or rewarding, and the demand or lure to be fiscally productive is strong, to the detriment of the child's and parent's mental health. Added to this there appears to be a temporary–ness about relationships with a certainty that a large percentage of children will experience their parents' separation and the trauma attendant to such separation.

I would suggest that an abortion history in the life of either parent or both, coupled with a societal mentality which lauds abortion and denounces large families, also contributes to this escalating war against the species. An abortion history in a family places a barrier between parents and children, and the barrier in turn distances those in the relationship. In this scenario anything is possible, including the most unspeakable holocausts.

What has driven this division between males and females? And what has changed the established "good" of society, that is, the family? I would suggest it is the liberalised sexuality, competitive sexuality, and sexuality no longer valued and sacred, but a sexuality which is considered an instinct and therefore to be used and abused. Women no longer value their advantages as women, spouses, mothers and friends of their male partner and mate. In their rampant promiscuity (to equal the male) and their concession to abortion, they have forfeited their exclusivity. The relationships and homes they make have now only a temporary nature and indeed the provisions and expectations are that marriage will fail.

Where in the past the uniting of a couple in marriage implied permanency, children, stability and longevity, today the most that is expected is that the man, woman, career, must be nurtured and protected, a child is not. An inconveniently conceived child does not warrant the same care and concern, and certainly does not survive where it is considered an intrusion into an existing mode of life.

Marriage, motherhood and fatherhood have become devalued to the detriment of all society especially children and the vulnerable. Apart from the temporariness of the married state, as deduced from the high divorce rate, escalating abortion rate, and a weakened parenting style, the impact on children who have been allowed to live is profound. The child or children may experience a deep sense of abandonment and failure. A deep sense of guilt emanates from the belief that they are a burden. Under these conditions children not only suffer psychologically but also spiritually. A child who cannot experience permanency, guidance, and unconditional love, in a two parent setting is cheated of an inherent right. Added to this is the knowledge that he or she survived in a culture where children are unwanted and disposed of, adding to the sense of foreboding. These children have survived the abortionists' instruments and live in constant fear of being found unworthy, and abandoned or disposed.

Professor Phillip Ney in his studies over many years has found that children born into a family where there has been an abortion live with a deep sense of fear. They have to constantly "prove" their worthiness and he believes that even where the child/children have not been told that a sibling has been aborted, they intuitively know, and this knowledge leads to behaviour which is outside of normal child behaviour. These children he calls "abortion survivors".

Another type of abortion survivor is the individual on whom an abortion has been attempted and who has survived the attempt. In my own experience I have encountered only four individuals who have been told that an attempt was made on their life whilst still in womb. These three females and one male proved a challenge to work with because of a deep rage within them. Further, these individuals live with a sense of "unwantedness" a sense that they should not be alive and their whole life-style has been geared and lived entertaining a death wish. These types of abortion survivors exhibit the deepest sense of worthlessness, apathy and self-loathing. Indeed they vacillate between rage, sadness and a desire to complete the original attempt on their lives.

As parents, these types of survivors fare very badly with parenting styles, which at best are neglectful and at worst, abusive. Ann came to me after reading one of my articles on post abortion trauma. She had recognised in herself some of the symptoms and called to see me. Ann is married with three teenage children who, as she said, "were more than a handful and I don't like them. I can't be bothered with them they can do as they want." Ann vacillated between authoritarian and neglectful parenting styles, and the children reacted accordingly. She lives with the constant thought that she is unworthy of love or respect, yet when she does not receive these she becomes enraged. Today Ann continues therapy, and after many months not much progress has been made. The brick wall, for her, is the knowledge that she was never wanted; that there was a terrible violence perpetrated against her and that she should never have been here in the first place.

Since the sexual revolution of the sixties, the advent of public acceptance of and demand for abortion, and the disintegration of family life, children have been deprived of the most basic of human rights. Their right to be children, to be happy, to be protected, to be educated and to be valued has been eroded and all in the name of the so-called equality of the sexes. The living children of a society that demands and applauds abortion, are wounded children, and as wounded children can only become wounded adolescents and wounded adults. This then continues the suffering which began when a generation of men and women began to compete against one another (not complement) and decided that they did not need one another, and began to slowly but surely destroy sacred relationships and family.

12.

Mental Processing, Attachment, Dehumanisation and Atonement

To understand the reason for the occurrence of post abortion trauma and the manifestation of universally ensuing symptoms, it helps to understand the processes and their progression.

Mental Processing

Several theories posited for the processing of information are automatic and conscious processing. Automatic processing of information occurs without the application of attentional mechanisms. That is, the perceptual and cognitive faculties do not require conscious involvement in order to process ingoing data. This process is entirely subliminal and is not directed or volitional. Automatic processing is continuous and effortless and the processing of incoming data is guided by existing internal schema. Physical characteristics of incoming data are matched with existing material stored in the long-term memory and stored there for future use.

Semantic memory is the memory of collective general knowledge. It is our general understanding of "things", including terms and meaning, which have been ascribed to ourselves and our environment and which are universally understood. Semantic memory is the repository of shared information e.g., we all know what it means to eat or what the word or image of "dog" refers to.

Episodic memory on the other hand is an archive where individual experiences have been stored. Episodic memory, unlike semantic memory is private, and is conditional only on one's own experiences. For example, an abortion experience is personal to the individual who has experienced an abortion, and is not generically known by all. Episodic memory is definitely involved in post abortion trauma, and semantic memory, whilst being able to identify with pain, as pain per se, cannot relate to the abortion experience itself unless the individual has had the same experience.

Conscious processing requires both the cognitive and perceptual faculties to be intentionally employed. Attention must be given to information in order for it to be learned, stored and able to be retrieved later. Cognitive systems are alert to the processes of learning, and an awareness of the cognitive processes themselves is understood, e.g., rote learning used to memorise something. In this way the message of the cognitive process is that some particular information is to be processed in a particular way, that is, for storage and possible future retrieval.

Of the two theories, automatic processing of information occurs without effort or intention and is not necessarily revealed to the conscious mind. The conscious processing requires effort, energy and attention.

For the aborting woman both processes apply. At the automatic level, the external factors, such as: Where was she when she learned she was pregnant? What was she wearing? What were her immediate thoughts concerning this new information? Who was with her at the time? What emotions were present? At the conscious level: how was the abortion decided upon? What were the determinants? How did she feel? Who told her where to go for the abortion? Did she always want an abortion? Did she at any time not want an abortion? Who pressured her? How did she get to the abortion clinic? These questions occur at the automatic level and are internal. They occur automatically when a crisis is experienced, and we can be sure that semantic memory and automatic memory are used.

At the abortion facility both processes (automatic and conscious) occur. At the automatic level, the woman processes the sights the sounds, the smells, noises and the individuals, time, preparation for the procedure, and small peculiarities pertaining to this particular event. At the conscious level she processes the more pertinent details, that is, reason for the abortion, any one or a number of mixed emotions, but most importantly the processing of misinformation about the foetus.

It is very important to understand the processing of the misinformation about the "foetus" (baby), that it is a "clump of cells", "tissue", "menstrual extraction", in order to be able to go ahead with the procedure. The woman's semantic memory has stored information relating to pregnancy and its outcome. So at the intuitive level she knows that pregnancy means "baby", however, because of her need to go through with the abortion she consciously applies the misinformation so that her memory and knowledge of what her pregnancy really means is superseded by the new information. This new information is convenient because if her conception is not yet a "baby", then what she is doing is not wrong.

This manipulation of meaning lies behind the success of the abortion industry, and ultimately, behind post abortion trauma. Meanings and their ascribed images form part of an individual's narrative history. Meanings and images form memories.

It is the extent and depth of both the conscious and automatic levels of processing that will determine the extent that the person will experience post abortion trauma. Further, to the extent that recall of past knowledge (semantic memory) about pregnancy and childbirth is present at the time of the abortion and afterwards, will be the extent to which post abortion trauma will be severe. The depth of processing of information combined with fear will also determine the outcome and severity of trauma.

The combination of deep processing of the event, automatic processing of externals and fear attached to that pregnancy, form a cocktail guaranteed to create such strong dissonance that trauma is the result. The "fear" element is also important because fear as a negative emotion tends towards creating a belief that "something bad" has happened or will happen and will propel the individual towards eradication of the stimulus causing the unpleasant situation. Fear implies some form of punishment or some unpleasant outcome.

The emotions of shame and guilt are also present and contribute to the decision to abort, and then contribute to the development of trauma. Again, in so far as these emotions underpin the decision and are aversive and negative, so too will the event be negatively processed and stored, to be retrieved later; either actively, or suppressed at a conscious or unconscious level. Retrieval from the stored area will also be negatively influenced because it was stored in the memory as a negative event, so that a triggering event, such as an automatically processed piece of information (smell, noise, and colour) may act as a spark to the recall of the event. From my counselling experience, automatically processed data is just as important, (requiring to be dealt with) as consciously processed information.

It is interesting to note the amount of fine detail stored in memory when revisiting the day of the abortion. There appears to be a deep imprint etched in the memory. Most women remember the clothes they wore, the song being played on the car radio, the finest detail about the reception room and clinic, the words spoken by the abortion "doctor", the thoughts running through her mind, what the abortion procedure cost. In fact, women even keep their receipts. However, not many remember past lying down on the gurney and waiting. The wait always appears to them very long. At this point there is a determined blank (avoidance). This suggests that even where the woman has actively sought the abortion, the actual experience has not been positive. Something within her being has recorded permanently the script for future reference, but has sought to suppress that script so that it is difficult to retrieve. Perhaps it can be likened to the starting of a new file in a filing system. The amount of information recorded in this new file and remembered is the extent to which PAS will be experienced.

Memories lie embedded deeply within the memory system and for the most part remain inactive until a stimulus excites that particular memory which then acts as a catalyst for recall and perhaps behaviour. It is the stored memories which really dictate behaviour when presented with new stimuli. Where there are unpleasant negative memories, the triggering stimulus creates a situation where energy needs to be diffused in order to accommodate the new sensation. Continual accommodation of negative stimuli and negative memories leads to great vulnerability and ultimately psychological ill health.

The memories of a human being are the recording of his or her history. It is important for equilibrium and wellbeing. In some way, DNA perhaps, some memories are transmitted from generation to generation. This may account for inherited knowledge (or semantic memory) and even inherited mannerisms.

Memories, and the history which they contain, separate the human species from the animal kingdom and elevate us to the realm of creatures of free will, free thought and uniqueness. Memories, the intellect, soul and free will are the human's signature. Every individual's memories are unique, similar to the exclusivity of fingerprints, because no two individuals will have identical memories and therefore no individual will have the same history. When we speak of a uniquely designed individual, our inherited memories, combined with personal experiences and the freedom with which they have been experienced, contribute to the exquisite and exclusive life story.

Relatedness and Bonding.

Bonding is the process by which human beings (and animals) develop a connection, either positive or negative, to another individual. It is an acknowledged reality. Bonding ensures safety and a secure environment but more importantly, safety from external threats, and ensures the learning and nurturing of the emotional blueprint inherent in all individuals. The basic human need for warmth, closeness and touch is fulfilled and the emotional component strengthened, and the need for deep intimacy and communion satisfied.

The innate motives of individuals for bonding and attraction may be to form communion, in which to celebrate, protect and enhance relatedness. Neither society nor any individual can psychologically diminish an affiliation of one to another because we were not designed to "be alone" (Gen 2:18). The human person is endowed with communication faculties, which incline towards another and are designed to transmit and receive information so that cooperation, protection and communion are possible.

Without interaction with one another, society may not have survived let alone thrived. Therefore, bonding can be viewed as a means of survival, expansion and security for the species.

Bonding, whilst peculiar to infancy and early childhood, is ultimately a lifelong need and because this is so, other emotions are connected with it. Love, joy, happiness and grief are associated with attachment. Grief in particular is associated with the process of filiation and relationship building, and then separation accompanied with pain. The human response to loss is usually evidenced through sadness, depression, anxiety, morbidity and weeping, which is the created person's response to loss and is the mechanism which assists the bereaved to come to terms with the loss. Memories and images of the loved one also help to buffer grief and assist in the transitional process.

Post abortion grief is unique because no memories of images exist to cushion the loss. However, bonding and some attachment has occurred. This is seen in the profound grief experienced.

Understanding bonding and the human's need for this security permits us to understand why when an abortion has been acceded to, there would still be grief. Today foetology studies do indeed clearly show that interaction and communication begin in the womb; as the biological bonding and attachment (between mother and child) grow and become more intimate, so does their psychological relationship become deeper. In the mother's mind the realisation that there is a child within her leads in turn to her regarding it as her precious and special son or daughter. And an unplanned or even an unwanted pregnancy does not stop the attachment from forming. However the unwantedness or ambiguity or even perceived difficulties factor acts to intensify conflict and facilitates the decision to abort. Notwithstanding the decision to abort, at a deeper, subconscious level the mother of the baby cannot help but become in some mysterious way attached and connected with the life within her. Psychologically and physiologically the two (mother and child) are connected and dialogue together from the very beginning, and thus form continuing bonds.

From the instant of conception these two individuals interact for the psychological and physical health of both. In the design for the wellbeing of the child, the psychology and physiology of the woman are altered so that the spoken and unspoken dialogue between the two begins and continues to become strengthened. Under "normal" circumstances the discomfort caused by hormonal changes in early pregnancy is buffered by the joy of being pregnant, and the child who will be born. However, in the case of a pregnancy outside of the "planned", joy at the end of the discomfort is lacking. Indeed joy is completely lacking. The crisis (from the Greek word *Kairos* meaning decisive), bringing along with it difficulties and change, is most often exacerbated by those nearest to the pregnant woman. Invariably they act as catalysts to the final decision.

Long-term effects and the persistent lifelong need for harmonious bonding are associated with psychological wellbeing for the whole life of the individual and perhaps even a fulfilment of God's word that "it is not good that man should be alone" (Gn 2:18). Aloneness, and even insecure attachment to the mother in early childhood, lead to difficulties in intimacy and bonding in later life. So important is bonding that where this is unsuccessful there is found suffering.

The history of the aborting female or male provides a clue to the ease with which they countenance and then grieve over the abortion. Many hundreds of counselling hours with abortive females reveal the one emerging constant, the troubled relationship between mother and daughter. Many of the abortive women express a sadness, ambivalence, and emotional distance from their own mother, with the figure of comfort and warmth, for them, being someone else. I believe this insecure bonding with one's own mother also may contribute to the final decision to abort. Weak attachment leaves the young child vulnerable and needing to employ strategies for coping. Most often these coping strategies are immature (and remain so), and are at times aggressive, or alternatively overly passive. Further, weak bonding imprinted in the memory will determine whether negative or positive attachment is formed when the woman herself is faced with a crisis pregnancy. In the recesses of her memory there exists a script, which says, "I'm not ok. My mum didn't want me. My mum didn't love me."

The intra-uterine relationship begins with the knowledge that one may be pregnant. It is confirmed with the hormonal changes leading to an acknowledgement that a new pregnancy has occurred. These steps, which are negotiated continuously, though unconsciously, begin the attachment and bonding process. Even if the pregnancy is unwelcome the unconscious mind still negotiates the changes and imprints the knowledge that a baby has been conceived. Perhaps the greatest tragedy about abortion is the fact that it occurs during the time of crisis with the mother (and father) being at their most vulnerable; ambivalent and confused. Those who support or encourage the abortion, while perhaps well meaning, intrude into that sacred space called "moments of creation", and forever change the woman's design.

My contention is that if a woman has, during her brief pregnancy, ever thought of, or referred to the foetus as "my baby" or "a baby" or "having a baby", she will have humanised and personalised the infant. "Foetus", "product of conception", "clump of tissue", "bunch of cells", do not bring to mind an immediate picture because these terms do not register in most women's minds, however, they relate to and own, "baby" or "my baby". The woman (and male) knows the term and understands and can visualise it. Therefore if a woman (or male) has used these personalised terms, an image and imprint has registered in her memory and imagination, which the termination has not erased. An attachment has been formed and ownership (my baby) has been claimed, so that the relinquishing of the child, through abortion, whilst terminating the biological, cannot terminate the psychological or the spiritual.

The terms attachment and bonding have implications of affection, of intimacy, of relatedness. It is a relationship so close and so intertwined that it lasts for the whole life span and beyond. It is an eternal covenantal relationship between mother and child and cannot end even through abortion and death. Grief, following abortion, must be processed as any other type of grief. Failure to do so subjects the sufferer of post abortion grief to a life incongruent with her being.

Abortion removes the physiological. The interruption of the process begun at conception, and interrupted prematurely, leaves incomplete the developmental process of the spirit and only spiritual (combined with psychological) intervention can complete the cycle. So strong is the connection between the mother and child that denial and suppression can shadow the event, while the substance remains as a reminder that something is amiss and incomplete. It is the incompleteness which causes the grief and requires a conclusion both in the psychological and the spiritual. Reconciliation, as part of a healing programme, between mother (and father) and infant serves to bring to an end, and close the cycle. The covenant between mother, father of the infant and the infant must be renewed, reclaimed and then brought to a close, so that the mother and father and baby may each rest in their present status. Never forgetting, always remembering but letting the child go in peace.

Every human being touches other lives throughout their span of life. In turn others touch them. To do this is right and wholesome because we were designed in such a way. The aborted infant no less touches the lives of many, and in ways which will change others forever. This is also right and just because of the divine value inherent in every human individual. It is right that no one passes by unnoticed and unremembered by at least one other person. To pass by unnoticed would mean that the divine initiative for communion among the created order was selective, thus rendering the weakest of creatures dispensable and non-valuable. The grief, sadness, ambivalence, depression, weeping, literally do acknowledge that another human being has passed by briefly, and has left an indelible mark.

Dehumanisation

Dehumanisation means removing the human qualities of an individual. It means removing the characteristics that determine the human being. What then is dehumanised becomes impersonal, cold, distant, and non-human. What is dehumanised is seen as not being sentient, cannot meet the so-called established criteria of being human, thereby opening wide the gateway for perpetrating holocausts.

The human race has had a long, dark and inglorious history of dehumanisation and then extermination. We do not need to look further than the past century to see systematic destruction of human individuals: Lenin and Stalin's regimes, Hitler's regime and the concentration camps, Pol Pot's regime and the destruction of his considered enemies and undesirables, the Vietnam War and its napalm bombs, East Timor and the attempted brutal extermination of its citizens, and the Middle East and its ongoing disputes. The list goes on. In each and every situation the brutalisation of human beings was systematically contrived and almost successful. The so-called "enemy" must always be seen to be less than human in order to commit atrocities. Dehumanised individuals are not accorded mercy or justice. The greater the dehumanisation, the more it becomes possible to violate them and murder them without emotional expenditure.

Perhaps the greatest injustice against the pre-born was the attempted denial of its humanity by the legal constitutions of various nations, e.g., America with its *Roe v Wade* ruling. Only in this manner was it possible to ensure the open slaughter of in utero children. This denial of personhood served to release a certain malice inherent in humanity. The denial that the child of two human beings (who are the parents) is anything other than a human child has sounded the death knell to millions upon millions of citizens – human citizens. The nature of the child doomed to abortion is human nature. Two human parents produce a human child. Two fish parents produce fish offspring. Bird parents produce bird offspring. Giraffe parents produce giraffe offspring. Each species reproduces its own kind with its inherent nature.

So it must be assumed that human parents would produce human children having a human nature. Removal of the humanity or human nature of the child in the womb, in effect, removes its protective shield by declaring it to be a lesser species or worse still non-species and therefore not entitled to full protection. Whilst certain members of the animal kingdom have been accorded full protection in order to preserve them from extinction, the human child has become classed as a parasite or pest and worthy of culling. Mankind has descended to an all time low.

Dehumanisation within the abortion industry, including its employees, did not occur instantly. The process began long before the first abortion was carried out, and continues past the abortion, with the selling of foetal parts for profit. This newest endeavour really sets the tone for the level of dehumanisation to be found in this macabre industry. Human spare parts sold for 30 pieces of silver.

Insofar as technology has improved the lot of the medical profession and therefore humanity, it has also been used to diminish the value of life. The mystery, which was "life", has been reduced to a process, which can be manipulated at will. By making the wonderful "mystery" into a process only, the human being is then no longer a uniquely designed masterpiece from the vast desires of God, but a collection of amino acids, jumbled nerve endings and tissue. A "conceptus" or "a potential human" or "bunch of cells" is considered not deserving of wholehearted protection and recognition of personhood.

Dehumanisation of society in general and the abortion industry in particular, accounts for the absence of empathy towards the baby. Whilst a false sense of sympathy is extended to the presenting woman, empathy for her child is decidedly absent. Empathy is an emotion, which requires energy. To "feel as the other" requires an expenditure of a part of self. There is a world of difference between the two terms "empathy" and "sympathy", and the difference between the terms is the place which has been invaded, in order to introduce dehumanisation. The sacred space invaded is a place of total communion.

Sympathy is the sharing of an emotion (e.g., weeping together) whilst empathy is the "full understanding of the other". One (sympathy) sits side by side and weeps because the other is weeping. Empathy is entering into the being of the other and being able to understand and feel the same pain. One (sympathy) says, "I think I know how you feel", the other (empathy) says, "It is very painful. It hurts."

False sympathy is demonstrated to the presenting individuals whilst no attempt is made to enter into the very being of the infant to be aborted. To enter into his/her being would mean that humanity would have to be accorded to it. In the abortion industry the sympathy offered can be equated with the voice of Satan whispering words of false consolation, whilst "empathy" is the silence of Jesus as He stands before the accuser Pilate awaiting recognition of his innocence, of his very being. Yes, these two terms have become so intermingled as to appear as co-existing. However, they are worlds apart.

For the mothers and fathers presenting for an abortion, the process of dehumanisation has begun long before the actual abortion day. The dehumanisation had begun with a society whose moral fibre has been weakened. A society which has bought the lie that "if it feels good do it". A hedonistic society overcome with "me-ism" and a society which understands sexuality as an animalistic instinct rather than sexuality as the ultimate creative gift.

Language, that marvellous implement for communication, has also been manipulated to accommodate the dehumanisation process. The language of the abortion industry is especially deceitful. Every word, term and nuance is used to deceive and confuse. The maniacal march towards the dehumanisation of humanity uses every form of expression and technology, making demigods of the voices of hatred. Slowly but surely the language of lifelessness is being corporately heard so as to assist in interiorising the change, leading to a global notion of human beings as programmable machinery.

Ideologies alien to the human person who is created in the image of God, are being spread with justifying explanations "for the well-being of the individual" and even politico-religious rhetoric has succumbed with passivity to the new language of relativism.

The depersonalisation and dehumanising of the abortion procedure, and the baby, by pro-abortion lobbyists and clinic staff who have been trained in this craft, are monstrous. Their false concern for the woman, the language they use, "it's only tissue", assist the presenting woman to dissociate herself from her infant and she is therefore unable to protect it. The seductive yet flippant language of the staff, combined with the woman's distress at an unplanned pregnancy, ensures the fate of the infant.

While some personal dehumanisation had to have occurred before she even entered the abortion facility, the final severance of her relationship with her child takes place through the hands of the abortion providers. Their "counselling" of abortion for "your own good" is simply and absolutely demonic. It is the last point of dehumanisation for the baby and for the woman herself.

In many ways the dehumanisation of the infant through abortion is similar to the concentration camp internees whose dehumanisation was necessary for the compliance of those exterminating them. Likewise the compliance of the aborting woman is necessary for the procedure to be carried out, so the tactics of concern for the mother and the nonentity of the child are emphasised and a third aspect of the deadly triad, "fear", is presented and accentuated. Of course this results in a *fait accompli*, the death of the child, and the exchange of 30 pieces of silver.

Atonement

Ancient religions understood the idea of atonement to be a purifying process acceptable to their gods. The Hebrew people, the society into which Jesus was born, also practised rituals of atonement. For them atonement meant the purification of all that separated them from YHWH, and their sacrifices of atonement restored their covenantal relationship with YHWH. For the Hebrew people one of the most sacred and solemn feast days was the "Day of Atonement" (Yom Kippur). On this day the Jewish people acknowledge to God their guilt and anticipate his forgiveness of their personal and collective sins. The end of the Yom Kippur service is announced by the sound of the ram's horn (shofar), thus closing off the past year and forgiveness of the past year's offences and proclaiming new life and hope for the coming year. For the Hebrew people the words of Isaiah "though your sins are like scarlet, they shall be like snow" (Is:1:18) are a comfort and assurance of the presence of God and his forgiveness.

For the early Christian communities, the re-interpretation of Jesus' death, in the light of past sacrificial offerings involved the integration of the suffering by way of the Cross and the sublime joy of the Resurrection and salvation. The early communities (and following) developed and understood the meaning of the Cross as the instrument of atonement with which Jesus atoned for the sins of the world and thus restored the relationship with God. His once and only bloody sacrifice brought to an end the tradition and need for animal sacrifices for sin. From this we see that the notion of atonement reaches back into antiquity and was understood as a way by which sins were acknowledged, recompense made, forgiveness asked for and new hope experienced.

The "atonement" child is a recognised symptom of post abortion trauma. The "atonement child" is a pregnancy sought in order to alleviate the existing grief. At times an abortive woman believes that "if I have another baby I will be able to love it so much that I will be able to make up for the death of the other one" (Sandra). The operative words in this comment are "make up for" or in other words "atone for" the death of the other child. Sadly, to achieve this, she may embark on promiscuous behaviour and when a new conception occurs the same difficulties exist which led to the first abortion. Inevitably a second, third and fourth abortion occur. Multiple abortions are often the result of the first abortion and a desire to "make up for" the first aborted child.

I believe that a woman countenances multiple abortions only when the first abortion has been very traumatic and resisted. Individuals whom I have encountered with multiple abortions clearly exhibit signs and symptoms consistent with terror, regret, grief and sorrow, especially over their first abortion or even where there has been other sexual injury. They appear to remember their first abortion so clearly. They remember every moment from conception to termination, yet ensuing ones are shadowy figures. Their first abortion has clearly so traumatised them that unconscious reparation has been attempted with the other conceptions. Multiple abortions also have inscribed within them other "pain" which the woman is seeking to have someone bring to the surface. To help her to not be alone in her pain. A good counsellor will hear what is not being said and help with this.

Where an "atonement child" is brought to birth they encounter new difficulties which, because of the unresolved past abortion or abortions act to impair the relationship between mother and child. A further difficulty often experienced is that when a young unmarried woman has one, two or more atonement children, she in fact places herself and her child/ren in a position of vulnerability to lifelong financial disadvantage and struggle. Her guilt at terminating her infant will propel her towards over-compensation. Her coping skills will be compromised on a financial and day-to-day level.

Research into this area has produced astonishing results, which clearly indicate bonding problems, caring problems between the mother and her "atonement child". These bonding difficulties clearly show disturbing behaviour in the parenting of "wanted" children. One would wonder why this might occur since "atonement" children are the "wanted" replacements following abortions. It is not surprising that this is so, because the "atonement" child or children not only cannot replace the aborted child, but in fact act as a constant reminder of the other child that is no longer.

Atonement children, or maybe even replacement children, face enormous difficulties not only as abortion survivors but also as constant reminders of a violent act. These children are in many ways stifled of their potential, or alternatively, deprived of a fair, normal, child-specific parenting. They unknowingly undergo their own post abortion suffering.

Pregnancies following too soon after an abortion will prove to be very unhealthy and perhaps even dangerous because they tend to exacerbate the unresolved guilt/grief. Any joy in this new pregnancy will be absent or conditional. Further, after the birth of the new child (a trigger for Post Abortion Syndrome) the mother will place unrealistic expectations on both herself and the infant, thus beginning a cycle of suffering for herself, her baby and her family.

Today, with abortion available for any reason and the inconvenient disposed of, we have developed a society with an insidious and odious notion of atonement. On the one hand, the society, which summarily disposes of the inconvenient, on the other hand practises a false kind of "atonement". There is an almost palpable sense of collective guilt over behaviour with one group of children (aborted). In reparation (atonement) for this, the living children are spoiled and pampered to their own detriment. The families and societies which wantonly kill "unwanted" children then proceed to outrageously pamper the living ones ("wanted").

Where the littlest one was aborted so as not to interfere with a career, financial lifestyle, reputation, the surviving siblings are either monstrously spoiled or alternatively emotionally neglected or abused. The big house, the car, the career, designer shoes and clothing and unlimited entertainment are the "atonement" price to appease and silence a troubled heart and mind.

The individual and collective guilt over abortion exerts its influence in deadly ways. The destructive and violent behaviours of children at seemingly younger and younger ages attest to this.

As I observe the youth scene and watch their frenetic lifestyles, it has occurred to me that the drugs, promiscuity, youth suicide and sense of nihilism are evidence that the young are turning inward on themselves. There is a sense that we are witnessing a tragic introversion, and there appears to be an overshadowing by a spirit of deep self-absorption. Do the young ones sense that it is unsafe to be young? Do they sense that children are not valued, welcomed or wanted? Do they sense that to be infirm, young, helpless and tiny is unsafe, therefore it is better to be none of these? Are the drugs, promiscuity, recklessness their cry to be loved, welcomed, valued, nurtured, guided, and directed? Are the dangerous paths embarked upon a rebellion against their perceived lack of value? Are the young unconsciously atoning for the unjust deaths of millions of their siblings? Has the societal message been "children are not important"? Self, career, freedom and money are important. Children are disposable.

Perhaps the worldwide phenomenon of youth self-destructive behaviour, suicide, hopelessness and artificially induced "happiness" is a sign that we have reached a new all time level of abandonment. It is ultimately a symptom of the absence of the Sacred and therefore absence of security, hope and future.

As a concluding thought, the death of Jesus "atoned" for humanity's sin against God. Society is "falsely atoning" for the death of millions of infants by according existing children a sense of values alien to their design. Children need to have restored to them a sense of dignity and worth. We need to banish the notion that abortion is only a minor procedure and that infants in the womb are a bunch of cells. This dehumanises children, and when children are dehumanised they resort to self-defeating measures.

13.

Eugenic Abortions and Hard Cases

Look at the birds in the sky: they do not sow or reap
or gather into barns; yet your heavenly Father feeds them
*Are you not worth much more than they are (*Mt 6:26)

The term "eugenics" comes from the Greek, *eu* meaning good and *gen* meaning produce that is, producing good offspring by manipulating the genetic makeup of the individual. This field of so-called "science" has a long and dark history. Ultimately those involved in its advocacy envisage a society made up of flawless individuals – *a Master Race.*

The twentieth century has seen, I believe, two well known proponents of this theory, Margaret Sanger, founder of Birth Control League which later became International Planned Parenthood Federation (IPPF), and of course the diabolical white supremacist, Adolf Hitler.

Both Sanger and Hitler were lifelong eugenicists who believed in the supremacy of the white race and the extermination of individuals, races and cultures which were deemed defective. Ms Sanger's notion of isolation and sterilisation of the "feeble minded" would ensure that ultimately those with "faulty" genes would eradicate themselves, and that no genetic imperfections would be passed on to future generations.

Hitler's attempted implementation of these ideologies was almost successful. However, the global outcry against his ideologies, post-World War II, brought the eugenic theory into disrepute and sent its devotees underground, at least for a time. Ms Sanger's original Birth

Control League became IPPF and the sales spiel was changed to one with a more palatable flavour. From now on family planning was to be seen as something desirable, especially where women were concerned.

Slowly, surely and subtly, IPPF and the introduction of the birth control pill set about changing the face of fertility. It has been an interesting situation watching the subtle and insidious progression from "crime" to "compassion" in only one generation. The world has deplored Hitler's attempt to exterminate the Jews, and to sterilise, destroy or experiment on other "undesirables". Yet, over the past fifty years, the same strategies have been quietly employed to eliminate from the so-called "gene-pool" those of who may be thought to "contaminate" that pool and not so much as a whimper has been heard.

Today, between technology and ideology, we have unleashed a monster onto the human race. Technology, which can diagnose from early pregnancy, is now used to determine who lives and who dies; which gender will be disposed of, and which accepted. Prenatal testing has not served humankind well; rather it has ensured the death of future citizens. "Compassion" was/is supposedly the motive underpinning these new technologies and ideologies.

These horrors were unleashed onto society under a mantle of "love, care, concern", with even the suggestion of the monstrous notion that it is kinder and better for a disabled infant not to live. The bait has been cast and society took not only the bait but the hook, and line and sinker as well.

In my experience I have encountered 27 women who have aborted their babies due to foetal abnormalities, and their grief is manifold. Each of the women spoke of the medical profession encouraging them to abort their disabled child. I believe we have reached a stage where it will become mandatory to abort defective embryos and even those who have passed the embryonic stage. Hitler and Sanger would be proud.

In my experience those women who aborted because of foetal abnormality have to deal with many grief issues all at various levels and at the same time. Most often the aborted baby had been a "wanted" baby. The ultrasound images had been longed for. The mother and the father had been looking forward to "seeing" for the first time their baby, to having the first picture to place in their baby album. The mother had been experiencing hormonal changes and most often morning sickness. Hopes and dreams for the future had begun to coalesce. Names had begun to be entertained. Families had received news of the impending birth. Much energy had been expended on this still unknown, unseen infant. However, though unseen, the parents had already identified "our baby" or "my baby". The bonding processes had commenced and progressed.

While the medical profession encourages abortion for foetal abnormalities, studies clearly indicate that the psychological trauma associated with abortion, for this reason, is enormous. Consistently studies show that abortion for foetal abnormalities or for maternal health reasons results in outcomes pregnant with psychological difficulties. Many studies can be cited; however it seems to me that what the women themselves have to say is much more important.

"I should have given my baby a chance," said Marie, who aborted her child because it was found that her little girl was Down Syndrome. "I should have allowed my baby to go to full term and given birth to it and held her in my arms so that I could tell her that I loved her. I should have believed in her. I didn't. I shouldn't have made the decision for her to die. I should have allowed her to go in her own time. I could then have known that I did the best I could for her. In this way I didn't even give her a funeral. I don't even know what happened to her" (Katherine, aged 28). Again the list is long and the statements do not differ much. Certainly the pain is not different.

Perhaps one of the saddest realisations I have experienced was that Ms Sanger's (International Planned Parenthood Federation) and

Hitler's hopes for a clean master race, may be coming to fulfilment. As I looked through a crowded shopping centre recently I had to admit that there were not too many mothers pushing prams and on a busy Saturday morning one could not spot one Down syndrome child.

Among the strongest reasons, often touted, for legalising abortion are the so-called "hard-cases", that is conception as a result of rape, incest or violence. The pro-choice, pro-abortion lobby parade these cases as prima facie evidence for the need to enact abortion laws.

Again in studies by the Elliot Institute and David C. Reardon, Professor Phillip Ney, Vincent Rue, and other researchers, over the past thirty years, it appears that the real number of conceptions resulting from rape or incest is minute. It is believed that this is so because of the stressful nature of the encounter, thus rendering sterile the forced intimacy. However, studies by the above-mentioned researchers and others, and my own practice experience, have found that where a conception does occur the mental health outcome of the woman is more positive with the delivery of a baby. Indeed I have known of two children born as a consequence of difficult conception (rape) are who are loved and cherished as children.

Both rape and incest are violent actions against a usually vulnerable individual. In both cases much more than physical wounds are inflicted. There is a deep sense of abandonment experienced, which is abandonment by one human being of another. It is a loss of such magnitude that I do not believe that it is ever possible to completely recover. It is possible to forgive, but the memory of violence, abandonment and distrust, always remains.

In rape, the violence, both physical and psychological, assaults the "me", the very real essence of "who I am" as an individual. The exclusivity of that individual is forcibly penetrated and violated. That very same place where God and creature communicate is the place that is assaulted through rape, and this, I believe, is the reason for the deep trauma resulting from this type of encounter. Further, the anger, sadism and cruelty of the assault ensure that imprinted on the woman's memory is an experience so alien, so distressing, that her whole body revolts against its association with the encounter.

Incest, also a crime of violence and hatred, is the nearest kinsman of rape. This type of rape is probably more aptly called soul rape and is usually more seductive and perhaps even more destructive because the perpetrator is known and a "supposed" near loved one. The violence has been systematic, secretive, persuasive and subtle and the result of this type of abuse is usually the death of trust. From the moment of the first violation, trust freezes. Thereafter the woman (girl) is unable to trust again, because the person who was meant to be trusted and who was meant to protect her actually violated her. A sexually abused person has no sense of self-trust because she has not learnt how to trust. Her development was arrested at the moment the sexual abuse began and therefore she has no schema on which to base her trust. She cannot trust God, humans or self. Sexual abuse whether by incest or by an outsider is a blasphemy. Abortion is a blasphemy. Both of these acts deface and distort the image of God and render the victim powerless. The consequence of this is that future relationships take place against this background, which is decidedly unhealthy and dysfunctional.

Sexual abuse, incest and abortion are the crossing over of invisible boundaries. This confusion of boundary lines occurs, I believe, because the girl/child has to comply with the abuser because of the power held by the abuser. It is usually a power relationship, that is, father, brother, grandfather, uncle and on rare occasions female members of the family. This leads to a real loss of the sense of knowledge of what is right and wrong. What is *her right and her wrong?* She will see future actions requiring decisions (e.g., abortion) through a lens of distrust, a lens of confusion.

Despite these considerations, abortion because of rape or incest can never be justified, because the child conceived even under these circumstances, is himself or herself innocent. The child thus conceived is still conceived and designed by God. The child is innocent. He or she has implanted in the womb because it was fertile "soil" and because God has designed this new initiative for a specific purpose, perhaps even to bring healing to the wounded spirit. A child conceived under these circumstances is not "guilty", is not an "invading parasite" and certainly it is not the woman's "enemy". This child is innocent, having the same innocence as the victim of the assault. Like its mother, the child is also a victim. This child's life also hangs in the balance, as its mother's psychological and spiritual life hangs in the balance. The child that is the result of a "challenged union" is not itself challenged or tainted but unique, different, precious and worth more than silver and gold. It does not warrant a death sentence because of the identity of its father.

An abortion of a child conceived from rape or incest ultimately destroys not only another human being but also the proof of the action. Perpetrators should not escape the penalty for their action but all measures of the law should be employed to ensure that justice is done. However, justice does not mean that the baby should be terminated. There was no justice in the assault on the mother by the perpetrator and there is no justice in the assault on the child by its mother or significant others in the life of the mother.

Perhaps it can best be summarised in this way: the story of each individual human being is tied up with countless others, some acceptable and some regrettable. However, there is a link which binds and connects all of us. Even a child conceived through rape or incest has a history going back into antiquity. This child has an eternal connection to God and to others of the human community.

There is a biblical story, which rarely ever makes the homily list but I think it is highly applicable to our time, generation and specifically to this topic. The story is found in Numbers (11:31-35) and is about greed, gluttony, lawlessness, and horror. More than this, it is a story of lack of faith in a God who had shown Himself to be faithful and just.

In this story God is feeding quail to the people of Israel. However, in their greed they over-feed in fear that the Lord may not provide enough. Seeing this, Yahweh God becomes angry and allows them to over-indulge in their gluttony. The place is called "Graves of Craving" or Kibroth-hattaavah, because there they buried the people who died through over indulging.

Abortion for foetal abnormality, or rape, or incest is countenanced because we live in a society very similar to those cited in Numbers (11:30). We live in a society which is gluttonous for sensory pleasures, greedy for instant gratification, ravenous for selfishness and seriously forgetful of God's mercy and friendship and providence. It is only because of these that it has become possible for a call to be made to kill a child inconveniently generated.

The story of the "Graves of Craving" is symbolic of failure to trust in a merciful God, to believe that He will always provide and take care even when it appears impossible. This story also points to the human urge of self-gratification and self-seeking. It points to human attempts to find answers to difficulties without due regard to God and when this happens the solutions proffered are usually monstrous. In this regard abortion because of foetal abnormality, rape, incest or violence is the human solution to the problem, and the fuel propelling this solution is idolatry of self, that is, seeking to remedy the situation "in my way", not God's way.

Idolatry of course means not honouring God but honouring or worshipping something else, e.g., self, cravings, desires or another. When we worship another, of course it means that the worship due to God is withdrawn and given elsewhere, thus turning completely away from Him. Idolatry and idols demand human sacrifice, and most often the human sacrifice of a child. Moloch (Ezek 16:21-22, Lev 18:21) the god of the ancient Canaanite peoples was offered children for his satisfaction. The Israelites even participated in this type of ritual for a time (Ezek 16) although it was banned by Yahweh God. God the Almighty Father does not want infant sacrifices. He abhors such practices.

While rape and incest are acts of intended malice, hatred and destruction, so is abortion. With abortion there is also malice, hatred and destruction. A woman who is raped cannot ever go back to a time pre-rape, and a young woman, whose sexuality has been compromised, confused and violated, cannot return to a time pre-sexual abuse. So too a woman who concedes to abortion will never be able to return to a time pre-pregnancy and pre-abortion. In all of these areas there is a sense that at the very deepest level what it means to be "me" or to be a human being has been violated, never to be completely healed. For the woman who aborts because of such a situation the abortion is her own act of violence or revenge, not against the attacker, but against herself. This then completes the trilogy of violence against herself. Assault, loss of innocence and trust, loss of life first through the abortion and then loss of her dream "future life".

Whilst the abortion of a baby conceived under these extreme circumstances is most often encouraged, it is my opinion that it is the cruellest of the trilogy. This is because the mother herself must decree the child's death. Where in the past she has been the victim and innocent party, in this case she herself becomes the perpetrator. She mixes and aligns her wounded and broken "self" on a par with those who assaulted her. She enters into a realm of violence previously unknown to her. She commits something akin to the destruction committed against herself and while it may sound justifiable, the result is not healing or removal of the rape or incest, but impressing an indelible mark of this particular event (abortion) for perpetuity. From this point onwards there will be two deaths to remember each time a triggering event is encountered. Her psychological and spiritual death and her baby's literal and physical death.

Janette & Martin's Story

My name is Jeanette, I am married to Martin and we are the parents of three children and a fourth one Thomas Michael who has returned to God.

At about 16 weeks gestation I had some spotting. I was extremely concerned due to the fact that spotting in a previous pregnancy had resulted in a miscarriage. So we went to the doctor immediately thinking the worst. An ultrasound concluded that the baby had two serious genetic abnormalities: Anencephaly and Spina Bifida. Anencephalic babies have 100% mortality rate. After many consultations with doctors and specialists, we learnt the specifics of the abnormalities. Anencephaly derives from the Latin meaning 'no skull'. Basically the baby had not developed a complete brain and hence could not survive on its own outside of the womb. The doctors gave us the hard statistics that most babies simply did not survive birth and if born alive would die a short time after. Therefore the natural thing to do "of course" would be to abort this child. The doctors had even booked me in for a termination the next day. At this point my husband said "what if we decide to continue with this pregnancy?" Now this was a shock to say the least…

None of the staff we saw had even considered that this was a human life! This "foetus" apparently was not valid? None of the staff we saw were rude, on the contrary, they were very caring and compassionate, but only because they knew what had to be done … From here we went home and researched anencephaly. There was a great deal of information on the Internet and my husband even looked up pictures of anencephalic children to prepare himself for the birth. We also found that there were some cases where anencephalic children had lived for a number of days after birth. We discussed all these matters with our families, our community and our catechists and we were determined to go ahead with the pregnancy and birth.. Despite this abomination (to the medical profession) and the opinion of most people we spoke to, we concluded after much anguish and prayer that we could not be the ones to decide or control the end of this baby's life. God had created such a unique and special child, it was entirely in his hands. One thing that we did immediately was to name our son to assure ourselves and others that he was real, valid and a child of God. Thomas Michael Jones. The pregnancy was the single most difficult period of our lives but it was also one of the most blessed.

We lived our lives fully not pretending at any stage that our lives were supposed to be easy, because it was difficult, especially knowing what was to come. Our son Isaac was happy to know that soon he would have a little brother and our daughter Rachel although too young to comprehend knew that there was a baby in mummy's tummy. I needed to have on-going ultrasounds as I had also been diagnosed with placenta previa, which presented a very real risk of bleeding to death during the delivery. I had ongoing prenatal care and the ultrasounds were very intense. We took the children with us and could see our son's heart beating, his little hands and tiny feet. I had the amazing blessing of carrying my son almost until full term. We invited our brothers and sisters and our family to join us at the hospital for his birth.

Thomas Michael died during the trauma of birth. This was heart wrenchingly sad, but we were overjoyed to experience and bear witness to God's love. With our families and brothers and sisters present, Thomas Michael was born directly into eternal life. A priest who guided us through the entire pregnancy said to me "how does it feel to be the mother of a saint?" Every member of our family was proud to hold Thomas Michael. Many photos and mementoes were taken. It was very difficult to let go of Thomas but we were blessed enough to spend two days with him in the hospital. More than one hundred people participated in Thomas's funeral to bless God for

His wonderful deeds. We celebrated his life and death in a beautiful service. My husband and Thomas's father carried his tiny coffin into the church and at the end sang for Thomas a beautiful hymn.

When we are born we know that one day we will die and hopefully go to heaven. Thomas Michael was lucky enough to go straight there. Our job as parents to him was now complete. After Thomas Michael was born into heaven we were advised that in having any more children the same could happen again. One-and-half years later Michaela Maree entered this world and two weeks ago turned one. Now my husband and I have 3 children and one in heaven who knows and prays for us.

In loving memory of Thomas Michael Jones born into eternal life 19 December 1999.

Joshua

Excitement was in the air. We were expecting our third child and before we knew it, it was time for the twelve-week ultrasound. We could not wait to see our precious little baby, so off we set with two children (15 months and three-and-half years) in tow.

The lady doing the ultrasound was very quiet and finally stopped, faced us and said, "there is a lot of fluid at the base of the brain." Still unsure of what she meant or implied I watched as she went away to "crunch some numbers." When she returned we were told that there was a one in three chance that there was a chromosomal abnormality with our baby. I think it was about this point that my world began to crash down around me.

The rest of the afternoon was a haze of doctors, nurses, receptionists. I had a CVS, which was the most painful procedure I'd had ever had. They took a sample from the placenta. We then had to wait two or three days for the results of the CVS.

The days passed slowly and painfully. Often crying, praying, begging God for good results and heartache. The news came via a phone call. TRISOMY 13 that was the result. We went straight to the doctor's surgery where we were given more information. The long and the short of it was that with Trisomy 13 the organs and basically everything else do not form properly. My baby had no chance of survival. The pregnancy was likely to end in a late miscarriage, or the baby would be stillborn and if it did make it through, the lifespan of a trisomy 13 baby was 4 days. We were told he would be in pain (he ... it was another little boy...) and they would pump him full of painkillers until he died.

My heart ached and my mind was a blur, my body numb. My beautiful, precious baby. We had wanted another child and we thought we were blessed to fall pregnant so quickly. We were told that we had to decide what we were going to do. Our heads were swimming with medical terms, odds and facts. Our only thought was of our child being in pain and we wanted to stop his suffering. Our decision was to terminate the pregnancy. We would end his suffering and just try again. So simple and yet so foolish.

Five days later the pregnancy was terminated. My life had become a series of actions. No feelings. Numb, numb and numb. But now my beautiful Joshua was gone. I gave him a name and place in my heart. I guess that that place in my heart has been there since the day that I found out that I was pregnant It was a happy place, but now it is a place of torment, pain and suffering.

Perhaps this is where the real torment began. Life around me went on as normal. We told people we had lost the baby, as everyone knew that I was pregnant. Conversations replayed in my head like re-runs of television shows. Then the nightmares began. Each night my two living children died in my dreams in every imaginable way. The paranoia began over the welfare of these children. I found myself checking them over and over again. I cried all day and all night. I wanted my baby back. What had I done?

I wished we had made another choice. I had wanted to keep my baby boy and hold him in my arms even if he died. My husband disagreed. He felt that we had made the right decision even though it had been very hard. It was here that we somehow lost each other. For the first time in our life together we did not share the same opinion on something that really mattered. I felt my life spinning out of control. I couldn't and didn't sleep. I had no patience with the children, I cried all the time and I found myself wishing that I were dead just to stop the constant aching in my heart. The pain and the guilt were more than I could bear.

I began to see a counsellor (Anne) a month or two after Joshua's life ended. It has helped and it has also helped my husband and I work through this together even though we do not share the same views. He still believes that we made the right decision for our son but I know in my heart that things should have been different. Now I have to face life without my precious Joshua, never having seen him, touched him, never having held him in my arms even once. I have to live with having no ending with him, no funeral and no grave to visit. Almost as if he never existed. I have to wake up each morning and look at myself in the mirror and know that I had a choice and I/we made the wrong choice and took the wrong path. I thought it was the easier path, the best choice but it turned out to be exactly the opposite.

I heard a line from the movie "Message in a Bottle" and thought of Joshua. "I should have held on to you so tightly that not even God could have taken you away." Each day this is how I feel.

14.

The Future and What It Holds

Oh! To have a crystal ball and be able to peer into the next twenty-five years. We live in interesting times said someone a long time ago. Indeed we live in times that are not only interesting but also dangerous. I would suggest more dangerous than interesting.

The pro-abortion pro-choice lobby has gained much ground over the past two decades. There seems to have been a rapid escalation of activity leading to the global legalisation of abortion and abortion to 40 weeks gestation. Infanticide. Or maybe the new terminology proposed "post-birth abortion" So that now the availability of anti-life mechanisms has mushroomed into a deadly feast of toadstools. The network of intensive activity in death peddling now includes abortion, mass sterilization, contraception on demand to young girls as young as twelve and thirteen years of age, euthanasia, embryonic stem cell research. A further item that I believe should be added to this list of death-dealing topics is cloning and same-sex legitimisation and demands for same-sex marriage. This latest initiative may be the last offering to the god Baal before God intervenes.

Understanding these particular anti-life strategies will allow us to understand the strength, power and hatred behind them. Each of these anti-life issues, abortion, euthanasia and cloning, relate to life, authority, power and love. They all relate to the divine prerogative. Polluting and corrupting these three and adding the demands for same-sex unions legislation and their legitimation, authority, power are ultimately about a personal assault on God, the creator. Sin has always warranted divine judgement. However, the sins of anti-life warrant it more so because (as in the Garden of Eden) they attempt to usurp power from God and in the case of same-sex couplings flout God's creative works.

The twentieth century appears to have crowned past anti-life activities with the cloning of "Dolly" the sheep and "Tetra" the chimp. The century began with devastating visible wars, continued with a vicious war against the unborn (invisible wars) and concluded with a war against the natural order of things (cloning, demands for SS coupling). On the one hand we have abortion and the destruction of over 50,000,000 babies per year, and the spectre of human cloning on the other. One side terminates babies with impunity and the other attempts to manufacture them artificially or to certain specifications. Will the ungodly dyad of abortion and euthanasia joined by the third malefic act, cloning, be the catalyst for God's judgement upon humanity?

How did we get to this stage? It came very quietly and subtly. When world wars and then localised wars distracted the world's attention, the agents of wickedness burrowed into the psyche of society, which slowly began the change. It was not difficult because of the weakened state of humanity as a result of wars and rumours of wars. The sexual revolution and contraception appeared on the world stage as mankind's saviours from the tyranny of control and over-population. Where contraception failed, abortion became the accepted backup method of disposal of an implanted so called "parasite" – not a new baby but a parasite (its new term).

Massive sex education programs outside of the home ensured (through schools) not a sexuality that is sacred, but a sexuality that is mechanistic or simply an instinct. More sex education did not ensure less sexual activity but more exposure at a younger and younger age, which has meant more and more sexual activity. The campaign to bring about change in the natural order entailed a well-managed, all-encompassing strategy. There had to be an all out, all-pronged attack on God and his creation. It could only work if the attack came from all sides and concurrently: contraception, the drug and violent music culture, abortion, immorality, breakdown of the family, loosening or abandonment of religious beliefs and practices, suicide, euthanasia and now embryonic stem cell research and cloning. The all-pronged attack has been well stage-managed.

To assist in the all-out attack on life, it was imperative that anti-life proponents engage governments in the debate. To this end family planning organisations sought out sources of law, upon which to base legal reforms in matters concerning the status of women. The reforms needed to include areas of so called "women's rights", which would include an absolute right to abortion to all stages of pregnancy, easier family laws including divorce, ready availability of contraceptives for all women including young girls, and the right to sterilization even against the will of the individual. "Women's rights" were meant to mean a better deal for women. However, it has not necessarily resulted in their betterment. Ultimately it has meant the right of women to destroy their own children freely and without fear. Women's rights have led to lobbying for changes in the moral order in order to accommodate the "new rights". Women's rights have ultimately meant the "rights of a selected few", and enslavement to pain for the rest of womanhood.

To enact all these changes, governments were encouraged to take control of the reproductive areas by funding these services. Naturally, government facilities were to be staffed by specially selected personnel, trained in these areas. Ultimately, total control of life and death matters was to be handed over to them. The implication is that what belongs to God alone has been handed to Caesar. Today, public opinion is verbose and has persuaded governments worldwide to take up control over beginning of life issues, end of life issues, and practically whether there will be any life issues at all.

The systematic attempt to change, at a global level, government control over reproductive matters has been very successful. The agents of change beginning with Malthus and Darwin followed by Hitler, Sanger, Family Planning Associations, population controllers, secular institutes with an agenda to fulfil, all appear to have done their jobs in an exemplary manner. So well, that today there is engagement in rampant sexuality even by the very young. Abortion on demand at all stages of pregnancy includes full term or near full term (partial birth abortion). The call for embryonic stem cell research, to be sold under the guise of "wellbeing of humanity", follows the demand for euthanasia.

All appears to be going according to schedule; but then again Noah's boat was being built according to schedule. The people were eating and sleeping and working on schedule. Everything was going according to schedule. Until...

Cracks have started to appear in the system. Women who have aborted children are beginning to speak of the pain and sorrow of their loss. Men who took their child to be aborted are beginning to speak about the pain over their loss of son or daughter. Grandparents are beginning to speak about the loss of grandchildren and their great anguish of never having been able to hold their grandchild. Siblings of aborted children are rebelling at the death of infants, and their rebellion takes the form of self-destructive behaviours. These siblings do not want to go on living, knowing that millions of babies are killed annually. These siblings don't want to live knowing that their parents could kill a baby. These siblings lose respect and honour for their parents and refuse any obedience. These siblings live in fear because maybe their own value, and their own worthiness, will be found wanting.

Cracks are appearing in the veneer. These have not been noticed in the past but are being noticed now because they are increasing in number and in intensity. Cracks are beginning to appear in the legal system with post-abortive women who have suffered physical and or psychological trauma being recompensed for their suffering, especially where they were not warned of possible psychological effects. There is a groundswell in the pro-life movement. Doctors, former abortionists, religious leaders, lay people, religious and non-religious, legal professionals, are all making noises. These noises appear to be gaining momentum. Perhaps we are seeing the beginning of a new day – a day when not one baby will be killed through abortion.

Of course we can dream the dream of every lover of life. Before the dream becomes a reality I think we will encounter much more suffering.

Today in many nations there is legalisation of abortion to full term with no set restrictions. The demand for this was hard fought by the pro-abortion lobbyists and won because of the politicians' own lack of moral strength. Imagine making abortion legal to 40 weeks and it's not called "murder" but the termination of a pregnancy because the woman demands it. Imagine children being aborted born alive and not assisted, and left to die because the woman has demanded "a dead baby". Since the new abortion laws passed in Australia in 2008 over 60 babies were born alive and left to die without assistance yet we attempt to call ourselves a civilised society. We started down this road because certain women wanted the right to abort freely and without fear of recrimination and in one biblical generation opened the door for full-scale death of pre-born infants up to full term.

Giving ground to pro-abortion thinking does not save infants, but ensures the mass slaughter of them. Further, when pro-lifers begin to negotiate with pro-abortionists, then the downhill slide of the pro-life movement has been started. The pro-life movement and the pro-abortion movement have no common ground, and can never have any common ground. It is never a level playing field when dealing with evil and evilly intentioned individuals, and it should never be seen as a level playing field. The essence of each other's argument is poles apart. Each side cannot negotiate because to negotiate would weaken their stance, and if their stance were weakened this would weaken their own movement. Further to this, the pro-life movement cannot negotiate to even allow one child to die through abortion, because to allow one child to die in this way is to repeat the words of scripture, *"it is better to have one person die for the people"* (Jn 18:14). These words did not come from the mouth of Jesus Himself but from those who called for his death.

The enemy's voice can at times sound so melodious (or is it malodious?), especially when he is trying to sound reasonable.

Today, I believe, we are living at a time of crisis in the abortion business. Something new is about to happen. It cannot remain at this juncture because there is too much disarray both for the pro-life and pro-abortion groups. Pro-life gained momentum for a time and then lost it, the seemingly impossible happened and full blown full term abortion happened everywhere. What happened?

It has been suggested that pro-life gains (financial payoffs for psychological suffering) and a gathering momentum of voices speaking about suffering post abortion and the very real risks inherent in an abortion (e.g., breast cancer, PID, long term psychological trauma, sterility, etc), will curb the abortion momentum. Initially this may be so and they may stem the tide for a while. However, I can only foresee this for a very short time. The abortion industry is too lucrative to be abandoned. So as one facility may close, two others will open, this time better resourced and self-protected. Legislation needed to be changed that will protect those within the abortion industry. It is Caesar that we are speaking about.

When we "obeyed" the wishes of Hitler, Malthus, Margaret Sanger and their colleagues, through the Family Planning Association's call for government control of fertility issues, we placed the matter of life not into the hands of the Author of Life, but the hands of Caesar. Now we are suggesting that this matter be wrested from him. This will not happen. Caesar will never give ground. The genie will refuse to go back into the bottle. What may happen is that new laws will be enacted calling for total freedom for the woman to abort whilst meeting minor conditions. When this is complied with, abortion on demand will continue as before. Only this time it will be legal, where previously it carried de facto legal status. Alternatively all out legal abortion, through all the stages of gestation will be available, leading to complete societal chaos and death which is indeed what has happened.

Liability for large amounts of compensation payouts by abortionists and their insurance companies may slow down the process for a time. More sophisticated staff will be employed, however, to ensure that the abortion procedure will be carried out. Screening for possible psychological sequelae may or may not be successful because ultimately the woman presenting for a termination of pregnancy will be "counselled" by well-trained individuals, whose task will be to "counsel" the woman towards an abortion decision while offering "alternatives". By offering the "alternative", the facility has carried out its duty to inform about other ways of dealing with an unplanned pregnancy and details concerning her pregnancy.

The informed consent issue has been hotly debated. There is a possibility that legal action may be taken against abortion providers because of neglect in informing the woman of her pregnancy stage, and the possibility of post abortion trauma. This is of grave concern to me because a woman presenting for an abortion cannot, I believe, give informed consent. Informed consent I understand to mean being in full possession of one's normal faculties. A woman presenting for an abortion, because of a crisis pregnancy, will not be in possession of all her faculties. These mental and emotional faculties will be compromised due to feeling pressured to have an abortion. No woman will present for an abortion because she has nothing to do one particular morning. There are always reasons, and at times very distressing reasons, for the abortion. Suggesting that during a time of stress a woman is able to take in all that is said to her and shown to her and then give informed consent is absolutely ludicrous.

Emotional stress impairs judgement. Threats impair judgement. Fear impairs judgement. Indecision impairs judgement. Insecurity impairs judgement. Loneliness impairs judgement.

It is so vitally important to understand that a woman presenting for an abortion is usually governed strongly by the difficulties which have motivated her to go to the abortion clinic in the first place. A boyfriend threatening to leave, a husband threatening to leave, financial pressures on the family, parents who insist on the abortion, career reasons. The list is endless. These very real difficulties in the life of the presenting woman will be highlighted by the skilled "counsellor". Although the "counsellor" will offer alternatives he or she will ensure that only the abortion option is attractive. Under these circumstances informed consent, I believe, will not be possible. Yes, she can be shown the gestational length of her child, she can be shown an ultrasound image, she can be told of other options but these pale into insignificance (at that time) in comparison with the very real and present difficulties.

Fighting the abortion issue via the medium of the law will not bring an end to this modern scourge. Fighting the abortion issue via the medium of financial gain, by suing for damages may work for a time, but this also will be an option that closes. This avenue may also open up a new and more diabolical method for the destruction of infants by callous men and women. This new method is most frightening because it would clearly give rise to a way of making financial gain, through promoting pregnancy and then abortion. Attempting to stem the tide by outlawing abortion will not succeed, because too many voices will rise in uproar over the so-called, long fought for, long called for and now attempted compromise of "women's rights", and of course the stories about "backyard abortions" and the so-called "thousands of deaths of women" unless they have available legal abortion. Further, Caesar has never been known to surrender any of his "rights". So how will it be possible to stop this modern plague? With great difficulty, but it can be done.

Society is on a downhill slide towards dehumanisation and mechanisation of its citizens. We know this because more and more technology is being used to attempt to show that the process of life is only a matter of amino acids and DNA, which can be manipulated. The more science and technology devalue the nature of life and reduce it to a process, the more it becomes possible to experiment with and discard human life. The more there is an interchange of organs, tissue or parts from animals to humans the more it becomes easier to see the human being as nothing more than another beast, and therefore suitable for experimentation and if need be, for culling. The more there is a toying with the genetic makeup of animals or humans for the sake of experimentation the more it becomes possible to experiment abominably. The more foetal parts or foetal matter are sold for large amounts of money (the new macabre industry which has emerged as a result of the abortion industry), the easier it becomes to see human beings as nothing more than tissue and cells and not worthy of defence. The more the beginning of life is demoted to below animal status, the faster the end of life will be seen as a costly encumbrance to society, and therefore disposable.

As the beginning and end of life are dishonoured, so too the so-called "quality of life" aspect will be considered and dealt with according to the prevailing ideology. That is, disposal. We reap what we sow

It is of course possible to reverse all of the above. It is possible, though not probable, that it will happen. A complete change can only come through God's intervention and our co-operation. God's intervention alone does not require our co-operation, because if his intervention becomes necessary, then we must accept whatever comes to the guilty and to the innocent, for in this life and death battle we have all, in one way or another, participated or remained silent. Alternatively, a united corporate effort at returning to the known "goods" values, norms, certainties and past beliefs about the value of human life. In the past, family and religious beliefs were valued, including an understanding of the meaning of motherhood and fatherhood. The need today is a reversal of the contemporary, disposable mentality and a return to, and recapturing of, at least some of the past certitudes.

A full-scale change of values must occur before abortion, euthanasia, or any other anti- life activities can become outlawed. Morality must undergo a radical *upgrade* (not downgrade). Just as surely as the morality of humanity upgraded when it recognised that slavery was unjust and inhumane and abolished it, so too morality must upgrade when humanity begins to recognise again that every embryo is a unique human person with inalienable right to life. The recognition that every in-utero baby killed is murder of another individual, may ultimately lead to recognition that such a permissive society was vain, barbaric and primitive.

The laws of a vain and barbaric society must also by definition be unjust. Not long ago the indigenous populations of a country were considered subhuman, yet today we are appalled by such an understanding. Not long ago women were considered of such little value that they were not allowed to vote. Such is unthinkable today in most Western nations. Discriminations in the past appear now as monstrosities in these enlightened times. Perhaps there will come a time in the near future when those inhabitants of earth will look back to this period of history, and be appalled that a society existed which killed its own children for no reason except that they were unwanted. What is currently condoned has the potential to become condemned.

There seems no apparent way to end the holocaust called abortion. This is not so. All efforts towards the reduction of this scourge should be employed. All strategies, whether spiritual, legal, medical and rhetorical, should be engaged in concurrently. A continuous all-pronged attack should prevail. At the forefront should be a re-education of both society and specifically its younger members. Abortion has become so accepted and commonplace because of two reasons, loss of faith or belief in God (irrespective of denomination), and the manipulation of language and ideologies.

Loss of faith appears to be a specifically 20th-21st century phenomenon. No past civilisations have been known to reject the notion of the sacred and of worship. Excavations clearly indicate the place that honour or "worship to a deity" had in the life of those peoples. The human race in the immediate past and current century appears to have deified itself (to the exclusion of the unseen God), and when self becomes deified, such a society creates a monstrosity, just as surely as the one in the society worshipping a god which demands human sacrifice.

Loss of faith has meant loss of value of the creature because of the rejection of the creator. Without an eternal Creator, there can be no creation made in his image. This loss of faith has led to loss of hope for a "future" life, and without future life all is focussed on the "now". Self-satisfaction becomes paramount and everything and anything is possible. Loss of faith has meant loss of long-standing beliefs, definites, values and hopes, which are part of that belief system. In its place the "me" society encounters and negotiates with the disposable society.

Manipulation of language and ideologies via all forms of media has ensured that a slow reinterpretation of past certainties has slowly taken place. Indeed so slow and so meticulous has this change been that it has generally passed unnoticed. Re-education of the masses has taken place without even as much as a murmur. Internet, television, film, music, theatre, radio, computers and computer games, magazines, all forms of print media, have contributed to the changing of past "good", by presenting these past "goods" as antiquated and superfluous. Past values and norms have no currency in today's society.

Modern language assures us all that with modern technology we are able to see that what was considered important in past times (e.g., conception and pregnancy, baby) is really only a matter of misunderstanding and ignorance. Indeed it was only a matter of tissue, cells, or embryo. Language today tries to assure us that an abortion is not the death of a human being but a "menstrual extraction" or removal of "tissue," which has aggressively implanted in the woman's uterus. In fact at times this aggressive little "monster" is considered an aggressive "parasite" that has invaded the woman's sacred space, and is unwelcome and deserves violent removal.

Manipulation of language serves to change reality. The reality that a pregnancy brings forth a child is clouded by the imageless words employed to distract. Abortion on demand has become possible because society has been lulled into believing the "newspeak" of the late 20th century and early 21st century. This new language has sanitised the very real monstrosity, abortion,, which ultimately is the killing of a very tiny infant at its most vulnerable stage.

So deeply has this language of confusion penetrated that I believe it will not be possible to overturn it. However, if we want to begin to make a difference then this is what must be done: reclaim our descriptive language and call a "spade" a "spade" and not an ambiguous "digging implement". A pregnancy means the birth of a baby and not an imageless "tissue" This dehumanising agent of change, combined with sense of temporariness and loss of faith in a transcendent God, has so speedily facilitated the abortion industry. The abortion industry must have willing clients who insist on handing over money for the removal of an invading "attachment", not a baby but an aggressively attached invading parasite. The abortion industry could not survive without willing contributors. These willing participants have deluded themselves (via non-descriptive, imageless language) that what is being removed is similar to menstrual material.

Reclaim our children and their right to be children; their right to develop and learn as wholesome children; not as some perverted individual or organisation would wish them to develop and learn. Reclaim and protect our children's innocence from the purveyors of smut, pornography, drugs and depravity. This will not be easy because the film and television industry will not co-operate, as money is their "god". It will mean fighting against the ideologies of the world. However, it must be done because the abortion issue will never be resolved unless a sense of value of human beings is instilled in children from a young age.

Our hope in reducing (if not eliminating) this abortion scourge is through the younger generation. Those who still have wonder in their hearts and eyes. Through the school and education system must all effort be made. Those who are already out of the school system and into the tertiary system or out into the secular society may be too difficult to reach and to convince. They will have been secularised and will by this time be convinced of the ways of the world. Physical, psychological or spiritual damage will not convince them that abortion is wrong. Not even the spectre of breast cancer or long term psychiatric care will convince them that abortion is wrong. The humanity of the child will not convince them that abortion is wrong. Only God's intervention will achieve this but even then there has to be a softened heart to accept his whisperings.

Education of the young about the value of all life is essential. Education of the community about the value of life, and the very real and possible dangers of abortion is essential. So is the re-education of the medical profession, legal profession, and all professions involved in the life issues. An all out effort is needed to bring God into the equation again. The Church *absolutely must* preach about the evil of abortion. There must be a reversal of the trend of a faithless generation. A re-education of seminarians, priests, bishops, pastors, and rabbis, about life matters and about abortion and its aftermath, and ultimately to return to God what belongs to God, and to Caesar what belongs to Caesar (Mk. 12:17). Anything short of this will not suffice, as the issue has become too widespread and requires drastic measures to facilitate change.

Abortion is ultimately about violence done to another individual by a more aggressive one. Carried out at the whim of an individual or society, it is violence against a newly generated human being that has not yet reached the stage of being able to survive on its own. It has however, reached the stage of "love" because it has implanted (with love) itself in the womb of its mother, and is formed initially by her (womb/compassion) love. However, due to its being unwelcome and its hidden development, its love source is terminated.

Conception always means love. It means the incarnation of another for the specific purpose of setting it out on its journey to fulfil its destiny towards God and for the purpose of extending "love" on this planet. Conception means that an uttered "word" of God comes to fulfilment. "Be fruitful", speaks the Word of God, and there was "fruit". Abortion means death. It means the thwarting and ending of another's life journey and the deprivation of the love story, to which this human was entitled. Abortion means that the uttered "word" of God was refused and rejected. Abortion means that the loving tug towards the ultimate destiny (God) has come to an end. God constantly calls but always there is the perfect freedom of choice to refuse or accept. Abortion ensures that the individual cannot hear and follow the path of love, and thus follows a path leading to non-fulfilment.

Conception continues and extends the mystery of the words "be fruitful and multiply" (Gen 1: 28). Abortion fulfils the words "you will surely die" (both physical and spiritual) (Gen 2:17). The Tree of Life and the Tree of Knowledge of good and evil are paralleled through conception and abortion. There is a profound contradiction between these two trees and they come to a confrontation at the moment of conception. The instant of conception is critical because powers from above and those from below must contend for supremacy over life and death, and further, if conception is successful the same powers must contend for the life of this newly created being. It is no wonder then that the garden is rocked by the confrontation between the two trees.

Perhaps the greatest and strongest warriors against the enemy of life, abortion, and against abortion providers, will be those individuals who have submitted themselves to the procedure and allowed their baby to be destroyed. Men and women who have experienced an abortion and who know the pain, loss, loneliness, regret, guilt, shame, will slowly surface. With a loud voice they will condemn governments, abortionists, societies and individuals who have lied to them, when told their baby was not a baby and there would be no after-effects.

If enough men and women stand in solidarity, and condemn those who have called for liberalised abortion laws leading to the belief that abortion was trivial, then perhaps there will be a reversal of the holocaust in our midst. This is not impossible because the hidden abortion wounded list is legion. Always it must be understood that the most sincere and most genuine voice against abortion slaughter will be those who have experienced the trauma. Those who have not participated in an abortion can be sympathetic, and may genuinely want to see this abomination stopped. The most powerful voices, however, will be those who have known the pain.

Abortion providers know that the voices of the women and men who have been wounded by their abortion experience are the voices of experience and truth. They know that it is not an occasional woman who has been psychologically and spiritually wounded, but whole generations, because when a mother is damaged through such an experience, this affects her future mothering, and indeed other generations are affected by that one decision. Various estimates suggest that over one billion infants have been aborted over the last 30-50 years. If so, then it is no wonder that our society has become a society which has eaten bitterly of the tree of knowledge of good and evil. It is also a society which has covenanted itself to destruction rather than to life.

Ultimately the challenge that we are now called to face is to either accept the status quo or "go with the flow", or do something about the situation. Too many opposed to life have held centre stage for too long, it is time that the pro-life sentiment is loudly proclaimed from the rooftops. The war against children, future, life, can be won but not by apathy. It can be won because God wishes it to be so. All that will be required are some willing workers with passion, unafraid to proclaim that enough is enough. The rest will follow.

15.

The Church

*"For the lips of the priest should guard
knowledge and people should seek instruction
from his mouth, for he is the messenger
of the Lord of Hosts"* (Mal 2:7).

The Catholic Church, together with other mainline Christian denominations and orthodox religions, deplores the taking of human life. In their belief each individual creation has its own intrinsic value. It is to be accorded the respect due to it because of its divine origin. They acknowledge the personhood and humanity of each created being and from conception to natural death, the individual is deemed to be of inestimable value. Each individual is unique, and unrepeatable – even those infants destined for abortion.

This having been said and understood, it is important to also understand that the Church has the most important and vital role to play, if the elimination of the moral leprosy of abortion is to be achieved.

Secular society cannot defeat this savage beast since this is waging a spiritual war. As a spiritual war, it must be defeated with a spiritual army and spiritual means. It is the same war of life and death as played out in the "garden". The same protagonist leads the fray and is at the head of the army. The contest is about the same trophy, which is, God's uncontested authority over all creation.

The Catholic Church has from the very beginning spoken out against abortion. One of the earliest extant documents *The Didache* was very specific about this instruction and command, *"you shall not kill the embryo by abortion and shall not cause the newborn to perish."* Throughout the centuries the Church has continued to defend and protect life from the instant of conception to natural death. At no stage in its 20 centuries has the Church slackened this belief or watered it down. This is one of the many beliefs which it has steadfastly refused (and rightly so) to even countenance as deserving negotiation. The right to life of every individual, according to this Church, is non-negotiable.

The Catholic Church under the leadership of Pope John Paul II, and continuing with Pope Benedict XVI, has openly spoken against, and encouraged the fight against abortion. These Popes have never failed to speak against this crime in whatever situation they found themselves, and have called for a united effort in order to fight this scourge, which seems to have assailed late 20th century humanity and is continued into the 21st century.

In particular the long serving Pontiff John Paul II has not only strenuously and continuously spoken out, but he has also written on life matters in ways which can never be understood as ambiguous. In his *Crossing the Threshold of Hope,* and *Evangelium Vitae,* the Pope is both direct and charitable when speaking about the issue of abortion. In no way does he diminish the reality that abortion is a heinous crime and a sin against "Life". However, he also speaks with great compassion and mercy to those who have fallen prey to this sin. John Paul II in *Evangelium Vitae,* offers words of hope, love and encouragement to those who have acquiesced to an abortion. He offers an olive branch so that they may be able to return "home". He appears to understand that often there are many circumstances leading to the abortion decision, and that following the abortion, men and women experience profound suffering. To read *Evangelium Vitae* (99), is to read and hear the voice of God. Only He could offer such gentle mercy to a sinner who already knows that they are or have placed themselves outside the ambit of mercy. *Evangelium Vitae* came as a breath of the Holy Spirit. It came (like *Humanae Vitae*) at the most appropriate time. It came at a time of great pain and a time when abortion was being, and is being, touted as something trivial, or worse still, as a human right.

Evangelium Vitae is both encouraging and hope filled. It is encouraging because it shows much understanding of women and circumstances – whilst not condoning the abortion – and the pain they now experience. It is hope-filled because a lifeline is thrown to them with the words "your child is living in the Lord" (EV 99). The hope is that the aborted baby, whom they thought was "lost", is actually not lost but "living in the Lord".

Today there is a clear understanding that post abortion trauma exists, and affects a large percentage of males and females who have participated in this procedure. Part of the pain and trauma is the deep fear which takes up residence in the individual's psyche. It is a fear which has neither name nor face but strikes terror at the knowledge that the individual has participated in the death of a child. This fear is so palpable that to alleviate it tends to the withdrawal from the Life of God, and to immersion into self-destructive behaviour. It means to live in exile wandering through a desert of pain and being fearful to turn back to look on God and be healed. God often invites the return.

He enters the Holy Ground of suffering to lead the captives out. However, out of fear and dread the person fails to listen, and ignores Him. To take off one's shoes and enter into the Holy Ground of suffering is to acknowledge hearing the love-filled Voice, which desires a response. This Holy Ground made up of suffering and love is the womb where redemption and healing can be found. The *go'el* (redeemer) has entered this territory. It is the place where God calls, and human beings either respond or turn their backs and walk away. The *go'el* responded. In this space of suffering and love has trodden the Saviour in his redeeming Work. It is a holy and sacred space that requires acquiescence, silence, respect and response.

However, for the believers of the Catholic faith and indeed for some other Christian denominations, the issue of baptism of aborted babies, has until recently remained a stumbling block. In *Evangelium Vitae* (99), when the Pope wrote the words "living in the Lord", he outwardly uttered words that had been hoped for by abortive parents, who had no way of acknowledging such a desire. Some abortive parents, who have come to an understanding of what it has all meant, had longed for a sign that would tell them that their baby was/is with God, and not in some place of pleasantness without a hope of ever seeing God. Many older mothers shared with me their anguish of having a baby in "limbo" because it was unbaptised. Pope John Paul II's words in *Evangelium Vitae* came like the balm of Gilead, words and healing direct from God. These words in this encyclical, I am sure, have helped to return many a mother and father towards their baby and God and their heavenly destiny.

In order not to appear to diminish in any way the need for water Baptism as the principal and initiating sacrament of salvation, it is important to try to understand (as best as we can) both baptism and God's mercy.

No particular passage of Scripture clearly outlines or states definitively the fate of infants who have died before receiving the sacrament of Baptism. These are the words of Jesus: "Go into all the world and proclaim the good news to the whole creation. The one who believes and is baptised will be saved; but the one who does not believe will be condemned" (Mk. 16:16). The words of Jesus' commission appear to preclude eternal salvation for the unbaptised. However, for infants who have died in utero, without even the possibility of hearing the Gospel preached, and without the possibility of "being born of water and Spirit" (Jn 3:5), perhaps a deeper level of meaning could be found. Jesus said that the Gospel had to be *preached*, that is, *spoken* and *heard*. Salvation follows acceptance and Baptism. Condemnation follows rejection of the Gospel and rejection of Baptism. For the in utero victims, the hearing of the preaching cannot occur, nor can rejection of the Gospel or Baptism. These children cannot and are not permitted to hear and to make a choice for or against Jesus.

For the in utero victims, the preaching and the hearing cannot occur .... unless ... Jesus Himself brings the Gospel to them. We can glimpse this possibility from the parable of the Labourers in the Vineyard (Mt 20:1-16). This parable tells of the hiring of the labourers at different times during the day. We sense a hope that at the "eleventh hour," Jesus goes out looking for, and searching for these souls whom no one has wanted (Mt 20:7) and offers them safe passage (Gospel – his call, his word) "into my vineyard" (Mt 20:8). The potential labourers (aborted infants) of his vineyard are as equally graced at the "eleventh hour," as are those labourers who have laboured for a lifetime (a full day's work in all the heat (Mt 20:12). For the unwanted souls, the Master of the vineyard takes great care to be extra generous because "no one has hired us" (Mt 20:7) that is, they were considered of no value by their parents and by their society, however, they are of immeasurable value to their Lord and Master. Truly the Master is generous to some, whilst not being unjust or unkind to others.

We cannot presume to know God's ultimate designs and will. We cannot confine God's infinite mercy to human thinking and understanding. Nevertheless, the issue of baptism or lack of baptism, of aborted or indeed miscarried or still-born children, always remains to torment the human heart and mind and for this reason it is hoped that definitive comment may be received from "Peter" whose word, in faith and morals, is assured to be the word of Jesus Himself. God is more than capable of devising a covert rescue mission for the unbaptised; still, to the human order of things, baptism appears vital to the salvation of and initiation into the Body of the redeemed. It is the means by which the fruits of Jesus' redemptive work on the Cross are applied to the individual being. Jesus has purchased the right (atonement) for every individual to access eternal life and God; and by the Sacrament of baptism that access is claimed. This particular sacrament restores the direct link to the Father, and is necessary in order that the other sacraments of the Church can be applied to build and strengthen the pilgrim child on its journey to its Father. Baptism is the infinitely divine initiative, which bridges the present and eternal.

Each baptised human being is baptised into the death and resurrection of Jesus, and severs forever the connection with the sin of Adam. Never again can a baptised person return to a state of Original Sin, even when mortal or serious sin is present. A sinner may never merit heaven due to serious unrepented sin; however, if baptised will always remain free of the sin of Adam, that is, Original Sin. Jesus cancelled this particular sin for he is "the Lamb of God who takes away the sin of the world" (Jn 1:29). The fruits of redemption apply to individuals who believe and are baptised. The Saviour passed judgement on the sin of the world.

The Sacrament of Baptism is therefore an obligatory pre-requisite for entry into the body of the redeemed. However, where it is impossible to administer this form of baptism due to reasons beyond the control of the one to be baptised (e.g., aborted infants, miscarriages, stillbirths), it is understood and believed that a Baptism of martyrdom (blood) or Baptism of desire is efficacious. This is because baptism of martyrdom or desire ensures eternal life because the individual dies for another, (martyrdom) as Jesus has so clearly outlined as true love, and/or baptism is greatly desired by another for the miscarried, aborted or stillborn child.

By Baptism of martyrdom the person being martyred (aborted child) imitates the passion and death of Jesus and performs the greatest act of love outlined by Jesus Himself since "no-one has greater love than this, to lay down one's life for one's friends" (Jn 15:13). The aborted babies have laid down their lives (for their parents, society) like their friend Jesus, "the Word became flesh" (Jn 1:14). This army of martyrs, "slaughtered for the word of God" (Rev 6:9), die just as surely for "the

Word", as indeed "the Holy Innocents" around Bethlehem (Mt. 2:13-18) died when the "Word", was born into the human condition. The aborted infants died because "the word of God" finds no rich soil (Mk 4:8), is unwanted and instead falls on rocky ground (Mk 4:5). In this arid land the cry of the innocents and oppressed is stifled. Life loses its sacredness and the blood of the martyrs flows freely.

The Holy Innocents (Mt. 2:13-18 who perished at the hands of Herod died because "the Word" had arrived. He was born. Something new and never experienced before had occurred. All of creation would change because of this new birth (as happens with every new birth). There was a new song and a new expectancy in the air. *There was also a new threat to the Prince of this earth.* The innocents who perish through abortion die because the word falls on deaf ears of parents and society and onto "stubborn and rebellious heart" (Jer 5:23). Therefore both sets of sacrificed innocents die as witnesses to "the Word" (Rev 6:9), and as victims of Satan's hatred for the "word" – Jesus. Satan, through Herod, acts to destroy "the word became flesh" (Jn 1:14) as soon as he is born. Again Satan, through abortion perpetrated by modern day Herods, destroys the future images of the "word", and ensures that the uttered word of God will not be born of flesh. Satan attempts to kill and destroy what belongs to God and is of God. In his fury to achieve his ends he continues the Passion of Jesus Christ through God's own creations, the aborted babies who suffer a cruel death, because they are bearers of the likeness of Jesus.

St. Thomas Aquinas in his *Summa Theologica* (q.66) speaks clearly about baptism and the individual's assimilation into the Passion and death of Jesus. He comments further that when an individual is conformed to Christ Jesus in his martyrdom (Baptism of Blood), the same martyrdom which is experienced by aborted babies, then this death confers on them the required Baptism. The death of Jesus on the cross completes his own Baptism by blood. The death of the babies on the cross of the sin of disbelief, and murder, also confers on them a baptism of blood, just as surely as baptism by water. Martyrdom for the sake of Jesus "the word made flesh" (Jn 1:14), unites the aborted infants intimately to Jesus Christ at the moment of his immolation.

This type of baptism (blood) completes the redemptive work of Jesus and is the pinnacle of his sacrifice. For the aborted infants, baptism by martyrdom initiates them immediately into the divine life of Jesus. The *blood* of the new Covenant opened up our access to our heavenly inheritance (Col 3:24), and for the aborted infants the heavenly inheritance appears assured. Moreover, their reflection of Jesus "the word" in his (and their) moment of agony, guarantees for them a place of rest and eternal life. Aborted infants have surely earned for themselves the white robes (Rev 6:9-11) with the same baptism of blood as their divine Lord, and their own martyrdom must surely be a crown adorning their heads.

The greatest concern, however, should not be for the infants who have died as witnesses for the Lord but for their parents and society that have passed the unjust and cruel judgement upon them. While the children die because of lack of fertile soil, and the "word" fails to take root, it can also be seen as a prophecy being fulfilled. Truly because of the despising of "the word" in these days, the prophecy of Amos is being fulfilled:

> *The time is surely coming, says the Lord God*
> *When I will send a famine on the land:*
> *Not a famine of bread, or a thirst for water*
> *But of hearing the words of the Lord* (Amos 8:11).

The famine of hearing the words of the Lord brings with it its own fruit, a society with a "culture of death" (EV 50) mentality. It is a society whose value systems cater for the temporarily convenient, ultimately a society doomed to destruction because on its altars of sacrifice are burnt offerings for Moloch (Ezek 16:20-22). The innocents who have washed their robes in the blood of the lamb and who are "now living in the Lord" (EV 99) are securely anchored to Jesus and in Jesus. The society whose ethos has decreed their destruction and martyrdom hears these words: "Woe to you Chorazin! Woe to you Bethsaida! For if the deeds of power done in you had been done in Tyre and Sidon, they would have repented long ago in sackcloth and ashes" (Mt 11:21). For a society, which has the mystery and miracle of the Eucharist and the Gospel preached, and still persists in human sacrifice, "it will be more tolerable for the land of Sodom than for you" (Mt 11:24).

I have laboured over the issue of baptism because from my experiences with those I counsel and especially Catholic mothers, the issue of baptism and their infants' eternal fate is singularly the most distressing point. The general consensus is that "my baby can't go heaven because he/she was not baptised, so I really don't want or deserve to be forgiven and I certainly do not deserve eternal life." Tears of anguish and hopelessness follow this comment.

The Church is both human and divine in its origins and life. It is human because it is made up of human beings whom it is mandated to gather and lead to God. It is divine because Jesus Himself instituted it, in order to continue and complete the works necessary to bring home the whole body of the redeemed. Indeed it is the Mystical Body of Christ, the People of God. The Church exists in time, to "be fruitful and multiply" (Gen 1:28), to fill, first the earth with heavenly creatures, and then heaven with earthly creatures in the image and likeness of Jesus. The Church is the earthly womb from which will be born into eternal life citizens for heaven. Therefore, if the Church is "Mother" and "womb" then surely this heavenly womb gathers to itself the infants rejected by their earthly mother, and gives birth to them in the eternal realm? We *know* that every child conceived (including the aborted one) is never an orphan, even if abandoned by its own earthly parents, because every child has a heavenly Father (God) and earthly Mother (Church). Therefore even if the earthly human parents reject it, then assuredly the heavenly Parents will welcome the child home.

One of the greatest acts of mercy that the Church could do would be for "Peter" (the Pope) together with his apostles (Bishops) to call out to abortive women and men. They could speak to them about God's boundless, immeasurable Mercy towards their infants and towards them. They could assure them of God's love for their children and for them, and speak with authority on the fate of the infants. There is a longing to hear from "Peter" that their child has been "loosed in heaven".

Further, the Church through its priests must speak out loudly, bravely, consistently about the evil of abortion. It is important to speak fearlessly about this issue, because all other "rights" disappear into nothingness, when the "right" to life has been violated. No other human "right" is as important as the "right to life."

The Church through its priests and pastors must speak about abortion. It must do so not only for its own sake but also because it must call to men and women in the pews who have participated in an abortion, or who know of someone who has had an abortion, and offer them mercy and reconciliation. The Church can offer real reconciliation between the individual and God, and the individual and their child.

Silence cannot accomplish this. By their silence, those who should know better condemn women to a lifetime of solitary suffering. This type of suffering is not redemptive suffering but a scape-goating type of suffering. The women who will suffer agonies as a result of their abortion decision redirect their suffering into self-destructive pain. It is merciless. It is their belief that only their aggravated suffering will suffice to atone for the "killing of my baby". It is a demonic call to suffering, rather than redemptive. Marie, a client of mine, told me that for 17 years she went to reconciliation weekly. Even at times when she felt she had nothing to say to the priest. This she did because "I liked to hear the words 'I absolve you from all your sins'." However, whilst she regularly sought reconciliation with God and with her baby, she never spoke of, or confessed her sin of abortion, because she was so ashamed.

Although her need to hear the words of absolution sufficed for a time, the need for them arose again, because the sin remained lodged firmly in her soul. As she said, "I never felt quite forgiven; that's why I went so often." This marathon of reconciliation came to an end when she was able to come face to face with a very humble and loving priest, confess her sin of abortion, receive absolution and not judgement, and hear that her baby was "living in the Lord". This time she believed that she was forgiven, and her baby was safe with God. Her deepest, darkest secret was out. She was not pilloried, and Satan no longer could hold her captive. Her journey home had been long, and fraught with many distractions, but just as surely as Jesus set his face resolutely towards Jerusalem, so too now this mother's face is turned towards her God and her baby.

Priests, by virtue of their sacramental ministry, have the power to bring the healing of God to abortive men and women. However, this will not happen by their silence. In most cases the pastors remain silent, out of a lack of understanding, or because of the perceived compassion for those who have aborted, but it is a *false compassion*. It is the type of compassion Peter offered Jesus (Mk 8:31-33), who rebuked him soundly for his effort. It is the seductive and compelling voice of Satan who whispers "leave them alone they are suffering enough", while the voice of Jesus whispers, "come to me all you that are weary and are carrying heavy burdens, and I will give you rest. Take my yoke upon you, and learn from me; for I am gentle and humble in heart and you will find rest for your souls" (Mt 11:28-30). The rest found in and with Jesus will give rest to souls. The silence, which Satan offers and encourages, gives no rest but isolation, alienation and despair. The living waters of Jesus wash clean. The stagnant waters of Satan, poison.

Priests, pastors, Rabbis, please offer the Mercy of God to your congregations. Go into the vineyard and find these broken, weary women and men, and like the Good Shepherd lead them back into the fold. No less than this is asked of you. Remember that while the sin of abortion remains hidden and unforgiven it works its poison not only on the woman but also on her family, friends, community and society. "How does this happen?" you might ask. The answer is: guilt, shame, and fears. These negative emotions in heavy doses will alter her behaviour and impair her coping mechanisms. The myriad of ways that an abortion experience affects the individual are well documented. It requires massive amounts of energy to continually deal with these three emotions. This leaves the woman incapable of experiencing any joy in living. In her suffering, those around her and those who love her will suffer also. Thus is perpetuated the cycle of abortion victims.

The Church, in its battle against abortion has the charism necessary for the healing of post abortion trauma.

Since Vatican II and the subsequent dissent and/or abandonment (of the Church) by thousands of its religious and consecrated, and gradual abandonment by the laity, we have seen at times a Church rendered almost impotent. It has not been as fruitful as commanded by Jesus. This impotence has led to a phenomenon of absence of children, both at a physical level and a spiritual level. The characteristic of the Suffering Church of this age has been loss (through abandonment) of consecrated sons and daughters, and through dearth of vocations. Added to this, we have seen the massive exodus from the Church of young and old.

Analogous to this have been the deaths of millions upon millions of infants (through abortion), before they have seen the light of day, and the loss through the death of innocence of the young. Of course the ensuing empty pews only make sense when we can see the desensitisation that the blanket of death has had on society and the church. Death has visited the Church in these times, and its victims have been sons and daughters of heaven and earth. Today the Catholic Church, as indeed other mainline churches, suffers through lack of vocations. It is my belief and contention that the Lord God is giving us all the vocations needed to lead his people home. However, we are killing them before they are born.

Imagine: up to 50,000,000 babies annually die, yet we are crying out to God for vocations to the religious life. "Before I formed you in the womb I knew you, and before you were born I consecrated you; I have appointed you as prophet to the nations" (Jer 1:5). This clearly suggests that God calls and appoints an individual to a service long before the individual is even born – even candidates to the priesthood! Could it be that in his attempt to destroy the Church (the mystical bride of Christ), Satan has found a spectacular way, that is, by killing future priests, pastors, servants, long before they are born?

This is not new. We have a precedent. The birth of Moses and the birth of Jesus were both accompanied by the attempted extermination of the innocents. However, in both episodes it was the response of the humans involved that averted the intended slaughter of God's chosen One. Although with the birth of Moses, and Jesus, there was a slaughter of young ones, today the saving response to the slaughter of the preborn infants is not forthcoming. If there is a response it is only a whisper when it needs a mighty roar. Today the human response to the death of the innocents is that "it is a right" of the woman and, more grotesquely, a "human right".

Perhaps as a society we can interpret from the incidents of Pharaoh and Herod and the death of the innocents, in both Old and New Testaments, that God will not be mocked. He tolerates, He loves, He forgives, He is patient and kind, but He will not be mocked. His previous human and world changing initiatives (the Covenant at Sinai and birth of Jesus), were heralded by the death of infants and the land flowed with their blood. We know this, because there is a record of it. Are the deaths of billions of babies, through abortion (both surgical and chemical) the precursor to another dramatic encounter with God? May it be so.

The Church is supposed to be the most powerful and wholesome unit on earth. This is not because of its large numbers, but because her head is Jesus Christ whose Father is God. The Church is powerful. It can pray, intercede, rebuke, embrace, heal, but most of all it can dispense grace and forgiveness. The Church is the womb and the confessional where God and man meet to reconcile. In this confessional there is always mercy in abundance because God Himself dispenses it in quantities of plenty. The Church (as mystical bride and mother) has the power, strength and courage and will, to gather all her children (including the aborted, miscarried and stillborn ones) and present them whole to their heavenly Father. Leaving them without a known destiny and paternity is surely not the way, and consigning them to some place of "heavenly utopia" falls far short of the mercy of God and His beatific vision.

My wish is to always defer to the findings of Holy Mother Church and her visible head, the Vicar of Christ. In obedience I submit to his decrees with the full knowledge that the Holy Spirit guides, understands and in due time will manifest the Will of the Father with regard to his beloved martyr infants. Indeed for now may they "rest in the Lord" whose mercy will not be restricted by human barriers or human thinking.

16.

The Death of a Child

"I Slept but My Heart Was Awake"
(Song of Songs 5:2)

The death of a child is the saddest and most devastating event possible. At all times it appears incomprehensible and unfair. The death of a child always renders those left behind incomplete and this will remain so. Whether through an accident, sickness, or because the child is severely challenged, the death (even when expected) numbs survivors and questions the validity of life. Death always leaves behind unanswered questions. However, the death of a child freezes the human spirit and calls into question the reality of a "Just God". As the birth of a new child serves to alter the whole of creation in order to accommodate this new individual, the death of a child serves to shake violently all of the same creation. There is a rebellion. At the death of innocence on Calvary "the curtain of the Temple was torn in two from top to bottom. The earth shook, and the rocks were split" (Mt 27:51). It was nature rebelling at such a gross injustice; so too the death of a child causes to shake violently all that is created.

Whereas any death is an enigma, and seems to taunt us for being unjust and unexpected, the death of a child is much more so. Many reasons can be offered for this. However, the closest and most understood reasons would have to be that when a child dies, a family future dies; a tomorrow has died; future generations have died; hope has died. When a child dies a covenant relationship has been broken, which can never be repaired. This particular covenant has been sundered.

Death, the enemy of humanity and the legacy of sin, continues to randomly claim its own. The intentional death of "someone" can unhinge the human mind. Intentional, and at times unintentional, death leaves in its wake an incomplete, interrupted journey, which the perpetrator of the intentional death, at times, unconsciously attempts to complete. This false attempt at completion of the journey provides a sense of vindication or atonement for the interruption. When there is an interruption in the story, there is the experience of a beginning, possibly middle, but no end to that particular story. There must be a conclusion, an ending in order to finalise the story. Intentional death, especially the intentional death of a child, mirrors chaos. It is an abyss from which there appears no exit.

In listening to the stories and observing the at times unconscious mourning of those who experienced one or more abortions, I have learned about the profound meaning and love present at conception, even where it appears that this is not so. I have seen the intimate relationship between suffering and love, and the very real metaphysical connection, (either known or unknown) between a mother and her child. I have further seen the very deep pain of a father, suffering the loss of the child, whom he has generated. Observing a father's deep grief at the violent death of his child reminded me, or helped me to understand (just a little) how God the Father must have felt, seeing his Child die a cruel and violent death, and not be able to intervene to stop the cruelty. I have gained a new appreciation of the unseen bond that both a mother and a father have to their child, even though at times it appears that they do not know that the bond exists. Post abortion grief is a visible symptom of that bond, indeed a "Redeeming Grief.".

A key to the understanding of maternal and paternal grief is to first understand the relationship between a mother and father, and their child. This relationship does not begin at some magical moment after the child is born, but can at times begin long before the child is even conceived. The bond, or relationship, begins at a moment in the life of the man and woman when they have become, "one flesh". However, before the "one flesh", a conception has occurred, in the instant when a man and woman have said, even a non-verbal "yes", to one another, and in that "yes", each has longed for an extension of the other.

Today there is a superficial understanding of "love", but for a man and a woman, the "love", for one's own child, has been internalised over a lifetime. In fact, love for an extension of oneself has been programmed since time immemorial and has a connection to God as its original source of love. For men and women, the future always holds children, and especially their own child/children. The future is understood to mean children, and in the life of human beings, it is rarely thought of as an option that future children will be killed, or in some way will die.

A woman begins to see far into the distance as she slowly matures and comes to an understanding that within her rests part of humanity. A man equally sees prophetically into the future and knows that his likeness will be extended. He is happy for this extension. She is happy that she can be involved in this extension. The future holds a finer and more complete model of each of them, because both of them have co-operated with the divine design for regeneration and donated the very best of themselves towards this regeneration. Of course this is good.

The death of a child whether "wanted" or "unwanted", whether by natural causes, illness, or intentional (abortion), is followed by a time of deep questioning. The questioning is complex because it requires facing multiple issues. The death of a wanted baby introduces a new set of emotions, difficulties, a new level of previously unknown suffering, but the intentional death of a child introduces the dimension of personal, self-induced suffering and death. Intentional death (abortion) of an infant by its own mother and father introduces not redemptive suffering but destructive suffering. Redemptive suffering has a dimension which raises it heavenward. Destructive suffering catapults it downward and inward. Destructive suffering has as its end point – annihilation. Destructive suffering seeks saccharine sympathy, but it is only *saccharine sympathy* with a bitter aftertaste.

After the loss of an infant through death, various levels of emotional and spiritual pain must be felt and negotiated before homeostasis can be achieved. This is not a return to a time pre-baby, but a levelling of the existing situation. One must experience a transitional period (following the death), if emotional health is to be retained. This transitional period (if handled successfully) serves to reconcile the hopes, dreams, expectations and future to the reality of the death of the baby. At the beginning in this transitional period, the groundwork is laid out for coping with and negotiating the moments of abysmal pain. Even when a live birth occurs successfully, a woman (and man sometimes) needs to negotiate her relationship with the baby, now external to her. For a woman the growth of the foetus/baby within her body has been a time of intense emotion and unspoken dialogue. From the instant of its conception, the child has "spoken" to its mother, and together they have formed an indissoluble bond. No words have been needed by either of them, just emotional presence and secret knowledge shared by them alone.

The loss of a "wanted" baby, after so much psychological and spiritual investment, results in devastation, which paralyses the mother and father, especially the mother. The loss involves not only the physical loss of the baby, but also losses at multiple levels. There is the loss of the baby who was real and a part of the mother, father, existing family and future family. There is loss of a future, dreams, names, hopes, expectations and love. There is the loss of self-image, as wholesome woman and human being, who can bring to life a healthy child. There is the loss of the sense of "my uniqueness", as a woman, and "my uniqueness", as my husband's partner. There is a loss of self-esteem as woman.

With the loss of the "wanted" child, there is the experience of the whole gamut of emotions. Ultimately, it feels like the whole world has come crashing down, and nothing actually makes much sense anymore. The death of a child through abortion has the capacity to bring on a similar reaction, even though an active decision was made to terminate the life of that child. The decision, and the reasons for the decision, cannot change the wound in the psyche. It cannot fill the gaping hole left in the place where the baby should have been growing. Self-esteem is especially critically challenged.

All this turmoil happens with an experience of a neonatal death through miscarriage. Such experience receives understanding, as grief is expected and its intricacies negotiated. However, it is also my contention that the death of a child, irrespective of the nature of its death, including death through abortion, always acts as a sobering experience to humanity. We are not in control, and even when we believe that we are in total control (abortion), we find out that this is not so. Post Abortion Syndrome tells us so. Mourning the loss of a child is always complex, and made more so under particular circumstances.

Modern society perpetuates an untruthful myth that the bond between a mother and her baby, and a father and his baby, begins when the child is born. This myth has served the abortion industry well. By believing that the bond begins at birth, and continues throughout life, then what happens before birth cannot be of life-changing magnitude. The wide promulgation of this myth made it easy to terminate the life of the child, from conception to full gestation. It has been easy also to dismiss those who mourn (even after abortion) the loss of their foetal child. After all, if the in-utero child is not a child at all, then a bond, relationship and secret dialogue could not have developed. If one denies the foetal child membership of the human race, then grief and mourning over its loss is really an overreaction.

A woman who experiences an abortion equally needs to work through the complex processes of letting go. In fact, this woman has perhaps a greater need to work through the mourning process, because of the added dimensions of fault, volition, guilt and shame. Because of the bonding between a mother and her baby, from the instant of conception, she experiences mourning, whether acknowledged or not. It is the unspoken dialogue, the inward thoughts, and those toward the other. It is at times the unconscious wish for the child. It is the need to make a decision, and during the decision-making process, the utter focus on the object of the decision. It is the both conscious and unconscious attempt at self-extension, and the thwarted attempt, which causes the need to mourn.

Ultimately, understanding the bonding, from the instant of conception, will explain the mourning or post abortion grief of women, following a termination of pregnancy. The grief and mourning are symptoms that indicate that the woman knows that the abortion has meant the death of her baby. The one with whom she had developed a relationship, with whom she had silently dialogued, and to whom she gave a part of herself. Now that baby and that part of herself have died.

While society attempts to dehumanise the in-utero infant, the grief following an abortion, says that this is not possible. Even those women who actively sought a termination for what may be termed as self-seeking reasons cannot erase the dialogue engaged in with their child. Clear evidence comes from the numbers of women, and men, surfacing who mourn the loss, suffer regret, and whose mourning takes the form of wandering through life seeking what was lost through a moment of weakness.

One of the Beatitudes states, "Happy are those who mourn for they shall be comforted" (Mt 5:5). At first glance this appears odd, and maybe even a little mocking. However, as we understand more and more the need to mourn, and the relationship between suffering, mourning and love, it does not appear as an odd Beatitude, but one full of profound meaning. For the individual who loses a prenatal child (by whatever means), their need to mourn is the assured evidence that love and life go together. It is because love is so closely connected with life that there is a need to express grief and mourning when this holy dyad is assaulted.

The loss of a baby through death (irrespective of gestational period) renders all of us temporarily out of kilter. It is not the norm, and can never be treated as the norm. Abortive parents cannot treat the death of their child as normal, or even as a trivial matter, because any attempt to do so ultimately backfires and causes much suffering. We cannot change the human blueprint. It is not ours to change, and our blueprint decrees that with an intimate loss there will be a time of unspeakable suffering. Love and suffering are closely linked and the bridge of fear is "loss".

We can never be in control of "life". The blueprint has been pre-designed, and any manipulation will result in grotesque caricature. Failure to grieve over the loss of a baby, even through abortion, is impossible, because the blueprint has instructions to the contrary. Where temporary denial of grief is present, it is only as a temporary measure, so that the issue can be dealt with at a later time. There comes a time, a moment, a sigh, which remembers, because the physical death of the baby has not been able to blot out the memory that once one existed who was as close to "me" as one can ever be. Part of me died, and today I live a resonance of that death.

17.

Healing of Post Abortion Trauma

"My daughter" He said, "your faith has restored
you to health. Go in peace" (Lk 8:48).

The counselling and hopefully healing of individuals who suffer post abortion trauma is difficult. The difficulties related to this particular type of grief and witnessed by grief practitioners may vary, but the manifestations are similar. Researchers and practitioners in this field, such as Terry Selby, Professor Priscilla Coleman, Professor Philip Ney, and even in my own counselling practice, have noted the difficulties. Selby urges those counsellors encountering post abortion trauma to "cast aside our prejudices, preconceptions and politics". (p. 12). Only by casting aside prejudices and preconceived ideas about abortion, can a post abortion grief counsellor help the suffering individual. Post abortion trauma and grief demand solidarity because wounded humanity is suffering, in part for granting tacit approval to the abortive woman by telling a woman that abortion is good for her and a right. So now in solidarity both now suffer. Post abortion grief and its root cause: abortion/abandonment/abuse happens because society/community has encouraged the abortion, and now the same society/community must come together to grieve.

For the most part post abortion trauma and grief can be alleviated, and the sufferer supported through his/her time of difficulty. There is a light at the end of the tunnel, but this light of hope is very dim and requires co-operation and willingness to persevere until the end.

Terry Selby, Professor Philip Ney, Professor Priscilla Coleman and my own literature and the literature of others can assist counsellors in this area of work. I believe, however, that the most effective counsellors are those who have journeyed the same path, persevered, and reached the light at the end of the tunnel. Standard grief counselling methods can and do assist, but mental health professionals should be aware of the complicated nature of post abortion trauma and grief. They need to explore and nurture an extra dimension (spiritual) before achieving any sort of healing. Grief, loss and trauma recovery practitioners must be aware that abortion is very traumatic, *even* where it ostensibly appears that this is not so.

There is a reason for my belief, that a woman who herself has experienced an abortion, and suffered as a result of this, is better equipped to talk to someone else in this position. It is a fact that most often someone who has not gone through the same situation cannot understand the reason behind the behaviour. One can learn from textbooks how to identify certain characteristics; however, one cannot pretend to know what the emotions are, unless one has "drunk from the same cup". This suggestion is of course, for people/clients who do not have other psychological issues to deal with. In such cases, it is always important to refer on to other mental health professionals, where experience in this area is not available to the post abortion practitioner.

As I continue to journey the path of post abortion trauma counselling, I keep learning from those who come. Today I understand post abortion grief differently, from my understanding even one year ago, and certainly a great deal more differently from four and seven and eleven years ago. Today I no longer seek to instantly remove the suffering from the life of the individual. Certainly it is important to ameliorate or ease the pain, and help to alleviate the guilt and the shame. It is important also to understand that these can be very important for the healing and conversion of the individual. It could even be said that post abortion grief, endured correctly, and understood correctly, can become a redeeming type of grief.

It is important to clarify the statement that post abortion grief may be a good thing. In itself of course it's not a good thing. It's monstrous. It's debilitating. It's destructive. However, if and when captured and understood correctly, it can become the turning point in the life of an individual. It can become the first step towards a total reconciliation both with God, and the infant. Without this pain, the mother and others would not seriously consider the action taken (abortion). In fact, the abortion and infant would be forgotten. post abortion grief is the assurance that the baby will never be forgotten.

At times, especially when I have been speaking publicly, listeners have harangued me because of this opinion. Yet I do not budge, because I have seen that in post abortion grief there is a seed (even if mustard sized seed) for renewal. In the suffering, there is the possible ensuing journey through remorse, pain and discovery. Accepting the pain and hearing the call to repentance, especially through the guilt and shame, the Lord God may have the permission to work his miracle of transforming a bitter lemon into the sweetest lemonade. To misuse suffering is to waste the opportunity for healing. By beginning to at least gingerly bless life again, and to grieve for that lost life, it becomes possible to wish for its healing.

Post abortion grief and sorrow are the hope of redemption, after the assault on the Author of life and his gift of life. It is difficult to counsel women, without some faith in God, because, indeed, there has been an offence against God. Hostility has been towards the Author of life. This demands reconciliation with the Author of life. But also because there needs to be forgiveness and forgiveness is something "other" than the normal. The special suffering, which comes following an abortion, is the "special" cross which is put on our shoulders. This cross can either unhinge and break us or become the instrument of salvation. It's the means by which a new life can begin. A life devoid of false pretensions and false pride. Indeed the virtue most present in the life of a woman (occasionally even a male) after an abortion, who has understood the enormity of the act, is humility. A woman who has aborted her child and realises what she has done, understands the total ramifications of her action and can no longer claim pride for herself. No longer does she ever feel "better" than another. My act is always before my eyes.

Anna, an abortive mother of three children, understood that as a result of her abortions, she had broken all the Ten Commandments at once, beginning with idolatry through to covetousness. From this clear insight of spirituality and sin, it is possible to see that what Anna said is correct. Breaking each of the Ten Commandments is an assault on both God and man, divine and human. An assault against life is an assault against the Lord and Giver of Life, who brings into being the human person. Abortion violates life, not only the life of the intended new human person, but also the life of the already existing human persons. It is a far greater sin because it is a sin against the command, the "word" of God, to "be fruitful". It is against the commanded "word" breathed by God Himself. A pregnancy occurs not only because of the language of the body of the man and the woman, but also because of the language of God. God has uttered his "Yes" to this conception, and hence has permitted his image to be propagated anew. A new creation now bears his image and likeness. Abortion rejects this new initiative of God.

To conceive a child is to become pregnant with the uttered word of God. Not as Mary who became pregnant with "The Word", but it is a pregnancy brought about by a spoken, desired, word of God. To be pregnant and to have conceived means that God has entered into a creation covenant with the parents of the new child, and has trusted them to fulfil their part of the covenant. He has trusted human beings again. In the creation of each and every new child, God encounters humanity, and that is why abortion is so lethal physically, psychologically and spiritually, because it is a rejection of that encounter. God's ecstatic embrace, in which He beheld all in the image of his Son Jesus, is violated and rejected. There is rejection of "The Word" through whom and by whom all is created. Abortion is the ultimate rejection of God. It frustrates the divine plan and returns individuals, and slowly society, to a state of perpetual sin and closer to a beastly nature. The beastly nature is enhanced with the perpetuation of more and more sin.

The whole spiritual life of the abortive person has been disarranged. Understanding this, it becomes possible to see the "how" and the "why" of the psychological and spiritual damage. Further, we can grasp more importantly that true healing of abortion grief and wounds can only ultimately come from God. It is not human actions which can save us, but He Himself. Secular measures, whilst commendable, cannot bring peace and restoration. Further, pseudo religious attempts will also fail, and may indeed be more harmful.

It has been suggested that for healing to take place a heartfelt turning to God is necessary and all will be well. Though this is possible, I believe that there is more, and scriptures appear to confirm this. In the parable of the "Good Samaritan" there is a sequence of actions. A man is robbed and left for dead, on his way from Jerusalem to Jericho. There is the assault, the victim, those that help and those who walk away, the ministering to the wounded, the gathering of the wounded, and the placing of the wounded into the hands of someone who can complete the healing. Jesus can and does heal instantly if that is his wish. However, He normally uses the human mediator, just as He Himself acts as the human intermediary between his Father and humanity. He uses the means understood by the human person, and does not cause scandal or breach the normal order of things.

The re-integration both into the human and spiritual community is necessary, before a post-abortive woman/man can have a sense of healing. This reintegration cannot take place in isolation. Both the human and the spiritual community must participate in the ingathering, because both God and human nature have been assaulted and damaged. Abortion grief, sorrow and regret are connected to the sense of alienation, disunity and loss of dignity. The regret and the guilt are a leaning towards the re-integration and a call for help: "Make me whole again, please forgive me, help me, and allow me to belong to you again." These are the cries of the abortive women. These are the cries of those who have recognised the enormity of the sin committed. They may not even know what a sin is, but the law written on the human heart (Jer 31:31), and written by the Lawmaker Himself cannot be erased. It therefore exerts its influence.

The state of sin and brokenness, which follows the abortion, is a sign of the future state of disintegration. It is a foretaste of what hell may be like. In the sinning against the Holy Spirit the Lord and Giver of Life, much more than a debt is incurred. It is more than a transgression. It is an act in which the human person consciously, knowingly makes a decision to sever the connection with God. It is the human will saying, "I do not want you to be present in my life." It is an exercise of the free will, which seeks to act on its own volition, removed entirely from the will and design of God. A sin is the will's decision to act on its own without reference to God's own perfect will. God's will tempers the erratic human will into actions pleasing to God and to self. A human will without this buffer or connection with God, cannot decide for good because its inclination is towards evil.

The will of a woman thinking "abortion" while connected to the will of God will hesitate, stall and ponder and experience a dissonance. This woman or man cannot proceed with the abortion because there is present a sense of "other" knowledge, of "other" influence, and if she does override this dissonance and proceeds with the abortion, the aftermath is immediate. Post abortion grief and trauma will be so severe that psychological, psychiatric and spiritual care will become absolutely necessary. A will already disconnected from God's will through negligence, misuse, and years of ignoring the small still voice, will not be able to hear the echo of God's voice. Even if heard, it is unrecognised as the voice of the beloved calling to the loved one, who is heading towards danger.

A human will attuned to the divine will still has hope inscribed into its being and with hope is inscribed *future*. Alternatively a will detached from God will have inscribed despair, and its essence comprises *death*. An individual who *hopes*, believes that there will be a tomorrow – that something new is possible. Someone who despairs closes down all doors to the future and dies. Sometimes such a person literally dies or suicides.

I once read a poem called *A Touch of the Master's Hand* by an unknown author. I thought it was so beautiful that I have remembered it ever since. It is about a violin that was up for auction. The violin was battered, scratched, and dusty, and had strings which were loose, and in reality it did not appear worth very much. However its worth was inestimable when a Maestro violinist picked up the battered violin. He lovingly dusted it, tightened its strings, tuned it and nursed from it the finest melody. It no longer was worthless but an instrument of delight, immense joy and of incalculable financial worth. The master knew the worth. Only he knew the possibilities.

In this work of post abortion grief counselling, I encounter broken violins (human beings) regularly. They suffer in silence, and for so many, their lives are definitely out of tune. The person who is so depressed and so out of tune with life is slowly abandoned (forget it or get a life) by the thoughtless crowd, and descends slowly into a pain-filled world. Into this world of depression, drink, drugs and promiscuity Jesus desires to enter, sometimes in an extraordinary way, and effects the rescue. He mounts a covert rescue mission directly through the enemy's camp.

The "foolish crowd" (or so the poem says) cannot understand the abortion grief. They thought that it was "a good decision". It does not matter very much to them that she suffers for the loss of her baby. It matters not that the despair has changed the person to a mere shell of her former self. It matters not to the thoughtless and foolish crowd (or so the poem says) that the suffering individual in their midst is worthy of the touch of the Master's hand. It matters not that, transformed, this soul is beautiful. It matters not that the soul touched by the Master's hand is a soul who has walked the holy ground called suffering.

Anna had given up on God as she was sure that He hated her because of her abortion. Jesus went looking for her in the midst of her despair. After 19 years she stopped long enough for Him to touch her and she bloomed. She is no longer the insecure, frightened whipping body for all and sundry but an intelligent classy lady with a smile that competes with the sun. She, who had not been to church in over 20 years, returned to God and to the sacraments and He rewarded her trust in Him with an image of her baby. She was transformed. The child that she thought lost forever now lived with Him, and the child was beautiful and whole. All it took was for her to hear the words "Jesus loves you so much. In your pain you mirror Him."

The emphasis moved from her, to Him, and the need for grace of healing and restoration of the psychological and spiritual damage of abortion. Healing comes when the person gets in touch with the reality of the abortion, what it has meant, and the power that this act has had on him or her. Facing this reality, as bad as this may be, and then accepting the reality that the abortion was evil begins the transformation. Acceptance and acknowledgement of the evil is the "Yes" to stop evil in its tracks. Healing can then follow through forgiveness of the sin and the power of Jesus to transform the person to wholeness.

18.

Parables of Hope, Mercy and Healing

To the question, "who is my neighbour?" (Lk 10:29), Jesus responded with a parable. A parable is a story from the known, daily experience of the listeners. However, parables have a depth of meaning and application that is timeless. While the scenario may change (i.e., context), the essence, the meaning will always remain the same. Jesus used parables as a teaching strategy. By using day-to-day experiences, tools, scenery, life situations and infusing them with his special meaning, He was able to teach timelessly. He used parables, knowing that the message would reach the ears of those who needed to hear, and learn and would speak to all future hearers in their time and situation. We are even told that when the parable was too deep, He took aside his own people and carefully explained it to them.

In reply to the question of "who is my neighbour?" (Lk 10:29), Jesus applied the same principles of explanation, by employing the parable pedagogy.

In this particular parable the characters used by Jesus to illustrate his answer to the question, "who is my neighbour?", were mostly Palestinian peasants. Jesus used the imagery familiar to them. His intention was to create a climate of shock. The purpose of a parable is to shock or surprise the hearer, creating a certain tension, and leaving the story as a riddle without conclusion. This method of pedagogy then permits the parable to be timeless, and the hearer to apply the conclusion as befits his or her situation and time.

In my counselling of abortive men and women, I have found three parables especially helpful. These can easily be transported into the milieu of the twentieth and twenty-first centuries, without losing any of their impact. The first of these parables is *The Good Samaritan* (Lk 10:29-37), the second is *The Healing of the Crippled Woman* (Lk 13:10), and third *The Woman Who Was a Sinner* (Lk 7:48-50).

The Good Samaritan is of particular help in explaining God's mercy. This parable is most efficacious, because it speaks of woundedness and later of healing.

At times my listener does not know the story. In such a case, to make full use of it, I give a copy to him or her. I ask him or her to read it carefully during the coming week. We will discuss it at the next appointment, when we will share insights into the story and listen to each other's understanding.

For abortive women, it is important to listen to their anger, anguish, frustration and hurt. The content, characters and essence of the parable assist in bringing to the surface these emotions. One woman's interpretation of the Good Samaritan story provides a good example. She saw herself as the main character. She saw her husband, parents (as passers by) and the aborted baby as the wounded and beaten person. Among these people she could not recognise the "Good Samaritan". She saw herself, her husband, and her parents as the ones failing to help, save or tend to the wounded dead infant. She could not see a "Samaritan" in her life.

This of course is understandable, because her baby was "beaten and murdered" (her words), and she herself had been one of the "bandits", who actually assisted in the murder (by complying with the wishes of others). In her anguish she was unable to see the depth of the parable. She saw the characters only superficially. Whilst this woman previously stated that she believed she was forgiven for her sin of abortion, she did not believe it at the level of the heart. This was clearly evident from her interpretation of the parable.

Parables provide signs and symbols of God's activity and transforming actions in the world. They can also act as instruments of transference, that is, the one meditating on the parable transfers onto the characters her or his own feelings and beliefs. In the case above, the woman still carried much guilt and anguish and transferred these onto the characters. She intellectually understood her reasons for the abortion and believed that God had forgiven her, and those who encouraged the abortion. Yet at the heart level none of these had occurred.

A skilled Christ-centred counsellor can assist the counselee to move from this vision of the parable, with its death and beaten imagery, to one where she can see clearly who the Good Samaritan really is.

In this case I was able to review her Samaritan imagery with her and then to leave it behind. We then explored an entirely different scenario. Using guided imagery I retold the story replacing the main characters with ones from her own personal drama. For the victim, the man who was assaulted, we substituted the woman herself. The bandits were the mistakes and sins in her life, ultimately leading to the abortion. Those who walked past without helping were friends and others, who for whatever the reason couldn't or wouldn't help with her unexpected pregnancy. Finally the Good Samaritan was Jesus (this was the biggest surprise!) and the "inn" was her seeking help and/or her return to the fold of God and her church denomination (in this case Catholic). The "inn" could also be the place where God led her to find healing. In my office with me.

As we discussed and reviewed this parable with its new interpretation, the change in her demeanour was visible. It was as if the scales fell from her eyes, and she really saw the Mercy of God in her life. With the same imagery, she could see that Jesus had come looking for her, when she was broken and beaten. He had gathered her up and taken her to a place of safekeeping, a place of nurture. But over and above all of this He promised her that if anything was missing, on his return to her "He would make good" what was still needed. This lady walked out of the counselling room with her head turned towards life. Her journey was to continue towards God. On her "Road to Emmaus", a place of disheartened loss, walking away from pain, Jesus comes in the guise of a stranger and helps her to review her life (with my help) and then move forward knowing that she is loved and He has come looking for her.

Other parables which speak of great Mercy are the *Healing of the Crippled Woman* (Lk 13:10) and the *Forgiveness of a woman's many sins* (Lk 7:36-50). These parables also are useful and helpful when dealing with post-abortive men and women. The healing of the crippled woman (Lk 13:10) speaks of a woman bent low with disfiguring pain. She can be seen as being bent at the waist as if carrying a heavy burden (a cross). Jesus comes and lifts the burden (sin of abortion) from her. She straightens up and walks towards life.

Parables are an invaluable tool for healing. A skilled counsellor can lead the wounded one to see that Jesus always comes to heal. He never fails, because He does not know how to refuse a call for help and so he responds. If the sin of abortion could be understood and acknowledged as a sin, and forgiveness sought, then abortion can become the moment of turning for the return journey. The return to the Father's house (like the Prodigal Son) in the best possible way, with the unrecognised stranger on the road of life with Jesus as her companion.

Jacinta's story

I'm writing this letter to express my appreciation at the support and help you have given to me over the past 11 months. I also hope this letter can be used to bring out the truth of abortion. Your support and love have shown me it's ok to grieve for the baby I killed.

As you know I was in a terrible state when I first saw you in January 2006. The few weeks prior I had remembered terrible parts about the abortion that occurred on the 12th May 1999. It is the day I remember as killing my baby. To try and make things easier mentally I led myself to believe that it was just a medical procedure and was right for me at the time. I have never been more wrong in my life. I convinced myself that I would be better off not having my baby as I was young and my partner didn't ever want to be a father. The pain and despair I've felt for the past seven years has been my own private hell. I didn't realise that my behaviour for those past seven years was due to the suppression of the pain and guilt I had felt from the moment I knew I was pregnant. This baby I knew right from the start wasn't going to survive. I knew that my partner wouldn't accept the baby. But I didn't know it was going to be at the hands of an abortion. When I told the father of the baby he was cold and uncaring. He just told me it's not a baby and it's just a bunch of cells and that I'm going to have to get rid of it before it's too late. My heart and mind just was so torn, I didn't know what to do. I didn't want to have an abortion! It was his idea, and I felt that I couldn't have this baby when he didn't want it.

He told me that I would destroy his life by keeping this baby. He made me feel so guilty that I felt I no other alternative but to abort my precious baby.

No one knew of my pain. I fell pregnant 11 months after we met. The loss of confidence and self esteem is what prevented me from fighting. I held my belly and told my precious baby it will be ok. I won't let anything happen to you. I love you.

Two days later I broke my promise to my precious baby. My partner had badgered me to the point I couldn't deal with him anymore and the baby was the innocent victim in all this.

The hardest thing for me to accept for seven years was that I couldn't and didn't fight for my baby. The day that my baby died was a day I'll remember forever in its entirety. My partner bought me flowers the night before to try and say sorry for putting me through this life changing event.

At the clinic two days prior to booking me in for the abortion, my partner told me to lie about everything so they wouldn't suspect I completely disagreed about having the abortion or they may not allow me to have it. The way I was treated I could've said anything and they still would have booked me in for the abortion I did as I was asked and lied to the counsellor who had only graduated five weeks prior and wasn't much older than I was, namely 22 years. I saw no way of changing the situation In fact the pain and shame I felt has now been suppressed for seven years and it has been so strong it resulted in me having three breakdowns, a lost relationship, lost career. This is all due to the fact I couldn't continue denying why I had the abortion. I denied that it was a baby and only ever saw it as the procedure. I was told this pregnancy will ruin my life but it was the abortion that was ruining my life. My parents tried to save me from making this life altering decision but I didn't listen. I was consumed with my partner and making him happy, his happiness at the expense of my sanity and self-respect.

After the abortion I woke up and was staring at a brick wall. I had never felt so dirty and disgusted with myself. I got up and looked out the window and saw the rubbish bin and wondered is my baby dead in that bin. I remember looking out the window and seeing the trees and thinking, "Jac, you will move on from this and you will never let anyone do this to you again."

My life from that moment changed for the worse. I would drink myself to a point of hospitalisation and each time I was admitted I would talk about the abortion. The doctors and nurses would tell me I needed to see someone about my issues. They couldn't even say the word "abortion" to me. In one admission I wasn't allowed to leave the hospital as they had fears for my safety.. They had me speak with a psychiatrist before I left and he said that I was fine and I seemed to be over-reacting to the abortion and my work was the real issue. I looked blank at him and thought I'm just going to tell you what you want to hear so I can leave.

I spoke with many counsellors, nurses, psychologists and psychiatrists and none of them understood me. In my mind no one could help me get through the anguish of having had an abortion.

I drank to excess at every opportunity. Everyone just thought I was this party animal who loved to socialize and get drunk and I would work to excess during the week to keep myself busy. I knew the reason behind all the self-destructive behavior was the abortion, and I thought that's all my life was going to amount too. I was so angry at my now ex-partner, abortion clinic and most of all myself for allowing this abortion to affect me so badly, that I would deliberately put myself into positions of danger. I thought I deserved to be punished for the abortion. I would sleep around and not have care because I thought I deserved to be treated like a dog! I convinced myself my life is this way because I deserved to be punished so badly, and that no one will ever love me and I would never have an opportunity again to have another child.

Then out of nowhere I met the most wonderful man. But my destructive drinking behaviour was to be the catalyst for future problems. But the most rewarding part of our relationship was the birth of our son. However, I was again faced with the request for abortion but there was no way that was going to happen. The power I felt by saying no to abortion was uplifting. My baby was going nowhere and

I've never regretted my decision and neither has his father. He couldn't believe he'd even suggested an abortion when he saw our baby for the first time through ultrasound at 12 weeks. The characteristics our son showed in that ultrasound have carried through until now and he is two years old. He still sleeps with his hand on his forehead. He is the most precious gift I have ever received.

It wasn't until his father and I separated that I again had another breakdown. This time I had to do something about it. I had to think of my son and the impact my life was having on his development and emotional well being.

It was at this time I was put in contact with a lady at a pregnancy counselling service.

The lady I met was so wonderful. Her words, 'Your bubby is tapping you on the shoulder telling you it's time to heal', was the first time since it happened that I'd realised the abortion wasn't just a procedure, it was the killing of my baby. I was then hysterical with the sobbing over what I'd done seven years ago. This lady was nice, caring and sympathetic, but she knew I needed someone that knew what was happening to me. This is when I was told to contact Anne. I will never forget your voice on the other end of the line the day I called. I was so relieved to hear you knew how I felt and you told me I could be healed of the pain. I cried in happiness and sadness.

At first I was sceptical because I'd had so many people try and help me. Your kind, sincere and calming words were a hope for me to be rid of the guilt I'd carried on my conscience for so long. You asked me if I thought my baby would have been a boy or a girl. I didn't really think about it because I'd always pictured my baby to be a girl. Then you asked me what her name was? I was a little taken back and thought what are you talking about? My little girl doesn't have a name. I didn't even know her. Why would I give her a name? These questions were turning about in my head, and then it came to me. I would have called her Ashleigh. That name always bugged me and I didn't know why? I then remembered I'd thought about that name years ago and thought what a beautiful name. I now have a plaque on a beautiful memorial at a church in Melbourne. This finally gave me some closure.

It's only since I have acknowledged her and given her a name that I've been able to move on. The memory will always remain.

From that first phone call I knew if I put in the work Anne could help me back to happiness and eventually find God again.

I'm grateful every day that I had the opportunity to see you Anne and to still be seeing you. It is difficult for me to put into words the support and love you have given to me. Your passion and understanding about the pain I was going through gave me that light to push through, and now accept it as being a part of my life. Although I'll never forget what happened you've helped me to move on.

You have given me courage to break down my barriers and not to be scared of what lies ahead. My own world that I created to cope with my guilt was in fact destroying me little by little

You also gave me the courage not to be afraid of God and that he has forgiven me. I thank you for giving me back my faith. I know Our Lady is taking care of my darling Ashleigh. Knowing that has given me hope that one day I will be with her in eternal life. When you suggested reconciliation for the sin of abortion (I'm a Catholic) I was absolutely petrified. You gave me the courage to break through the fear of thinking I'd never be allowed back into the church and God hated me. You showed me that God forgives and allows us the opportunity to make right our wrongs. I will never have another abortion and I would like to try assisting and educating women and men about the trauma of abortion.

Anne your compassion for women who have been victims of abortion is what helps them. I thank God every day that you have been apart of my life. I will never forget the words of encouragement and love that you share with me every time I see you. Your smiling face, loving hug and kisses is what makes you so special and unique in your work. I don't even think you believe this to be work. This is your passion and God is with you every step of the way and will continue to be.

You have inspired me to change my life. I am very much looking forward to starting university next year and beginning my new life free from pain. I thank you for asking me to write a letter. Writing this letter has been a fulfilling and cleansing experience. Putting my story into words has made me more determined to fight abortion.

Thank you for going through your life experiences and finding God because that is what has led me to you for my healing. You are an extraordinary woman and one day I'd like to walk in your footsteps and be an inspiration and light to other victims of abortion. I consider you as another mother, nurturing, caring and protective I cannot say enough about you and your wonderful work. You are a rare gem that needs to be protected and cherished so others may have the opportunity of having you in their lives.

Thank you for giving me the guidance and support to allowing me to move my life into what it is today, a life full of love, happiness and peace.

Thank you Anne.

19.

I Have Kept Something Beautiful in my Heart

John O'Donohue wrote a beautiful poem called *To Keep Something Beautiful in your Heart.*[6] In it he encourages us to cherish something precious in our hearts, to allow the privilege of memory to rest there, safeguarding its beauty, exclusivity and its preciousness. *To Keep Something Beautiful in your Heart* reminds me of many things. It reminds me especially that there is always a place set aside which tabernacles the life of an infant who has died. It reminds me of wintertime and springtime, of fields covered in snow and hay bales. It reminds me of fruit orchards and almond trees in blossom. It reminds me of grottos with bunches of hastily picked field flowers left there for the guardian statue. It reminds me of the grape-gathering season and the winemaking. It reminds me of quiet evenings filled with the security of adult murmurings deep into the night. It reminds me of the warmth of the loving arms of God who whispered, *"I have loved you with an everlasting love and have chosen you for myself."* I have kept something beautiful in my heart and these memories are a perfumed ointment for me.

Blasé Pascal suggested that for difficult times one should keep something beautiful in one's heart. This is what I do. It is the beauty of the memories of times gone by, filled with laughter, and of course the times also filled with sadness. I keep times of sadness and times of insight, which do indeed, as the poet suggests, "save us in the end". We need to fill our memory chalice with all manner of life experience in order to avoid the gloom, the visionless twilight. Natural wisdom suggests that the way you are towards your life is the way that your life will be towards you (*Anam Cara*, p. 227). This appears such a wise and deep interpretation of life. An obstacle – is it an obstacle or a beautiful interruption offering not only a moment's rest but also a new vision? Is it a new road, a new opening? A gloomy thought – is it so? Or maybe a bright new insight into the gloom? One would see no light and another would see no darkness. It is the viewer rather than what is viewed that makes the difference.

To reach old age and to have known the sufferings of life, and yet still hold on to hope, would suggest a life lived looking upward rather than downward. To maintain one's innocence through all of life's challenges and sorrows suggests not escapism but rather a life lived embracing its offering. Such a life has energy surrounding it. Its vitality, its maturity, its serenity are the results of trust in Him. It is the result of treasured and respected innocence. It is the result of a life lived with something beautiful in the heart. It is a life lived both as blessing and being blessed. It is a life that has danced to the music of mystery. It is a life lived with the greatest friend of the soul; regret may be that friend, or as C.S. Lewis would say, "God whispers to us in our pleasures, speaks in our conscience, but shouts in our pain: it is his megaphone to rouse a deaf world" (*The Problem of Pain*, p. 74).

In a society which abhors silence, reminiscing, reflection and regret are anathema. Regret is considered wasted energy. Wasted time spent in imagination. Regret is considered unhealthy and best avoided. Yet regret is not about imagination or about what a past event might have been (or was). Nor is it about what a past event factually was, and the pain that it caused to some human being, either self, or others. Regret is the acknowledgement that something happened, or did not happen, and as a result of this, the one experiencing the regret feels diminished, and perhaps even the world is diminished because of the past action, which has caused the regret.

Regret is a negative emotion. Regret on its own is destructive, draining and time consuming. Regret is psychologically and spiritually challenging. However, regret can at times be the greatest friend of the soul because in the situation of abortion, regret can lead to a moment of life-changing grace. One's abortion may one day be viewed as the "pearl of great price". That pearl cannot be prised from its shell without one first having experienced regret, tears, sorrow. Perhaps it can never be found without first having the regret at the loss (baby) and the need to go looking for it.

During my time as an abortion grief counsellor I have seen an evolving theory about regret emerging, that regret at the violent loss of their baby and their part in the death is the "forget-me-not" of their child. After many counselling sessions, with the tears all but spent, it is possible to speak about the child and viewing regret through different coloured lenses.

I remember asking a client if she remembered her living children every day and what reminded her of them. She related a litany of things about her children, which constantly acted as a reminder of their presence in her life. Then I asked her about her aborted baby and what she regretted most about the abortion. Her reply was, "I regret that I never met my daughter and held her and bought her clothes and took her to school and loved her." Then I reminded her that as long as she regretted the loss, her aborted daughter, whom she named "Rose", would also live in her heart and mind and presence. I like to use this explanation giving the analogy of scar. The pain has gone but the scar (regret) remains to remind us that this once caused great pain.

The past is never gone, but remains hidden within the memory. For someone who experiences a great loss, especially where there is guilt, then regret may be the best and most merciful outcome possible. As I counsel and talk to men and women who have experienced abortion, they can see that regret is a memory tinged with both love and sorrow. It is a memory they wish to retain for as long as life exists. I thank God for that, in my own experience as well. To remember, even with regret, is a rare privilege and not to be despised. To remember means that the infant who was meant to crown their life with joy, but was refused, is now remembered. To no longer regret means a certain forgetting because it is in the pain that the imprint of the infant is indelibly etched.

However, to simply remain just at regret is somehow akin to stopping just outside the gates of heaven or maybe even between the gateways. Regret shows a deep sorrow over the consequences and outcomes of an act. There could even be a tinge of selfishness in regret. To remain at regret may also mean failure to understand the true nature of the sinful act. However, to move from regret to sorrow over the pain caused to the "principal" life giver, to God, and then to the infant, is truly the beginning of conversion. God was wounded first. His uttered Word is not only spoken, but in being spoken it is creative (baby), who was (in the rejection) wounded and cheated of its life. Anguish over this begins the journey back home.

20.

Violence: Fruit of Abortion

By its very nature abortion is a violent and soul-destroying act. This evil can only be equated with past crimes of human sacrifice and genocide.

The violence inherent in the very act of abortion manifests itself also in the physical, living realm of society. The act of abortion destroys an innocent child, through the various cruel and dastardly means available. Abortion is not a clean sterile procedure, where the child is anaesthetised, and then disposed of in some magical way, which does not cause pain. In fact, the mother is sedated, while the infant bears the whole violence, being still fully conscious.

The partial birth abortion procedure is particularly violent. The child is partially delivered. Scissors are then inserted into the base of the skull to create a hole. Then a tube is inserted into the hole, and from this the suctioning out the brain matter. This facilitates delivery of a dead child. Even with this barbaric procedure the child is not sedated, but the procedure, and other gruesome methods of delivering death, is carried out while the child is struggling and flailing. The abortionist who performs the abortion in this manner and cannot feel for the child is indeed a terrorist, no different from known terrorists. Further, a society, which not only condones but also considers it a "right" of the woman, to have made available the procedure for partial birth abortion and abortion to full term, must by its very approval have reached a state of violence and bestiality previously not imagined or contemplated.

The systematic, condoned, violence of the trade, that is, the slaughter of the innocents, is carried out unhindered every moment of every working day of the year. The violence inherent in abortion is a malignant type of violence, because it is deadly to all, including those involved in its advocacy.

The relationship between abortion and violence has many facets. It is violence against children, women, men, family and society. Certainly it is violence in its ultimate form against children. It simply kills them. There is no mercy, no discussion, no negotiation – just death. Abortion simply kills children, and destroys their families. It is violence against women. Acquiescing women develop malignant syndromes and such anguish of heart that their lives will never be the same again. It is violence against men. Willingly or unwillingly, the male who accedes to have his child killed, or participates in the killing of another's child, will change forever. He also loses his innocence and sense of maleness. His masculinity is fatally fractured. It is violence against the family. God's strategic and ingenious design for the family is to enhance the well-being of each person.

As we take a bird's eye view of our society we easily see how abortion, sexual perversions, sex crimes against women, men, children and boys have markedly increased over the recent 30-40 years. It would be easy to suggest that abortion is the only culprit leading to this miasma of suffering. If it is not the only contributing factor, it is the main one. This is so because women have been convinced into believing that their children are not children but tissue. Their value as women is only valid as an income producing agents, rather than a human who can produce masterpieces. Women have believed a lie, and have swallowed it whole. Women have been convinced that to have their child ripped from their bodies in pieces and broken is actually good for them and for their psychological well-being. Only a demonic influenced culture could be capable of this type of persuasion. Only someone who hates could conceive of such sorrow-producing action. Only someone who hates could suggest such a great violence, which is both psychological and spiritual, against humanity as a whole. The 'fruit' of such violence could only be death since perversion of the life-giving instinct can only result in the death instinct.

For the woman the violence done to her design is disastrous. It creates in her a new and flawed understanding of her being. The corruption of her feminine being must again bring a new fruit into being, that is, a caricature of her original feminine nature. This corruption then leads to the radical feminism of our times. This type of feminism is not "feminine", as it is not interested in women and their genuine well-being, but as a mechanised hybrid which lacks any of the original feminine qualities, meant to be the anchor and safety of society. This abortive society is now attempting to remodel "mother" from "nurturer", "carer", "wife", "lover", "love chalice", into the "commercialised" woman. This model finds and maintains her fulfilment through her value as a commercial asset. There is a reason for this systematic deconstruction and transformation of the woman and societal understanding of woman. Society is experiencing a moral malaise, and overcome by a spirit of apathy underpinned by guilt. The deconstruction of an existing system requires deliberate, methodical and tenacious players whose agenda is full of hate. Radical feminism has many such players.

Abortion is not only about physical violence, but also emotional violence. Abortion means humiliation, with consequent loss of belief of the value of self. Abortion means failure, which means lack of fulfilment. It means disintegration, a condition without hope, and silence, which means an agonising death. This is true not only for those participating in the destruction of a child, but also for the society standing by and accepting the norms, irrespective of their being right or wrong. Abortion is possible because of the silence and compliance of society. Ironically, those who call for, condone, accept and demand abortion are those who have themselves been allowed to live. Their "right" to life was protected and respected. Their violent intention in turn is an omen in itself. It heralds a future society of disposable, automated human beings whose value is estimated by the computer chip installed into their being. A desensitised society will provide the perfect opportunity for individuals with megalomaniacal aspirations.

Abortion is violence at its most grotesque because it assaults that mysterious instinct called "mother love", and nullifies its influence towards goodness. It (abortion) acts as a catalyst to turn in on oneself and one's own offspring. The sin of abortion and its ensuing guilt degrades the human person. The more guilt there is, the less conscious both individual human beings and society become of wrongdoing. This is true of a society, which "calls good evil and evil good". Guilt becomes the root of all thought and actions, and this involves society in the responsibility and suffering experienced by the whole world. This further leads to flight because the key symptom of guilt is escapism. We know this from precedence. Adam and Eve (Gen. 3:8-9) tried to escape and hide in order to avoid guilt and discovery.

The assault on the mother instinct is clearly visible with post abortion trauma and grief. An abortive mother's relationships change, whether with other children, husband, boyfriend, or family. Future children suffer because of bonding difficulties. Existing children suffer because of a barrier which now exists between a mother and her children. Again we stress that in the design of the woman there was no contingency for the intentional destruction of her child. The turning in on self is her response to her own sense of this evil.

The turning in on self is also apparent in the increase in malignant cancers associated with reproductive organs, that is, breast, and ovarian, uterine and cervical cancers. Are we seeing the very areas designed to form, nurture and sustain life become diseased and unable to carry out their function because increasingly society despises these organs and their work? A certain type of violence is taking place on the self, by the self. This is the result of confused and malignant messages, which the self has been receiving. It is almost like the warrior blood cells fighting among themselves rather than the enemy. Self is slowly becoming the enemy of self. Note also the enormous rise in mental health problems of women globally. We can ask the question, "Can a woman take her child to intentionally die and not be affected?"

A large section of society generally misunderstands the reality that abortion actually alters understanding of intrinsic worth. Temporarily at least, it values extrinsic worth. Wholesale acceptance of abortion (almost globally on demand) has not empowered, or liberated women. In fact abortion has turned them and children into expendable commodities. Women have come to accept this violence as their just "right". This has created a new, grotesque façade, which ultimately cannot continue for any length of time.

Evil has its consequences, both personally and corporately. Unless the evil is rooted out and stopped, it can, and will, pervade future generations. As grace can be passed on and flow from one generation to another, and blessings continue through the generations, so too can evil be passed on from generation to the next generation. The violence of wars and cruelty over the last 100 years has coalesced into the violence of abortion. Nations do not fight one another so often in a visible war. Nations are fighting themselves in an invisible and deadlier war. Deadlier, because nations are legally killing their children, their future, their citizens.

No major full-scale global war has been waged in the last half century, yet a more deadly war has been quietly going on and in this war there have been no prisoners. Not even one prisoner (abortion). These wars have been more deadly and more systematic and more horrific because the war has been one-sided (adults), and against one's own children. The wounded of this war are God and society as indeed the wounded on the first occasion of sin were God and society. With this satanic weapon called "abortion", virtually every nation, culture and creed has decided to participate. Hence virtually every nation, culture and creed comes to suffer sickness and weakness leading to an almost universal lethargy. Our time of peace from global warfare has not resulted in the enhancement of humanity, but has instead been used to mechanise the creature of God. True, scientific advancements have seen noteworthy achievement, but they may have hidden the slow rebuilding of the Tower of Babel. In our flight to conquer all manner of difficulties, we have traded in the value of human life. It has been a costly exploration into the unknown.

Anger and guilt are diabolical projections of violence. These (anger and guilt) are the visible manifestations of a particular kind of suffering pervading the world. They are primal signs of the impotence of sin and man. Anger and guilt and violence are the triad which characterise the flight from Eden. These alien emotions and behaviours set forth from Eden rolling, and gathering debris since time immemorial. No doubt they will continue to roll on unless there is a divine intervention of some magnitude.

We understand that love and sacrificial suffering always go together. Yet, our natural instinct is to try to escape the pain which often accompanies these. From this we know that there is a profound link between love and suffering. Deep, true love and sacrificial suffering are like two links in a chain. We could say that love is a need, and suffering is the permission to experience that need. We must treat the two areas of love and suffering reverently, indeed as Holy Ground. This is a place where we remove shoes before approaching. To live in the region of redemptive love is to enter a region of ultimate holiness. To misuse suffering is to miss the opportunity for great love and great healing.

Redemptive suffering is truly the human's only achievement and should not be wasted or dismissed. Dismissal of suffering following abortion as something trivial, or even as something unreal and imagined, fails to understand the nature of man and of God. The suffering of the holy ones of any society or generations are the sufferings that characterize the age. As many vacate the Church (mother – womb) in droves, so sadly too the wombs of women are being vacated in droves. As the Church mourns the loss of her children, so too women mourn the loss of their children, and both wombs refuse to be comforted.

Further, to refuse to allow grief after an abortion means that when a generation or people is prevented or forbidden to weep and ritualise its losses (as with abortion) then those who survive and follow on are entrusted with the work of passing on this work of weeping to future generations. Perhaps it is hoped that the future generation will look back kindly on those who failed to grieve for lost loved ones, and in an act of mercy complete the task of mourning which was forbidden or neglected by them. This is an act of collective connections, generosity and collective sorrow. Perhaps if someone can grieve for those who were neglected and abandoned in life and in death, then we can truly believe and know that we are from one flesh, one body, and one spirit. Indeed we can say that we are our "brother's keeper" and no one is forgotten.

21.

Penitence and Impenitence

Penitence and impenitence are two words which have lost favour, not worthy of use in modern society. Yet in these two words we may well find the very essence of what suffering and pain mean to the human individual. We see that these two words are the antithesis of one another, but there is something deeper than opposites. Within these two words and the deeper meaning they signify, lies the difference between legitimate and illegitimate suffering. Legitimate and illegitimate suffering and penitence and impenitence are synonymous with one another.

Proper and lawful suffering and penitence

Coupling these words helps us to focus on a specific type of suffering. The human person experiences this type of suffering (proper) primarily and precisely by belonging to the human family with all its sins and imperfections. Proper suffering is the suffering experienced because we are flesh, which can easily be wounded. We know pain, which can be psychic, physical or spiritual. We know the suffering of helplessness when it is impossible to do other than stand by and watch innocent suffering. Proper suffering is justifiable, and no penitence is called for, because already a penitence of humility is inherent and evident within that type of suffering. The suffering of a penitent is the suffering experienced by the spirit. This is a deep type of suffering. The sorrow reaches into the depths of the individual and begins the *metanoia* (conversion). Within this type of sorrow and pain lies also the key to the forgiveness of Jesus Christ. It is at this level where He judges, heals and forgives. Lawful suffering and penitence produce a fruit of healing because their experience is one that is turned towards understanding of a wrong committed. The person finds redemption at this juncture.

Conversely, unlawful, prideful suffering is the suffering experienced due to our fallen nature, due to the sin of pride, due to rebelliousness. This type of suffering despises penitence and embraces impenitence. Impenitence speaks a language of self-willed decision. It permits a hardness of heart so that redemption cannot take place. Impenitence relates to the freedom to choose but the choice is made without due regard to the other. It is the sin again of Eden. God does permit this course of action because in the freedom is the choice for or against Him.

Observing penitence and impenitence calls for an explanation of wrongdoing, which leads to either impenitence or penitence. Wrongdoing is not merely the beginning of a process of moral decay; it is also what happens and the repercussions for now, and for the effect on the individual, from that wrongdoing. Wrongdoing has repercussions and because of repercussions it alerts to outcomes affiliated to it. Penitence and impenitence emphasise dimensions of change, and the change is usually moral and lasting. It will affect future behaviour.

Impenitence is unwillingness to see a wrong and then at least attempt to set it right. This contributes to committing further wrongs, and renders an individual prone towards wrong responses. Continued wrong may not always happen, but the original wrong will leave a mark on the personality, thus changing it from its original design. One transgression will cause suffering and pain simply because it is contrary to the designed truth. Even only one transgression will have the power to leave an indelible mark on the individual psyche.

Suffering caused by moral deterioration is not suffering which is caused by another, but is the state of being of the wrong doer.

Individuals, when ontologically challenged, cannot remain untouched but must change in their very being. Moral deterioration occurs because it is impossible to knowingly and willingly commit a wrong, and hope to escape without damage to the moral stratum.

Sorrow and regret can lead one to repudiate evil. Moral deterioration is a condition irrevocably attached to error. It cannot be avoided and is related to the depth of the wrongdoing. Guilty suffering is not only a promise of error, but is the proper response to error for the world, humanity and the individual. In its original design God declared creation as "very good".

Another response to wrongdoing is penitence. This implies acknowledgement of the wrongdoing, its repudiation and conversion. The consequences of this course of action include moral change in the individual. The movement from error to right action also implies a break, and therefore, a form of violence from the present into something new. This then by necessity is an occasion of change, which also is an occasion of suffering.

Sorrow, penitence and moral deterioration are alike insofar as these all are a type of suffering. However, this is as far as the likeness goes. Sorrow and penitence, though they cause suffering, renew and return the individual to the order known as "good". Ongoing moral deterioration leads to deeper and stronger deterioration and an increase in ontological suffering. Penitence and suffering are self-evident. However, continued wrongdoing and impenitence suggest a hardening of heart, a moral opiate dulling the spirit and ever increasing the insensitivity to pain. We see this kind of suffering in the symptoms of change in a person.

There is a marked difference between penitent and impenitent suffering. Penitent suffering is the suffering in reparation for wrongdoing, with the recognition of error. There is recognition of pain. One recognises the pain in another, leading to a deep regret at having been the cause of the pain. Such suffering may be willingly accepted. Impenitent suffering is different. Hidden within this type of suffering is hardness of heart, which refuses to, or simply cannot recognise the pain of another. An impenitent person cannot experience empathy, because an impenitent cannot feel or recognise the suffering of another. Impenitence means refusal to see an error, and withdraw from the error, so that a change can occur. Impenitence does not allow for a moment of conversion. The penitent person, however, sees the small window, hears the still voice and ceases the wrongdoing. Impenitence cannot recognise error and therefore cannot refute it, continues to err, and hardens the heart.

The suffering related to penitence, whilst ostensibly limited, may however continue for the whole of the individual's life. Whilst penitence has restored the former relationship, the reality is that the reason for the need for penitence, and therefore suffering, may linger for the individual's entire life. Impenitence in itself cannot cause suffering because it cannot recognise its own contribution towards that suffering. Therefore it is unable to appreciate the suffering which it has been involved in causing. Impenitence cannot recognise cause and effect. However penitence does recognise cause and effect and so is able to effect a change.

An absence of the language of the symbolic in post abortion grief

Symbols, rituals and myth belong to the substance of the human being's psychic life. These three types of languages speak to the unseen in the human person whilst the "word" speaks to the cognitive.

Today more than ever before we have a need for a language which pertains to and warms to the psychic and the spiritual world of the human being and especially to the death experience, and the only language possible is the language of ritual and symbols. This language speaks eloquently, where words fail. Where there is unbelief and even where there is confusion.

The symbolic is vital for both psychic and mental health of the individual and wherever there is no symbolic or imagination or the imaginative there is to be found a deep disequilibrium.

Symbols, rituals, myth and mystery evoke within the human person deeply held and known realities. Deep longings for another life and the eternal. Symbolic thinking and understanding is consubstantial with the human being, preceding the faculty of language and discursive reasoning and above all the symbolic language is the language of God.

We know this because of the language of the sacramental economy. Through the symbolic, God takes an ordinary form and imbues it with Himself. This then transforms that symbolic item or action into an event of grace.

The symbol reveals certain aspects of reality. The deepest aspects, which defy all other modes of knowledge. Images, symbols, myths are not what one might call irresponsible creations of the human mind or human psyche, but they fulfil a need, and fulfil a function which is to unveil and to make present the most profound places of being.

The human imagination always comfortably and naturally finds its dwelling place in the realm of the anamnesis where it has its natural abode and it is in this abode where the symbolic acts as a bridge between God and the human creation.

The Elders and Keepers of ritual, myth and symbolic truth and life have always been religions but today there is even an attempt to rob these (religions) realities of this truth by an empirically demanding science of facts and figures (statistics) in order to attempt to lay bare and to make concrete the symbolic. This is impossible for it treads into the realm of the sacred and this empirical dimension, statistical data, is the place of the pragmatic.

Eternal Truth can never be objectivised without suffering some loss. This is because of the animosity of the scientific mind, which cannot accept the symbolic as a higher form of truth and can never do justice to it. The symbolic, via the medium of ritual, always has many meanings with the visual and the subjective meaning attached to it pointing to deeper unexpressed or even inexpressible realities.

The need for the symbolic and ritual at specific moments in the life of human being is vital. These types of symbolic events or rites of passage with their own signs and symbols point to a story of a past, and make present something otherwise absent, and then point towards the future, taking to that future a memorial of past. To our detriment rites of passage are being slowly phased out and this loss of "God consciousness" through the symbolic is not being replaced with anything of substance. Indeed it is being replaced with nihilism.

In the life of the human person there are many moments of sacred passage through which there is a crossing into a different stage of life, and the celebrations, symbols and signs which accompany these usually assist in the transition.

Amongst these many transitions is death, and whilst death is feared and avoided, it is the symbols and rituals which assist those dying and those to be left behind to move through these unique moments. To understand these transitions and to be really present in them with all the signs and symbols available, comforts the spirit and assures it of life.

To be with someone at the moment or point of dying is to be with them at the most intimate moment of human being's life. To be present when dying is to be consummately near. Abortion robs the woman and the man of this vital function. Abortion says there is no psychic life, no symbolic life, and no ritual; and because of the denial of this, the psyche of the woman and the man rebels against this offence. The spirit/soul of the woman who was aware of the conception and manifestly present in its earliest moment of creation, rebels at the intrusive violence which is abortion and will continue to make its anguish known until a satisfactory conclusion has been reached.

It is a great gift of mercy that human beings can weep. This we can know. Grief is a great gift. It is a merciful gift in lieu of loss. We of course can laugh, be sad, love, etc, but to weep is the soul's response to deep loss, to a deep wrenching separation. It is the soul's symbolic response to its loss. The soul is invisible, but its grief is made manifest through the tears, and heart pain, and the soul pain.

The expectation (as a society) is that we do not cry (over abortion) or express emotions but to put it away and move on. We need to weep, grieve. Grief is a profound response of the human being.

This is why abortion can be so utterly devastating not only because all manner of dreams become nightmares but because abortion cuts short the psychic language of life and love. And no symbolic ending is encoded or imprinted for such an event. Further, there is no ritual with its symbols which can help close the story of this stalled event.

When an infant is intentionally aborted for any reason and even for foetal abnormality, the previous dreams, expectations, hopes, assumptive worlds of the parents of this baby to be aborted, are rendered null and void. All the "normals" of this newly created life become abnormal. And after the pronouncement of its fate, words fail. After decision to abort, words not only fail but the psyche retreats into an unknown sphere. There is no word which can help. There is indeed no precedent written into the psychic fabric of the woman's life, which can adequately express the horror, so there is retreat into the unknown sphere.

When an infant is aborted there is no possibility for the ritual and symbolic to step into place as would have occurred with a "normal" death. The parents (most often mother alone) with shoulders hunched and bent low, turn and leave the place where the death of the child took place. They came in with a child in the womb at times still moving, (abortion for foetal abnormality) and leave with a discordant memory This is all. No body, no resting place, no headstone. No good byes. Nothing to speak, or words to say and a feeling of being numb. Nothing to comfort the spirit. Nothing to assuage the soul's pain as a result of this loss.

When a death occurs, each culture has its own ways of dealing with it, but all ways are visible and tactile, and emotional. The flowers, the burial, (or disposal of body) the words, the prayers, eulogy, wake, the headstone, and even manner of dress (black/white). These realities speak of an important event in the life of the individual, family, friends and society. A parade of funeral cars reverts an observer, even an unknown observer, to realities outside of the normal. There is an introversion and in inward looking moment. This death of an unknown person with its ritual and symbol of this event sets into motion a search for questions relating to the deeper meaning of life. When an abortion for any reason occurs, there is no room for the ritual and the symbolic, because this is the language of love and life and spirit. Abortion is a hidden event filled with shame and guilt and in this there is no room for symbols and rituals about death. Hence these absences leave a rupture and cause disequilibrium.

This is why I would strongly encourage continuing the pregnancy when discovery of symptoms of severe foetal abnormality, and with the excellent medical care available the child is helped to be born and then accompanied in love as it dies naturally. In this way all manner of ritual and symbolic work can be carried out. It is this temporarily painful work which will in turn help in the grief process and eventually to be able to make sense of this loss. Yes, there will be pain and grief because of the death of the child, but grief is good. The only time that grief is not good is when it becomes complicated through guilt and shame.

Michaela's baby kicked as she entered hospital to abort this child. That is her last memory of her baby boy who was aborted for severe abnormalities at 19 weeks.

Michaela can still "feel" the kick as she speaks about the day of the abortion. The "kick" is as real today as on the day of the abortion. Michaela's little son was left behind at the hospital, and she had nothing to hold on to. It was the work of symbolic and ritual which eventually helped her lay her little one to rest. It was the work of naming, claiming, place of rest, Mass (she was a Catholic) plaque with his name, toy sports car and toy kitten left at the burial site in the children memorial garden. It was the words of comfort and prayer and burial which the beautiful priest friend uttered over the name. This son of the family now had a resting place, where the other children could go and visit their brother. The other children, who had also been cheated of their brother, now had a place to visit him.

Mystery is the unfolding of an ongoing drama, accompanying the journey of return to where the desire is implanted and so the desire is the motivator of the journey. Symbols and rituals are the signposts along the way. The "lights" which shine on the arrow for direction. The cross which is a new clue to the direction, and the eventual mound of death and resurrection. Rituals and symbols are mysteriously placed to light the next stage and these are written as necessary for the journey. When absent, as with abortion, miscarriage, the psyche, soul, causes disturbance until its needs are met.

22.

Healing of Abortion Grief
and Other Stories

The healing of post abortion trauma must be the most painful and drawn out of processes. It demands time, energy, patience, love, compassion and the Mercy of God. Healing of post abortion trauma is ultimately about healing the memories of deliberately taking to die one's own child. The abortion was not accidental. It was intentional and the memory of it is lodged deeply within. Abortion grief may lay dormant for a time but in reality it persistently tries to arouse attention to its presence.

Manuals and PAS counsellors are beginning to abound as well-meaning individuals embrace this new "yuppie disease". In my opinion this will mask the seriousness of the problem. I share the opinion of Professor Phillip Ney and Terry Selby, Fr. Michael Mannion, Vincent Rue, Anne Speckard, Professor Priscilla Coleman and others that post abortion psychosis, grief, trauma is both real and serious. The process of healing must encompass the whole person. This implies understanding the theology which the body speaks, the theology of suffering and the theology of wholeness, wounded-ness and brokenness. In abortion, we are dealing with someone who has intentionally taken to be killed her own child, a part of her own self, and as this reality crystallises in the person, this knowledge can lead to physical, psychological, emotional and spiritual shut down. A fracture occurs in the emotional environment of one realising that an abortion has meant the death of her child and that she contributed to it. From this the defence mechanisms, which have helped to guard the individual's sanity, begin to break down. On the surface the woman or man may not have considered the abortion as a death, but she or he believes it ontologically. In the depths of her being this knowledge has been written.

Abortion grief counselling is an emerging type of counselling. The sheer number of abortions now demands that this type of grief be studied further and that strategies for healing be developed and implemented. It is important to understand, however, that those dealing with this type of counselling should not be pro-abortion. More specifically, only "life friendly" psychiatrists, psychologists, psychotherapists or counsellors should engage in this type of counselling. A woman nursing an image of her dead infant will not respond to a counsellor who denies that her infant has an image, and deserves the grief shown by its mother. Even with the best of intentions and the most professional behaviour, an abortion positive woman will see through someone who is not in union with her thoughts and beliefs. A pro-abortion or even pro-choice counsellor will fail to understand the acute grief experienced over the death. More especially such a counsellor will not appreciate the woman's role in the abortion decision.

Where there is abortion grief, there will also be found other anti-life events in the woman's history. These other events will fuel the severity, duration and strength of abortion grief. Other issues may at times require priority, in order to deal with the abortion issue itself. These issues could include sexual abuse, abandonment, physical abuse, alcoholism, suicide or attempted suicide and other abortions, all within her family structure.

The severity of past trauma, especially in the area of sexuality, in the life of a woman who has aborted, is a possible indicator of future abortion decisions. The decision to abort is then followed by the severity of post abortion trauma itself. I have found that where there are sexual wounds, almost certainly there will also be an abortion. Perhaps this is the final act of self-harm. From this point she will either seek healing, or slide into self-destructiveness. In my experience those seeking help for their abortion grief are in reality seeking help for all the other issues in their lives too. Finding meaning for their at times profound suffering provides a clue to their decision to abort.

Sexual abuse and neglect of a young girl sets the pattern for a life filled with anguish. The combination of abuse and neglect arrests psychological and spiritual development. It sets the girl on a journey of seeking her missing essence, and her lost "something". A young violated individual cannot have positive 'earthing' because he/she cannot hold onto reality. For them reality is too grotesque. An abused person cannot joyfully experience intimacy because intimacy is a reminder of past events. One who is sexually abused is robbed of the progressive lived material and experience for sequential psychological development.

Normal development requires that she carefully builds according to the model presented to her so that she can create her own history. Those without materials constantly try to gather building blocks in order to build the person that they believe they should have been. However, irrespective of the building blocks, they are always marked by the history of abuse, and eventually are like wounded gazelles, fragile in heart, mind and body. Sexual abuse, like abortion, attacks the life principle. In effect the victims attack their own lives or abort their own lives and lose their desire to live. There is an unreal sense that there is something grotesque about living with such violation. The person strongly entertains the thought of suicide, which becomes a reserved option. Self-mutilation and self-abuse in all manner of ways are indicators that abuse has been in the life of that person.

Abortion grief counselling and sexual abuse counselling can help someone to re-learn the purpose and meaning of his/her life (now), as it is, and not as it might have been. Life, post abortion, or post-sexual abuse, will not be the same. It should not be treated or lived as if the violation or abortion had not happened. This simply leads to continual suppression and denial. The best option is to help the individual to rebuild her life, incorporating the experience. This journey, while at first appearing difficult, has the potential of discovering God, his mercy and his forgiveness and a new love for self which did not exist before. It has the potential to lead to a new type of goodness, holiness not possible or present before. This is the other way. This is the new way home. It is not the original way desired and designed by God, but a different way home. The person may not recognise the way, and the journey may be hazardous. However, it is a way home. The three wise men, who went looking for Jesus when He was born, had to return to their own homes by a different way. It wasn't the known way but it was a safe way home (Mt 2:12).

The healing of post abortion trauma and grief *can occur* when we begin to understand the type of pain that it is. It is pain experienced as a result of the violation of that mysterious something, which we call "mother love". "Mother love" is etched deep within the heart of a woman. This is intrinsic to her. It could be said that it is intrinsic to the female of the species. You cannot find it in the male of the species, just as you cannot find in her what is inscribed into his being. "Mother love" ensures that humanity continues. It is the secret at the very heart of God and a woman. Just as surely as all of creation has a nuptial essence inscribed into its constitution, so too all of womanhood has inscribed within its ontology that mysterious element "mother love". This becomes clearly evident when encountering the grief and attempted self-destruction of the woman, on realising that she took her child to its death. This is also clear when we see the grief after a miscarriage or stillbirth, or death of one's own child. In both miscarriage and abortion, the mother has not seen the child and in most cases did not feel it. The child had not made its presence felt, other than hormonally. Yet the grief experienced over foetal loss clearly indicates that some mysterious dialogue had occurred between the child and its mother. The mystery of this dialogue leads to the need for recognition, then acknowledgement and claiming of this child who has refused to disappear into nothingness, into non existence.

When the light of God is not present in the mother, and a crisis pregnancy occurs, the psychological and spiritual environment is not conducive to reception and nurture of a new child. The Greek word for crisis is *kairos,* and crisis or *kairos* also means a moment of judgement. It is a moment when *the Word of God* challenges the human person to make a decision. A crisis moment is a decisive moment because nothing will ever be the same again from this moment onwards. Whether the child is brought to life or the child is aborted, God has uttered *the Word* in the child's favour. It has been an awesome *Yes* by God. God's word entails a new and untrodden path. Moreover, God's *Word* not only heralds, but also creates what it heralds. The response to God's *Yes* is vital, as it determines the path the woman travels home in God's company – his home, heaven. The secret of God is written deep within the mystery of fecundity. God writes this secret within the individual's biological reality. In the physical union of man and woman the seed is fertilised. New life grows from this. We learn from the way of the earth that rest, silence, ecstasy, almost the deep sleep of absence and secrecy, are essential for the genesis of life.

The woman who succumbs to the abortion of her child adds to Satan's revenge pool against God. In his attack against the woman and her child, we are reminded that in Eden Satan also approached the woman (not the man), in order to entice and lure her to his bidding. As in Eden, the woman is again asked to decide. She is placed in a state of *crisis.* For her, and for humanity, that is a challenging moment. Placed in a crisis moment she has to believe or not believe. She must decide for or against God's awesome *Yes* to life. Abortion, by its very nature *destructive,* is geared towards a big No, a movement away from God and the life principle (with its attraction towards God) and slanted towards annihilation. This destructive movement is a clear attempt to erase the perpetuated image of God in the human. In his ugliness, Satan no longer bears any likeness to God's image (Gen 1:26), and in his rage he seeks to destroy what he can no longer have, especially those who still retain the *Imago Dei.*

The suffering following abortion is a moment of mercy in which God ensures that the child designed and destined by Him cannot and will not be maliciously willed out of its intended existence or even forgotten. Instead, the memory (tinged with pain) will be a love given to that child, and it is a love in place of great loss. In this love is inscribed an echo of that destruction (abortion), resonating with the original violence and destruction in Eden (Gen 3:1-34). The response to the destruction is also a resonance of something past. It is calling into being the possibility of a holier creation, a creation forgiven and healed and renewed by God Himself. It is a creation that when renewed completely, images Jesus Himself (Gen 1:26), and like Jesus takes into the heavenly court the marks and scars of suffering.

A particular grace is evident when the sinner (abortive woman/ man) repents and experiences forgiveness. This individual is now marked with a sign of grace and protection (Gen 4:15-16) and is a witness to God's special mercy toward sinners. Those who experience and witness to Mercy are called to mediate for and on behalf of those who still remain bound by darkness.

The forgiveness and conversion of the post-abortive man/woman are visible signs of Magdalene. She is the woman who stands in silence awaiting stoning because of her grave sin of adultery. Jesus has written her name in his Book of Life and next to her name He has written, "Forgiven sinner". "Much is forgiven because she has loved much" (Lk 7:36-50). "Magdalene", "Sally", "Mary", "Sharon", "Anna", "Therese", "Anne", "Julia", "Rosemarie", "Faith", "Breeanna", "Judy", "Cherri", "Cheryl", "Susan", "Andrew", "Melissa", "Jodie", "John", "Roger", "Andrea", "Stephanie", "Jacinta", "Garry", "Matt", "Graeme", "Fiona", "Katherine", "Kathleen," "Heather," "Alexandra," "Annemarie," "Alicia," "Marlene", "Sandra", "Christine", etc. Jesus whispers each name and they hear his voice calling gently, "Come to me all you who are weary" (Mt 11:28-30). Each experiences the healing and forgiving power of God, in Jesus Christ. She responded to his call to meet her child, the one she aborted. Not in sorrow now, but in joy.

Sorrow over the abortion is good because it sanctifies the infant's life. Sorrow also changes the future through a life now focused on goodness. The one ingredient needed for this new life focused on goodness is love. The memory of the abortion remains salvific because it brings understanding of the individual's own life, history and action. Now there is a memory of the destructiveness of sin and the more spectacular reality of God's goodness and mercy. The memory embalms the sorry event with some good, though remembrance of the infant will always be heart-stopping, and the imagery always tinged with anguish.

The mind will have stored a memory of the existence of an infant and will be attached in such a way that it cannot forget. This should not be seen as necessarily to be removed, for the image rightly seen can become an image of grace. In remembering the broken body of the infant, we remember Mary holding the broken body of her son Jesus, broken for *this* particular sin. For *this* abortion He was prepared to die. In remembering the broken body of the infant, broken because of the selfishness of the "other", we can understand the anguish of Mary as she held the broken body of her Son, broken for the sin of the "other".

The journey to authentic conversion always begins at Cana (Jn 2) and moves resolutely towards Jerusalem. Between these two locations there will be sorrow, regret, suffering, penitence and hope. Without these, conversion and healing cannot occur. This journey begins with the revelation of sin (abortion). The ensuing sorrow is the first step in the journey towards the Father's house by the prodigal son/daughter. The new dimension in the relationship is born of the forgiveness of the cross and of the divine filiation, the mystery of the new familial relationship with God won for the sinner by Jesus Christ. This applies even to someone who has had an abortion. Even this sinner, through Jesus Christ, has hope of forgiveness and healing. The cross has restored the primal integrity, originally destroyed through the abortion, and has restored the innocence of childhood.

Hannah's Story

The story of my abortion is long and painful but maybe it's also the same story as other girls who have had abortions. Today I don't think that I am the only one who suffers as a result of my abortion because I know that many of my friends have had abortions and they too are always in sadness. I think that's the most important word, which is related to abortion. It is SADNESS. But you know it's a different kind of sadness. It's a sadness that feels like it will never ever go away. It's sadness almost like the whole body can feel. In fact its almost like people can actually feel the sadness simply by looking at me.

I have had two abortions. One when I was 22 years of age and one when I was 26 years of age. With the first abortion I was married at the time but I was married to someone who drank a lot and who when drunk was violent and I already had two children. It seemed to me that if I had this other baby then I would never be able to escape from this marriage and if I didn't escape then maybe one day he would kill me or I would kill him. In fact I had even started to think about ways of doing it. So I thought that before this really happened, and since I couldn't go back, I would leave the marriage.

Then I discovered that I was pregnant and things really became bad for me because I suddenly felt really tied and trapped again. Because I wouldn't be able to leave and still be pregnant and take the other children and look after them on my own.

I went to my doctor and he had treated me some times when I had gone to him after I had been hit and he knew what my marriage was like. So I told him about the situation and he suggested that I have an abortion. But in order to have an abortion, I would have to go and get a psychiatrist's letter which said that I wouldn't be emotionally able to look after another child and then I would be able to have an abortion in hospital. This I did that is I went to a psychiatrist that the doctor sent me to. The psychiatrist spoke to me for about 15 minutes and I told him my story and he wrote a letter and gave it to me. Then with the help of my doctor he booked me into a hospital and I went in had it done and got a taxi home. I think from the time that it was booked in, about 10 days after the letter, I shut down everything. I no longer thought about baby, it didn't exist, I wasn't pregnant. Nothing, nothing nothing. On the morning of the abortion I first took the kids to mum and said to her that I would pick them up later that night, then I went home called a taxi (husband was at work), went to hospital, had the abortion, got a taxi back home, and went straight into the shower and showered until the hot water ran out. I couldn't get out of the shower. I needed to get washed and more washed. After this I sat around for a while and then went to mum and had tea and biscuits with her and told her. I had had a good day quietly without the kids and thanks for looking after them. I took them home. My husband was already home, so I cooked dinner. I couldn't speak about anything. I remember not wanting to talk to him. I remember hating him so much because if he wasn't like he was I would never have had to do what I did. I think that after this I really did push him to hit me because I needed to be hit by someone because of what I had done.

Not long after I started to plan how to escape from home and it had to be done properly because he used to tell me that if I ever left he would find me and kill me. I don't know if he really would kill me but because he used to hit me all the time I thought that maybe he would one day kill me even if he didn't mean to. I was also scared because the kids were seeing the hitting.

It took me about three months to find a place two bedroom flat (cheapest I could find), get some government assistance and move into it. I also knew that from the time that I moved out I would have to carry through with the separation. There wouldn't be any going back. I also got a lawyer and she really helped me so I wasn't scared because I really was very scared of being hurt again.

Just as I thought, he did find me within a couple of days, and the threats started to come and in fact he threatened to kill me one night if I went out. I was terrified anyway so I didn't go out at night. But it was interesting because now I started to have nightmares and the nightmares were about dying and dead babies and I kept jumping off mountains into darkness and I also started to think that something awful was going to happen to my children. I always thought that someone was going to kill the children but I didn't know who the someone was. Just someone. Also I started to cry a lot but I just thought that this was because of the fear and threats and everything else and maybe this was it but also I realised that that I never could think about the abortion. I would never let myself think about. Every time a thought of anything about abortion or anything came in radio or television or papers I would turn it off and I could not listen or read about it.. I remember one day at the office where I worked as a part-time clerk (after about a year I got part time work) girls were whispering and talking quietly about another girl who was away for the day and it turned out that she had gone to have an abortion and when I heard this I started to cry and couldn't stop. The others thought that I was like this because I had a headache (that's what I said) but the truth was that for the first time I cried about the word abortion. After that time I kept away from the word. I was ashamed and there was nothing I could do.

My second abortion happened about four to four-and-a-half years after the first one. I had met a man who I thought was really nice. He was so nice to me and the children and I think I fell in love with him. I had never known any man to be nice to me. And when he was nice to me I fell in love. Except that when I got pregnant (I don't know how because I was on the pill) he told me he was married that's why I could only see him on certain nights because of his wife and family. You can imagine how I felt. Again I shut down everything. This time I didn't ask him to accompany me; I didn't think about it. I just went to the doctor, got a referral to a psychiatrist (we needed a letter from a psychiatrist in those days which said that this pregnancy wouldn't be good for us. Or to the effect that this pregnancy would cause serious difficulties) went to the psychiatrist who remembered me from the first abortion and said to me not to go back to her again because she would not give me another letter, and then booked for the abortion. Went in on the morning, by taxi and went home that night by taxi. I remember reaching home that night (kids were with a friend) and going inside my flat and it was dark and no noise – empty. And I went and lay down and got covered up tight and went to sleep. I remember I had such a heavy heart I think I really wrapped myself up tight for comfort and maybe I thought I might go to sleep and die.

However, I didn't die and my friend brought the kids home that night about 9.30pm and I had to get up and get them ready for bed and then I went back to bed again. Next morning I got up and looked after the children and I felt that I couldn't talk at all. I took day off work and just wandered around like someone who lived in different world. I particularly remember that I couldn't look at the kids that day. Every time I looked at them I cried and became angry. In due course (next day) I got up again and showered and got the kids ready for day care and went back to work. I passed my abortion off as a "curette" and nobody asked anything else.

My life changed slowly but I never once associated my sadness, erratic behaviour, uncontrollable crying, depression and unknown fear as being related to the abortion. I think I probably thought that it was related to being a single mother and always struggling with the kids and money and loneliness and everything else that single mothers 25-30 years ago experienced. There was little help for single parents in those days.

For me the triggering memory of the abortion was the birth of my best friend's baby. I suddenly remembered never having a little girl and having always wanted a little girl and I remember saying that maybe I did have a little girl but that I had killed her and that's why God couldn't trust me with more children or baby girls.

I was really lucky because God didn't abandon me (although I think He should have because I didn't deserve His forgiveness). Even though I had not turned to God in my time of need He still didn't abandon me and prepared some people who would be able to help me out of the sadness and loneliness and self-hatred which slowly began to overtake me. One day at the shopping centre I met a really nice priest and we started talking first about groceries and things and then about church and when he found out I was Catholic he started talking about Mass. He saw that I was uneasy and he seemed to have the wisdom not to continue but he invited me to go and have a cup of coffee and a chat with him and I promised that I would.

I must admit that I had no intention of keeping my promise but somehow everything happened in such a way that I had to keep my promise as I kept bumping into him and he kept saying that he was still waiting for me to go for that coffee. Eventually I did go and one thing led to another and I told him my whole life story including the abusive husband, the children, the abortions and everything else that I had kept deeply hidden. I expected him to send me away and be disgusted with me but he wasn't and slowly I developed a trust of him. We made an arrangement for me to go to him again and talk to him about the abortions. By now I trusted him and wasn't afraid so I went and pretty much the rest is history. He helped me to name my children, he said a Holy Mass for them and helped me to lay the children to rest. He helped me to really believe that the children are with God and that they will never leave God that they are with him forever and that they pray for me and their father(not with me) and their other brothers. He also told me never to forget the children and that I didn't have to forget them. He said that it was OK to remember them every day, but that it was not OK to keep grieving for them. He helped me to go to confession and to communion and Father said that God had forgiven me. He then assured me that God has always wanted me to be happy and to live the rest of my life as well as was possible.

Today I still remember the children. I wish that I had never ever, ever had the abortion. Today I wish that I had had the courage to have the children, but the fact is that things are as they are and I can't change them no matter how much I would like to. This regret is part of what I have to live with and this is OK. It's my memory of my children who should have been alive but are not because I didn't really know any better.

Christmas is especially difficult because for some reason I seem to remember more strongly. When I look at the set Christmas table I remember that there should be other children there but because I didn't know any better, and I certainly didn't trust God, today they are not sitting at their place at the table. For this I am so sorry. My aborted children fill a space in my heart which belongs to them alone. As much as I love my living children, the aborted children also are cherished. I cannot see that it can be any other way.

I saw for a short time a therapist who tried to tell me to get on with it and that it was the best decision that was possible for that time frame in my life but I realised that this therapist did not know a thing about grief and mourning. This therapist did not acknowledge that aborted children are important and therefore worth mourning over. This is the mistake being made. If someone doesn't believe that my aborted baby was a "baby" or "important" that simply says that they are not prepared to acknowledge my grief and pain and that means that they can cause more hurt than healing. Thank God that by "accident" I heard about Anne and her manner of counselling of abortive women and since going to her I have started on my way back home again and it feels so good. And more than this I am beginning to experience fleeting moments of absolute joy. Something I had forgotten about.

23.

"I would now like to say a special word to women who have had an abortion"

John Paul II, *Evangelium Vitae* (99)

With these words of encouragement the Holy Father, Blessed John Paul II, turns to women who have submitted themselves to an abortion. The Pope in *Evangelium Vitae* covers not only all matters of life, but also offers hope to those who have crossed the boundary. He calls out to those wounded and offers the balm of healing. He is the shepherd who ventures out to find the lost sheep.

Abortion cannot ever be anything but a sin and an immense loss, both a human loss and a spiritual loss. It is more than a loss *per se, but* is a loss of immeasurable worth and this loss leaves in its wake lifelong pain. It leaves in its wake recurring memories of the loss. This loss cannot ever be found again. It can never be bought back. The loss is unrepeatable. A blueprint has been lost forever.

Abortion today can no longer be considered harmless. Medical science has vindicated what religion has taught, that life begins at conception. Science also has taught and shown that the baby "functions" almost from the beginning. It dialogues with its mother. It sets up the conditions for its survival and when its environment is invaded, it objects. Screening of the infant in the womb clearly shows life pre-birth, and the ordered manner of life. And whilst modern technology assists us in previewing our child, the same technology (like all new inventions) is used to destroy the very same life.

Concluding a book on abortion grief and trauma is difficult because I am conscious of the amount still to be written. However, it is important to bear in mind that books can only give the reader a taste of what is out there. Readers must then pursue their own interest in the subject.

Post abortion trauma is real; we cannot dispute this today. The dispute is not about its existence, but about the extent, the severity and the reason for it in some individuals whilst not in others. My contention is that, not merely "some", but to some degree everyone who has had an abortion will be affected. To make a bolder statement, I would assert that not only those submitting to the abortion are affected, but those surrounding them, that is, family, friends, colleagues, abortionists, staff and society. On the basis of this stand, we can see that the whole of society is affected, because of the sheer number of abortions. Society is smeared with the crime of anti-life, when we consider the rate of surgical abortions, chemical abortions and the more sophisticated type of abortion, the creation of embryos for experimentation. Society can no longer claim ignorance because it is out in the open, and demanded as a "right".

Legal in some countries, it is pseudo-legal in others, and flaunted, demanded and protected. Today, society has washed its hands of the whole issue and is prepared to have the innocents' blood on its head (Mt 27:25). Today in its rhetoric, society is calling for swifter resolutions of problems in, and including, the illusory over-population issue. It is prepared to accept the deaths that it calls for. Yet there is an inconsistency because societies of the late twentieth and early twenty-first centuries have masqueraded as societies immersed in technology and every manner of health knowledge. This suggests that its members continue to look for that elusive fountain of youth with its magical elixir. At the same time society blindly refuses to see that a deep terror propels the need for the fountain of youth, longevity. The fear of ageing and death fuels the urgent desire to find the magic formula.

Blessed John Paul II has called the society we live in a society immersed in a culture of death *(Evangelism Vitae),* and rightly so. Violence is part of this culture of death and the more sophisticated the society, the more sophisticated the violence, the more sophisticated the manner of death. Abortion kills infants; euthanasia kills the sick and dying or elderly. Drugs kill all age groups. Suicide kills – self. Truth is killed in the service of me-ism, consumerism and materialism. Fast and hedonistic life styles kill through various ways and various diseases. So-called entertainment kills innocence. And all of these and more kill the urge and desire for a heavenly connection. There is a death of desire to know our creator God.

24.

Remembrance

The term 'remembrance' requires definition. It does not mean a 'memorial' of the abortion itself, but of the event. A memorial to the abortion would be blasphemous. The intention of a remembrance is the committing to memory of an event (abortion), which has served to change the individual's life. This event has caused a detour from the original journey in this person's life. Remembrance serves not only to acknowledge that the event happened, it was also outside of the normal. It was an unforeseen episode bringing with it some permanent changes.

The healing of abortion grief and wounds cannot occur without remembering. This is because this type of grief and sorrow (according to society's decrees) does not deserve support. Those suffering this grief must first recognise that it is a disenfranchised grief and then while assisted by good counselling seek to re-enfranchise it. Only by doing this can healing occur. Remembrance is the committing to permanent recalled memory the abortion experience. It holds in open memory the event, which may or may not have been suppressed. It acknowledges that it differs greatly from what had been expected. It acknowledges the making of a big mistake, and that this mistake has embedded within it a lifelong grief. Remembrance commits to memory an action embedded with guilt and shame. Making a memorial of this act serves to bring to consciousness deeply held beliefs and acknowledges the violation of these beliefs. Among them are beliefs about motherhood and fatherhood.

In acceding to an abortion there is no abandoning or rejection of fatherhood and motherhood. It means the abandoning or rejection of the mothering and fathering. post abortion trauma and grief clearly show that motherhood and fatherhood cannot ever be rejected because these are inscribed within the human person, in his or her very being. The ontology of a woman has inscribed within her the *knowledge* of motherhood. She is designed to be a wife and a mother; all else are additional accretions. A man has inscribed within his ontology the knowledge of fatherhood. He is designed to be a husband and father; all else are additional accretions. A mother cannot be a father. She can carry out some of the labours of the father but she cannot "father" her child. A father can carry out some of the labours of a mother but he cannot "mother" a child. Each gender has inscribed into its ontology its own gender specific gifts, attributes and talents and any attempt by the opposite gender to mimic the attributes of the other results in a caricature of the attributes.

An abortion decision made by the mother of the child and/or father or others cannot remove "motherhood" from the woman/girl. That is in her inscription. However, abortion does reject the mothering. No one can reject "motherhood" because this is inscribed into the being just as gender is inscribed into one's being. "Mothering" can be rejected. To mother even one's own child can be refused. To father even one's own child can be refused. "Motherhood" and "fatherhood", however cannot be refused or rejected because this is inscribed in the being of the male and female.

Post abortion grief and pain are located in that space between "motherhood" and "mothering". It is a regret at the loss of the opportunities, of what might have been. It is a sadness based on a misunderstanding of what it means to abort. The child has been terminated, gone and disposed of, but its presence cannot ever be forgotten because the design of the woman and man ensures that this would never happen. Isaiah rightly asked, "can a woman forget her nursing child, or show no compassion for the child of her womb?" (Is 49:15). At first we may accept the possibility of a woman forgetting her baby. On closer inspection we see why it is impossible for a mother to "forget her baby". Thankfully, just as it is impossible for a mother to forget her baby, it appears that for God it is still more impossible. As a mother's design is such that she can never forget her baby, even the one whom she refused to "mother", so too God's design is such that He cannot ever forget his "baby", even the sinner, the one who rejected her own baby. There is always the haunting echo of remembrance and its lifelong influence.

Remembrance, memorialising or the commitment to memory by the mother, father and significant others, help to bring to a close an act which has changed the nature of things, reversed the order of how things should have been. More importantly, memorialising assists in the closing of the chapter involving the life of the child. The remembrance literally does bring to the heart and the mind what one has suppressed and tried to forget. It brings to the mind the memory of the child and in the bringing that child to memory it gives the child a form of "mothering" and "fathering" only possible in the form of memory. Memorialisation validates openly the life of the child and gifts that child with a life story.

Conclusion

"And having been warned in a dream not to
Return to Herod they left for their
Own country by another road" (Mt. 2:12).

It is always difficult to conclude a book, any book, but especially a book about death of children and a violent and intentional death. Can anything good be said about the death of an infant through abortion? God who can make lemonade from our most bitter of lemons would surely find it difficult to find good out of that tragedy; Yet He does. He finds a way to lead his people home "by a different way" than perhaps He had originally designed.

Recently, for the first time and after many years of reading the above scripture passage, I actually understood what it meant, and perhaps how going home by a different way is the reality for all of us. I do not wish to imply that all have had abortions but I do wish to say that all of humanity is "going to their own country by a different way" (Mt. 2:12)

If I may explain. The original way designed by God was rejected. Adam and Eve ensured that the original route was "aborted". We can never know what it might have been like without their disobedience. We can never know how life would have panned out. How our relationship with God would have been. How our relationship with one another would be. We can never know what it might have been like because we cannot remember. There is an echo in our very being which at times resonates, however, in truth we cannot know.

But even if we cannot know what it might have been like without sin, we can rest assured that the second way, the roundabout way, the circuitous way is still just as good. The second way is not the way of Adam and Eve (pre-disobedience) but is the way of Jesus. It is the way of God Himself, so if this is the second way the first way cannot have been that different. God has had to devise the rescue mission and ensure that it could not be defeated and indeed He has done this. It is the other way.

For abortive men and women the "other way" is not the original way. It is not the way intended but it can be an equally good way and valid way. Just as the sin of Adam and Eve cannot be removed so neither can the abortion experience be removed. Learning and trying and retrying and relearning and continuing along the road until the end are what is asked. Except that upon the shoulders of abortive parents there is the knowledge that "I have done what I have done." The child has gone; the abortion has ensured that this is so; however, its memory remains to be carried forward. It will not be left behind. It demands that it is not forgotten because he/she belongs to the human creation, human family, and thus deserves recognition and deserves to be carried forward on our shoulders toward the heavenly kingdom. For the abortive parents the new way, or the "other way", will be more difficult and more wearying, however, it can still be a sure way home. And this is because of the suffering which accompanies those whose hearts have been not hardened, but whose hearts are touched by Mercy.

Indeed it is a way home but this way home means being carried in Mum's heart or in Dad's heart, an infant who was destined never to be remembered but indeed is now carried lovingly and as a treasure of inestimable worth. This is the other way home and it can be "very good".

A Prayer for the Healing of Abortion Wounds

(With Ecclesiastical Approval)

Eternal Father

We come before you
bearing the wounds of your Son, Jesus,
who, by his passion and death
we know has forgiven us.

We thank you Father for creating a special place
in heaven for our precious infants
who now surround your Holy Altar.

Father, on our journey home,
bearing the scars of our sin,
grant to us mothers and fathers
the grace of healing, courage and peace
so that we may be true witnesses to the world
of Your Love and endless Mercy.

Through the intercession of Our Lady,
the Mother of all Mothers,
we ask you this Our Father
in the name of Jesus Your Son
and in the unity of the Holy Spirit. Amen

Nihil Obstat: Very Rev. Peter J. Kenny D.D., Diocesan Censor
Imprimatur: Monsignor Les Tomlinson, Vicar General.
Date: 21 April 2005

Endnotes

1 *Catechism of the Catholic Church,* St Paul Publications, Homebush, 1994, nos. 2270-2275.

2 John Paul II, *Evangelium Vitae,* Encyclical Letter, St Paul's Publications, Australia, 1995, n.99, pp. 183-184.

3 Paul VI, *Humanae Vitae,* Encyclical Letter, St Paul's Publications, Australia, 1994, n.17, p.21.

4 *Catechism of the Catholic Church,* St. Paul's Publications, Homebush, 1994, no. 2207.

5 Kahlil Gibran, *The Prophet*, Heinemann, New York, 1928, pp. 49-50.

6 John O'Donohue, *Anam Cara: Spiritual Wisdom from the Celtic World*, Transworld Publishers: Bantam Press, 1997, p. 227.

Recommended Reading

Ainsworth, M.D.S. (1979). "Infant Mother Attachment", *American Psychologist*, 34, pp. 932-938.

Bowlby, J. (1951). *Maternal Care and Mental Health.* Columbia University Press, New York.

Brind, J., Chinchilli, V.M., Severs, W.B. & Summy-Long, J. (1996) "Induced abortion as an independent risk for breast cancer: a comprehensive review and meta analysis", *Journal of Epidemiology aand Community Health*, 50, pp. 481-496.

Burke, Theresa & Reardon, David C. (2002). *Forbidden Grief,* Acorn Books, Springfield, Illinois.

Clowes, Brian (1997). The *Facts of Life*, Human Life International, Front Royal, Virginia.

Coleman, Priscilla, K. Abortion and Mental Health, http://bjp.rcpsych. org/content/199/3/180.abstract?sid=f3a640ac-1664-489e-9f34-2ecc688a6d52, accessed November 2011.

Dillon, John J. (1990). *A Path to Hope.* Resurrection Press, Williston Park, New York.

Doka, Kenneth J. (1989). *Disenfranchised Grief: Recognizing Hidden Sorrow.* Lexington Books, New York.

Fergusson, D.M., Horwood L.J., Ridder, E.M. (2006). "Abortion in young women and subsequent mental health", *Journal of Child Psychology & Psychiatry*, 47 (1): pp. 16-24.

Gissler, M., Hemminki, E., & Lonnqvist, J., *Suicides after Pregnancy in Finland, 1987-1994*, BMJ, 1996.

Lewis, C.S. (1943). *Mere Christianity*, Macmillan, New York, p. 86.

Lewis, C.S., *The Problem of Pain*, HarperCollins, London, 1940.

Major, B. & Cozzarelli C (1992). "Psychosocial Predictors of Adjustment to Abortion", *Journal of Social Issues*, 48 (3), pp 121-142.

Miller, W. (1992*).* "An empirical study of the psychological antecedents and consequences of induced abortion", *Journal of Social Issues,* 48 (3), pp. 67-93.

Ney, Philip G. (1997). *Deeply Damaged.* Pioneer Publishing Co., Omaha, Nebraska.

Reardon, David C. (1996) *Making Abortion Rare.* Acorn Books, Springfield, Illinois.

Reardon, David C. (1987). *Aborted Women Silent No More.* Loyola University Press, Chicago.

Rue, V. (1981) *The Psychological Realities of Induced Abortion: Post-Abortion Aftermath.* Sheed & Ward, Washington D.C.

Selby, Terry L. & Bockmon, Marc (1990) *The Mourning After Help for Post-Abortion Syndrome,* Baker Book House, Grand Rapids, Michigan.

Speckhard, A.C. (1987) *Psychosocial Stress following Abortion.* Sheed & Ward, Kansas City.

Speckhard, A.C. & Rue, V.M. (1992) "Post-Abortion Syndrome: An Emerging Public Health Concern", *Journal of Social Issues,* 48 (3) pp. 95-119.

Worden, J.W. (1983). *Grief Counselling and Grief Therapy: A Handbook for the mental Health Practitioner* (2nd ed), Routledge, London.

Zolese, G. & Blacker, C. (1992). "The Psychosocial Complications of Therapeutic Abortion", *British Journal of Psychiatry,* 160, pp 742-749.

Diagnostic and Statistical Manual of Mental Disorders. (1987). Washington, D.C., American Psychiatric Association, 3rd ed.

Biblical Quotations are taken from the New Revised Standard Version.